SECRET AGENT'S HANDBOOK
of SPECIAL DEVICES

WORLD WAR II

SECRET AGENT'S HANDBOOK
of SPECIAL DEVICES

WORLD WAR II

Introduction by Mark Seaman

PUBLIC RECORD OFFICE

Public Record Office
Richmond
Surrey
TW9 4DU

© Crown Copyright 2000
Introduction © Mark Seaman

ISBN 1 903365 00 7

A catalogue card for this book
is available from the British Library

Printed by Cromwell Press,
Trowbridge, Wiltshire

Back of jacket:
Wartime "Boys' Adventure Stories" illustration commissioned
by the Ministry of Information (PRO, INF 3/502)

Contents

Publisher's Note

This publication brings together the two parts of a catalogue compiled by 'M.0.1 (S.P.)', a bogus War Office branch that served as a cover name for the Special Operations Executive (SOE), issued in 1944 and 1945 respectively. The main pages of these two documents (HS 7/28 and HS 7/30), which may be consulted at the Public Record Office, Kew, have been reproduced photographically from the original catalogues.

The 1944 catalogue included both a detailed Table of Contents and an Index, whereas the 1945 catalogue included neither. The Index of Special Devices and Supplies at the end of the present publication is an amalgam, consisting of the Table of Contents from Volume I, subject to some minor adaptation, with the addition of similar entries based on the headings and captions of Volume II.

INTRODUCTION
by Mark Seaman

Introduction

The story of espionage throughout the ages has been marked by the regular use of secret devices, disguises and concealed weapons. However, it was in the Second World War that such gadgetry reached new heights of ingenuity and technical sophistication. Fiction, rather than fact, has since fuelled the public's interest, with each of the James Bond films invariably featuring several fantastic devices produced by 'Q' and his department. The provision of such weapons and communications equipment became an integral part of the plot of each film. Although the movies ultimately took the inventions to absurd levels, their inspiration lay in real equipment encountered by James Bond's creator, Ian Fleming, while serving with Naval Intelligence during the Second World War. The origins of these secret agent's gadgets that so fascinated Fleming, his readers and generations of moviegoers lay in the first days of the realization of a threat from Nazi Germany and fears of another World War.

Early days

In the late 1930s the War Office and the Secret Intelligence Service (SIS) paid increasing attention to the potential of clandestine warfare in a future conflict. The military were particularly interested in guerrilla tactics and 'secret armies', while SIS began to consider the destabilizing impact upon an enemy of 'dirty tricks' such as subversion and sabotage.

Consequently, in the spring of 1938 the War Office appointed Major J C F Holland of the Royal Engineers to prepare a report on irregular warfare. His appointment as GS(R) constituted little more than a one-man research department, but his resulting report was sufficiently well received by his superiors for him to be instructed to develop his work and engage the assistance of two other experienced officers, Major C McV Gubbins and Major M R Jefferis. Over the following months they were to be joined by other officers, and on 27 June 1939 GS(R) was renamed Military Intelligence (Research) or MI R. Holland and his team enjoyed a very broad remit, including the formation of a research and development office to look into new weapons and technology. At the outbreak of war in September 1939 this subsection, designated MI Rc, comprised Jefferis, Captain R S Macrae and Staff Sergeant W Bidgood.

While Holland was progressing GS(R) and MI R, a parallel organization was created in SIS. On 1 April 1938 Major Laurence Grand, another Royal Engineer, was seconded to SIS to carry out an investigation of the potential of sabotage and subversive warfare. Having submitted his report 'Preliminary Survey of possibilities of sabotage', he was then asked to extend his stay with SIS and oversee the implementation of his proposal that a special section be formed. The resulting department was known as Section IX or, more theatrically, Section D (for 'Destruction'), with Grand adopting the symbol 'D'. The report had identified the need for the formation of a team to research and develop the special devices and equipment needed for clandestine operations. Like Jefferis's MI Rc this was to be a small group, headed by Commander A J G Langley RN and supported by C A Meek and Dr H D H Drane of the Research Department of the Royal Arsenal at Woolwich. The Section D team was later supplemented by two scientists from the academic world, Dr F A Freeth and C R Bailey of University College, London. Grand laid down important guidelines for their work, emphasizing the clandestine nature of their undertaking, the need to ensure that acts of sabotage might appear as simple accidents, and that devices be small and concealable rather than large and elaborate. The first important device to appear was the Time Pencil Fuze, designed to initiate sabotage devices after a prescribed period of delay. Other types of fuses and incendiary devices followed and new explosives were tested, such as the 'plastic' type then undergoing trials at Woolwich. At the same time, contacts were made with industrial firms and research establishments that might be able to render assistance as occasion demanded.

MI R and Section D did not work in isolation from each other. Although pursuing parallel courses, their objectives differed sufficiently for their endeavours not to be a wasteful duplication of effort:

> 'Jefferis was to run a more or less legitimate outfit which was to produce unusual but respectable weapons, the gentlemen concerned all being in uniform and therefore not to be confused with saboteurs, whilst Grand & Co would get double the money for running a Cloak and Dagger outfit. That was reasonable enough.'[1]

However, the link between the two organizations was such that as war loomed MI R joined Section D in the latter's offices in Caxton Street, Westminster. Then on the outbreak of war they both relocated. MI R returned to the War Office and Section D moved to Bletchley Park, SIS's emergency war station in Buckinghamshire, where they had already established a laboratory and a small magazine housing their stores of explosives and incendiary devices. But the evacuation of the whole of SIS from its London headquarters and its subsequent overcrowding at Bletchley Park resulted in Section D taking up alternative accommodation at the Frythe, a requisitioned residential hotel near Welwyn in Hertfordshire. Meanwhile, the experimental team acquired their own property, Aston House, near Stevenage, in November 1939. The subsection, which had Commander Langley as its first commandant, became known both as Station XII or – under another cover name – the Signals Development Branch, War Office. Intriguingly, a surviving document[2] refers to a 'Brown Book of Devices' being published at the end of 1939, but the work does not appear to feature amongst SOE's files. However, mention of its contents offers confirmation that, even at an early stage, Langley's team had already begun to follow Grand's dicta and had developed explosive devices camouflaged as pieces of coal or logs of wood.

Station XII's work was divided into two departments: D/D dealing with research and development of an engineering nature, and D/X (also known as the Laboratory Section) dealing with matters of a chemical or physical aspect, in particular explosives and incendiaries.

MI Rc was also on the move, taking over the premises of the International Broadcasting Company at 35 Portland Place, in London, as its workshops. Later it moved to a more suitable property, the Firs, at Whitchurch, near Aylesbury, in Buckinghamshire:

'The Firs was an ideal place for us. The large house could provide both offices and sleeping accommodation. There was extensive stabling, which could readily be converted into workshops. There were several cottages on the premises and, best of all, included in the property were levelled sites where buildings to serve as stores and so forth could be erected. There were also fields which could be used as firing ranges and where experimental demolition work could be carried out.'[3]

The Special Operations Executive (SOE)

Both organizations continued their work through the 'Phoney War' period, but the German onslaught in the west and the fall of France were to have a radical impact upon them. Europe was now in large measure occupied by Nazi Germany, the British Army had lost most of its vehicles and equipment in France, and the nation now faced the prospect of invasion. In this state of affairs, irregular warfare took on a far greater importance and, in recognition of this, the decision was taken to create a new organization to coordinate clandestine warfare against the Axis Powers. Consequently, after weeks of discussion, political manoeuvring and behind the scenes deals in Whitehall, on 16 July 1940 Prime Minister Winston Churchill instructed Dr Hugh Dalton, the Minister of Economic Warfare, to take control of Britain's subversive campaign. The new organization, the Special Operations Executive (SOE), was given its charter on the 19 July and its formation was approved by the War Cabinet three days later.

SOE soon acquired a host of cover names, including the 'Inter-Services Research Bureau' and the bogus War Office branch 'M.O.1. (S.P.)'. Its headquarters were in Baker Street, in London, and its operational structure was built around 'Country Sections' working into specific territorial areas. Staff officers (where possible, with fluency in the language of the relevant country) were appointed to run these offices, but few British citizens were considered suitable for employment on undercover tasks. The agents were usually drawn from the ranks of the armed forces of the Allied Governments-in-Exile or volunteers recruited from the refugees who had managed to reach Britain following the German occupation of their country. Inevitably there were exceptions to this rule. No less than five Sections worked into France, with F (the Independent French) Section electing to utilize as its agents British citizens capable of passing themselves off as French men or women. And although RF Section was primarily a liaison agency with de Gaulle's Free French, it too sent British personnel to France. Other sections, in particular those operating into the Balkans and the Far East, pursued extensive paramilitary activity with uniformed British Liaison Officers (BLOs) supporting local partisan or guerrilla groups.

One of SOE's most important tasks was the training of its agents. This was not achieved overnight, and a substantial outlay of resources was expended in building up a variety of training establishments in the United Kingdom. Fortunately MI R and Section D had made substantial progress with the recruiting of staff, acquiring premises and developing syllabuses. By the end of the war, SOE had built up a large and highly effective system of Special Training Schools and holding stations for its agents in the United

Kingdom. Reflecting SOE's global perspective, similar training centres were developed in the Middle East, Canada, India and Australia.

It was clear that even the best trained and equipped of agents were worthless without the means of inserting them into enemy territory. Consequently, the Royal Air Force was reluctantly persuaded to devote aircraft to 'Special Duty' work, parachuting personnel and supplies and, where circumstances permitted, employing light aircraft to land and pick up agents. The Admiralty was inveigled into making a similar contribution but, like the RAF, frequently jibbed at the diversion of men and resources from their primary operational tasks.

SOE assumed many of the assets of MI R and Section D, but the two founding fathers of these departments were not amongst them, and Holland and Grand returned to conventional soldiering. The former enjoyed a dignified exit from the shadow war, while the latter engaged in a brief, acrimonious and futile struggle with Dalton to retain control of his organization. The transfer of staff and duties from the old set-up to the new took some time. MI R was broken up, and was formally wound up on 2 October 1940. Many of the innovative schemes devised by Holland's team were adopted by the War Office and other government departments. MI Rc found itself elevated to the unusual and prestigious status of coming under the immediate control of Churchill himself:

> 'This was therefore no time to proceed by ordinary channels in devising expedients. In order to secure quick action, free from departmental processes, upon any bright idea or gadget, I decided to keep under my own hand as Minister of Defence the experimental establishment formed by Major Jefferis at Whitchurch.'[4]

Now known as M.R.1, Jefferis's team pursued a variety of projects for the rest of the war but continued to contribute to the design and development of clandestine equipment.

Meanwhile, SOE was developing its own research and development section from the rump of Langley's team. It was fortunate to be placed in the safe hands of Major F T 'Tommy' Davies, whose pedigree as a businessman was matched by his service in the clandestine world. He had been a pre-war member of MI R and took part in its Mission to Poland in September 1939. A former director of Courtaulds, he had shown great audacity during the fall of France by removing hundreds of thousands of pounds worth of platinum from its Calais factory shortly before the arrival of the German forces. On the creation of SOE, Davies had been chosen by Sir Frank Nelson, the organization's first executive head, to be one of his two assistants. Soon after, Davies was entrusted with the Directorate of Research, Development and Supply – bearing the SOE symbol AD/Z – and given a seat on SOE's Council.

In addition to the limited amount of material that had been issued to Section D agents for operations on the Continent, the new special equipment was made available to the Auxiliary Units – small groups of specially trained civilians who were to fight as guerrilla forces in the event of a German invasion. In the summer of 1940 they were given crash courses in sabotage and clandestine warfare and provided with weapons, explosives and incendiaries cached in secret operational bases throughout Britain. In turn, sabotage material from secret stocks was used by Commandos on their raids on the recently occupied coasts of Continental Europe.

Nevertheless, despite the legacy of MI R and Section D, it was to take some time before SOE was ready to mount operations. On 5 October 1940, Gladwyn Jebb, the Chief Executive Officer, reported 'for the moment, and probably for some time to come, we are simply not in a position to effect any sabotage operation to Western Europe'.

By the summer of 1941 the increasing responsibilities of SOE as a major instrument of war resulted in major changes. Davies remained in overall charge of SOE's Research, Development and Supply Directorate, but on 9 June Professor D M Newitt was appointed Director of Scientific Research (DSR). A month later, research and development of equipment (D/X Section) was moved to Station IX at the Frythe, while production, routine inspection, packing and dispatch of stores remained at Aston House. Myriad cover names continued to be allocated, and on 12 May 1941 Aston House had been given the additional designation Experimental Station 6 (War Department) or E.S.6 (W.D.). During the course of the war, Station XII attained a remarkable level of activity. Its staff rose from 119 on 30 June 1942 to 524 military and civilian personnel on 30 June 1945. Although SOE devised and developed its own equipment, orders were usually placed with outside contractors for its manufacture and an increasingly large burden fell on DSR for trialling and testing supplies. Because of the need for security, some devices were only made in component form and then constructed at SOE workshops. The output of material was impressive: no less than 6,667 tons of stores were issued from 1941 to 1945.

When the United States entered the war, its intelligence gathering and special operations agency, the Office of Strategic Services (OSS), drew heavily upon SOE and SIS know-how. Training, methodology, personnel and, not least, equipment were shared with the fledgling American organization. SOE's training establishment in Canada, Camp X, near Toronto, became an important centre where OSS staff were given an initiation into the techniques of clandestine warfare. Inevitably, as the war progressed, the United States' customary ingenuity, technological skill and production capacity resulted in the OSS developing some of its own equipment, while at the same time adapting SOE material to their own needs and specifications.

It was not just the manufacture of equipment with which SOE was concerned. In November 1941 a camouflage expert joined AD/Z. It was soon clear that the job required more than one man, and in January 1942 a small workshop manned by a modest complement of three men was established at Station IX. The following month larger workshops were opened at the Victoria & Albert Museum, in London, and the staff was trebled. Under the command of Lieutenant-Colonel J Elder Wills of the Royal Engineers, the Section attracted a variety of civilian and army technicians and craftsmen, many of whom (like Wills) had formerly worked in the cinema industry. Special purchases were procured by a 'buyer' from a film studio, while a range of plasterers, carpenters, metal workers and painters were deployed on a succession of challenging and ingenious projects.

In June 1942 the main workshops were moved to the Thatched Barn, a 1930s-built roadhouse on the Barnet Bypass, north of London. This establishment became known as Station XV, while the premises at 56 Queen's Gate (Station XVA), in Kensington, took on a primarily liaison duty with its customers – the Country Sections. There was much to

The Thatched Barn, designated by SOE as Station XV. It was here that the Camouflage Section had its headquarters and main workshops. (PRO, HS 7/49)

commend this move. It offered much-needed space, easy access to Research and Development facilities in the area, and proximity to the film studios at Elstree. A Photographic Section (Station XVC) was absorbed by the Section and situated at 2–3 Trevor Square, Kensington. It provided photographs for use in the production of false documents, and its prodigious output resulted in no less than 1,620 agents being photographed between 1 March 1943 and 15 November 1944.

Unusually for such a secret organization, it was decided to set up a Demonstration Room, the venue being the Natural History Museum in South Kensington. An internal history of the Camouflage Section recorded that it was created 'in order that the Agent should receive every possible help and avail himself of "food for thought".' However, Section heads became concerned that the massive range of equipment on view would beguile agents to such an extent that they would seek to avail themselves unnecessarily of the full inventory. On the other hand, it was also recorded that attendance was really quite low and relatively few members of SOE took advantage of the opportunity of examining the latest gadgetry. Nevertheless, it did serve as a very useful asset in SOE's public relations, and King George VI was only one of the dignitaries to visit. Another of them, Sir Robert Bruce Lockhart, the Director-General of the Political Warfare Executive (PWE), wrote in his diary:

'Friday, 10 November 1944 . . . the South Kensington Natural History Museum where in six sealed rooms they have an exhibition of all gadgets (uniforms, wireless sets, hand grenades, tiny motor-cycles etc.) used by their agents. Most interesting and very well done. One exhibit showed ties, shirts, underwear, etc. of continental manufacture

The Main Gallery at Station XVB, SOE's Demonstration Room housed in the National History Museum. Although this was a secret establishment, it nevertheless proved very useful for SOE's public relations with Whitehall. (PRO, HS 7/49)

showing the difference from British makes. Likewise shoes. Most ingenious, too, were the blocks of wood, spars of ships, petrol tins etc. used for concealing radio sets and even tiny but useful motorbikes, not to mention arms, tommy-guns etc. Also very ingenious containers and one-man submarines, also many kinds of disguised bombs and explosives which stick to ships. Wonderful dummies, too, with dreadful faces and dressed in the different German uniforms. A good show.'[5]

In 1944, at the height of its activities, the Camouflage Section boasted four main sites: Station XV comprising the headquarters and main production; XVA working on prototypes, clothing, and ageing of new items; XVB (Demonstration Room); and XVC handling make-up and photography. By June 1944 over 90,000 articles were being issued by the Camouflage Section each year, and an average of 16 agents were equipped each day. The complement of staff had risen from its original three men to over 300, with subgroups established in Italy, Algeria, Egypt, India and Australia. In January 1945 yet another branch was created in liberated Brussels, to service the requirements of agents being sent into Germany.

The defeat of Germany resulted in little diminution of SOE's commitment to produce material for SOE operations against Japan, but after VJ Day all orders for manufacture were cancelled and the winding up process began. By the end of October 1945 Station XII had become the primary centre for the residual elements of SOE's equipment and supplies.

The Property Shop at Station XV. Here newly manufactured material was artificially 'aged', concealing devices were prepared, and consignments packed for operations. (PRO, HS 7/49)

The remnants of Station VI (Small Arms) and XV (Camouflage) had already moved there and were soon to be joined by Stations VII (Radio), IX (Research) and XVII (Training).

SOE ended its existence in much the same way as it had begun. Dedicated members of the organization struggled to save it; vengeful bureaucrats sought to settle old scores; and other government agencies fought to acquire selected elements of its duties, personnel and equipment. Its winding up proved to be slow and complex, with the formal end coming on 15 January 1946.

But SOE left a tangible legacy. It had made a significant contribution to the Allied victory; and the innovative concepts of clandestine warfare that it had fashioned, supported by the supplies and equipment it had developed, were to feature strongly in many, if not most, of Britain's post-war conflicts.

The Catalogue

Both MI R and Section D produced manuals and instructional booklets, although only a limited number have been released or have survived. One of them, the *Handbook of Special Ammunition*, contains neither a date of publication nor any mention of its origins, but it can safely be assumed to be of Section D derivation. The Germans are mentioned as the foe, although at least one of its illustrations rather disconcertingly depicts a French tank as a target for a mine. What is clear is for whom it was intended, as stated in its foreword:

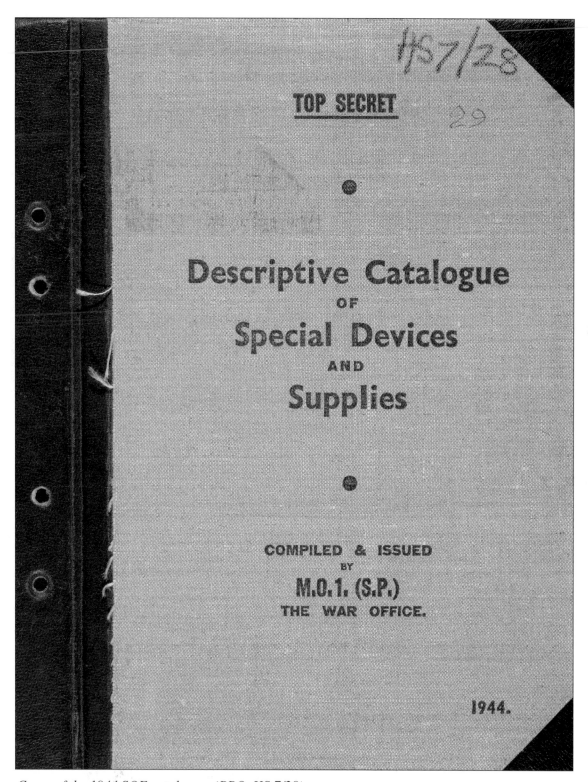

Cover of the 1944 SOE catalogue. (PRO, HS 7/28)

The Compositor's Shop at Station XV. Printing tasks ranged from secret codes to instructional booklets and the replication of foreign labels and packaging. (PRO, HS 7/49)

'Whilst this book is primarily intended to facilitate the training of the men who are going into the field, it should also be an aid to those whose task it is to plan and direct operations. In order successfully to solve the problems which are presented to them, they must know their enemy, know their men and, above all, they must know their weapons.'[6]

SOE's surviving files reveal the existence (if not copies) of a *Technical Newsletter* that was replaced in November 1943 by a quarterly *Technical Review*. This latter publication was intended to appraise 'operational and stores branches of missions and groups' of new equipment, modifications, research, technical literature and notes on wireless, training, camouflage and operations.[7]

The files also record that another catalogue was in circulation in 1944 'to assist officers in selecting equipment for agents by making available, in convenient form for reference, a representative list of types of stores available'. Its author(s) exuded confidence – for, in addition to material already manufactured or in use, it was emphasized that 'given sufficient time, almost anything can be produced'.[8]

A small instructional booklet was compiled, too, for the use of members of Resistance groups to whom supplies were dropped. Each pamphlet consisted of 32 pages of instructions, printed in English and five other European languages (French, Dutch, Norwegian, Danish and German), with illustrations. The booklet described the types of weapons and sabotage material that would be found in the parachute containers and how to use them. Far less sophisticated than the SOE Catalogue, the booklet nevertheless gave the reader the opportunity of ordering standard containers: 'When ordering a consignment of Containers you need only say "Send X H5 and X H3" for example.' The instructions are detailed and clearly expressed, and would enable any literate man, woman or child to become a saboteur. The booklets were packed into the containers and distributed in their thousands. Although they contained no 'secret' information that was not already known to the German security forces, they must have left SOE's adversaries in no doubt about the range of British weapons and explosives and the damage they might inflict.

By the end of the Second World War the Special Operations Executive had taken research and development of weapons and equipment to previously undreamed of levels. Material could be ordered from stock with the same ease as selecting a new suit or a pair of shoes from a mail-order catalogue – but it should not be forgotten that, unlike fashion accessories, the equipment described in the SOE Catalogue had a dangerous, and frequently deadly, history. The following seeks to offer a few examples of the equipment's use at the 'sharp end' of the clandestine war.

Agents' equipment

When planning an operation, SOE usually exhibited exemplary diligence in providing an agent with their requirements of clothing and equipment. The Camouflage Section was responsible for providing appropriate clothes – usually second-hand items, either purchased from old stocks in Britain or obtained from recent refugees arrived from the Continent. Tailors produced new items of clothing where necessary, but strictly in accordance with the details of the agent's cover story. Recently-manufactured clothing could be artificially aged to conform with the correct level of rationing in Occupied Europe, while agents waiting to be sent on their missions frequently wore their new clothes for extended periods to get used to the feel of them. One F Section agent, Richard Heslop, wrote after the war of the impressive arrangements to prepare him for his mission:

> 'Everything I needed I got. I was fitted with two good suits cut in the French style, with padded shoulders, and I lived up to my school nickname of "The Square Man" when I was wearing them. I wore them regularly on trips to London so that they would not look too new when I arrived in France. The labels of a well-known French tailor were sewn in, and I memorised the name of the tailor and the place where I was supposed to have bought them.
>
> My French wardrobe was complete down to pants, vests, socks, shoes, ties, razor blades, pocket-knife, fountain-pen, and pencil. I was given French matches and lighter, cigarettes, and cigarette papers – essential for the smoker, for in France at that time you never threw away a dog-end.'[9]

The Catalogue reveals the availability of German Army uniforms amongst its stores of clothing, but although SOE sent some agents into the Reich dressed as members of the Wehrmacht, its agents in Occupied countries usually tended to steal their requirements from laundries and cloakrooms.

Station XV's Textile Shop, where work on textile containers and the alteration and fitting of special clothing, such as uniforms, were carried out. (PRO, HS 7/49)

During their training, agents were given instruction in how to alter their appearance using quick and relatively simple methods. There would be little opportunity in enemy territory to indulge in elaborate disguises, and even the dyeing of hair might cause future problems. The French agent Pierre Brossolette had been a well-known journalist and broadcaster before the war, and therefore took pains to grow a moustache and dye his hair before his clandestine return to Paris. When he was eventually captured, in February 1944, his false papers left his captors in ignorance of his true identity, but the longer he remained in captivity the greater the risk that a very distinctive flash of white in his real hair colour would be revealed. In the event, the interception of secret messages unmasked Brossolette and he committed suicide lest under torture he betray his comrades. Certainly some agents felt the need to have a more permanent change to their appearance, and the Camouflage Section's files record:

> 'Nasal operation carried out on a Student [Danish] to enable him to return to the field without fear of recognition.'

Perhaps the most famous example of disguise through surgery was that attempted by Sir James Hutchison, the one-time head of SOE's RF Section. A veteran of campaigns in France, Gallipoli and Palestine during the First World War, he yearned to leave Baker Street and return to active service. He therefore volunteered for service with the Jedburghs – teams of uniformed Special Forces who were intended to parachute into France at the time of the invasion. Hutchison was concerned that his identity had become known to the Germans and he decided to have his face altered by a plastic surgeon prior to embarking on his mission. However, despite assertions in his autobiography that not even his own daughter recognized him, fellow members of SOE have recalled that the surgery achieved no discernible change in Hutchison's appearance.

Most SOE agents were inserted into enemy territory by parachute – the X-type being the most commonly used, especially after unfortunate accidents with the A-type. The 'Striptease' jump suit (so called because of the rapidity with which the wearer might disrobe) proved a great success and was adopted by other clandestine organizations, such as SIS, for their own parachutists. White snow-camouflage versions were issued for operations in Scandinavia, but the bulk of those manufactured used heavy-duty windproof material printed with a unique green-and-brown camouflage pattern. The primary aim was to protect the parachutist from injury and enable him or her to emerge from the landing with their civilian clothing clean and intact. Thus bandages were supplied to support ankles and other joints, overshoes were fitted, and a spine pad was placed in a special pocket of the voluminous jump suit. Other pockets were provided for a knife, pistol, emergency pack and spade – with the intention that an agent could cut the shrouds of the parachute if it caught in a tree, defend him/herself against attack, survive until located by friendly forces, and bury the parachute and 'Striptease' suit before vanishing into anonymity.

In addition to the 'Striptease' jump suit, SOE developed the Parachutist's Watersuit Mk V to provide waterproof protection and buoyancy for agents deliberately parachuted into water. Opinions of its efficacy vary. An SOE staff officer, Donald Hamilton-Hill, claimed that the suit proved a great success when used by a Dutch agent who parachuted into the Zuyder Zee:

Bill Pickering, an SOE wireless operator in Italy, wearing his 'Striptease' suit and parachute, 1945. (Imperial War Museum, HU 48173)

'The water proof jump suit with Mae West attachment worn by our Dutch friend had proved itself one hundred percent effective. It had, of course, been tried out by our instructors previously but this was the first occasion on which it had been used by one of our 'specials', and on a night drop. This was another good mark for our SOE technical backroom boffins, who comprised some of the best brains in invention and manufacturing of their kind in Britain.'[10]

The Parachutist's Watersuit was also used by the Norwegian saboteur Max Manus as a wet suit. He was under no illusions about its quality: 'I knew the Germans had rubber suits with webbed feet and oxygen masks, but we had only a little poor equipment which at the very best could keep us warm in the water.'[11] The voluminous suit had at least one advantage – namely that a substantial amount of air might be trapped in it, thereby imparting a degree of buoyancy to the swimmer. Manus described how on one occasion he and a fellow saboteur prepared to swim on their backs to their target ship, but as he pushed off from a jetty he sank like a stone. He managed to pull himself onto the wharf and cycle back to his safe house with four or five gallons of water still in his suit. Examination of the suit revealed that the limpet mine had worn a hole in the fabric, into which the water had flooded. In spite of this near disaster, Manus and his companions later returned to the water for another attempt.

Amongst the wide range of equipment available to agents were several types of incendiary briefcases and suitcases. These were intended to provide security for compromising documents and at the same time to constitute a booby trap for any overly inquisitive enemy policeman. Although very few accounts have survived of the issue of the incendiary briefcases, at least one particularly graphic description of their use (or misuse) has been published. After service behind enemy lines in Albania, David Smiley joined the Siam Section of SOE and parachuted into Thailand on 30 May 1945. On 23 June he and his party were warned of an impending Japanese raid and prepared to flee. Smiley placed his codebooks and other important documents in his incendiary briefcase, but as he was

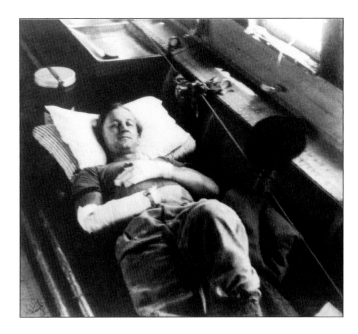

David Smiley aboard an RAF Dakota during his evacuation from Thailand. His bandaged arms bear witness to his encounter with an incendiary briefcase. (Imperial War Museum, HU 65755)

completing this task the case exploded (perhaps as a result of an electrical short circuit) and Smiley was showered with blazing thermite:

> 'I had shut my eyes at the moment of the explosion, and my face was so burnt, with the skin black and hard, that I could not open them again. I was burnt on my arms, knees and hands; all the nails were burnt off both hands, and the flesh was burnt to the bone on four fingers of the left hand.'[12]

Smiley's aides did what they could for him with the limited medical supplies available to them, giving him morphine for the pain and rubbing coconut oil into the burns. An aircraft was arranged to collect him, but this was delayed and he endured terrible suffering before he was eventually brought out to India, where he could gain proper medical attention. Typically, when he had recovered from his wounds he returned to duty in Thailand.

Explosives and incendiaries

SOE benefited from the availability of recently developed powerful explosives, especially plastic explosive (PE). Usually light yellow in colour, it had the consistency of dough but after being stored for some time would harden. Vaseline might then be mixed with it in order to return it to elasticity. It was very safe to handle and would not detonate even if hit by a rifle bullet. Other types of explosive were also used, such as Nobel's 808 and gelignite, both of which had some unpleasant side effects on the SOE personnel who handled them:

> 'Jenkins and I spent all next day in preparing the gelignite: it had to be taken out of wooden boxes and the sticks moulded together and repacked, which not only gave us both a splitting headache but made me sick as well. It is a known fact that handling gelignite in some way poisons one through the pores, with these unpleasant results.'[13]

Plastic explosive did not possess similar properties. Moreover, it could be easily moulded into a desired shape and packed into a variety of casings, and even camouflaged in exotic disguises such as oriental carvings and statues. It required a detonator to initiate it and, in order that a saboteur might safely withdraw after planting a device, needed either a slow-burning fuse or a delay fuse. Thus Langley's Time Pencil was a significant advance, and it became a standard part of the saboteur's equipment. However, it was not always entirely accurate, due to variations in temperature and the metallurgical characteristics of the retaining wire. John Goldsmith, an F Section agent, wrote of some of the difficulties he encountered when using the Time Pencil in France:

> 'Reliable from the point of view that they nearly always functioned, I never knew a single one of these detonators [sic] to go off on time, a weakness I took pains to impress on Resistance fighters when later I had to instruct them in France.'[14]

Whatever its occasional failings, the Time Pencil was a standard piece of SOE and army equipment both during and after the Second World War, with nearly 13 million being produced under the auspices of Station XII alone.

The Time Pencil had its origins in Section D, while one of MI R's most impressive legacies was the limpet. The latter stands as an ideal example of the British qualities of eccentricity, enthusiasm and expertise. It was the brainchild of the editor of *Caravan and Trailer* (soon to be Captain Macrae of MI R) and the owner and chief designer of the Low Loading Trailer Company Ltd (later Major C V 'Nobby' Clarke of SOE). Using a variety of improvised materials and facilities that included tin bowls from Woolworth's, children's magnets, aniseed balls, prophylactics and Bedford Public Baths, the two men produced a serviceable limpet mine that could be clandestinely fixed, below the waterline, to the hull of a ship. Macrae and Clarke's Mark I limpet was improved by SOE's scientists and technicians, and the Limpet Mark 6 became a standard maritime sabotage device for the latter part of the war, some 38,500 being produced by Station XII. Arguably the most spectacular and effective use of the Mark 6 limpet was Operation JAYWICK, a sabotage raid on Japanese shipping at anchor in Singapore harbour. On 2 September 1943 a team of SOE saboteurs sailed from Australia in a captured Japanese fishing boat to a lying-up point near their target, whence three two-man canoes launched their attack on the night of 26–27 September. Limpets were attached to several vessels, with the result that 30,000 tons of enemy shipping were sunk. The mission achieved a successful conclusion, with the entire party returning safely to Australia a fortnight later. Tragically, a repeat attempt was made the next year. Operation RIMAU proved a disaster, with the entire party killed in engagements with Japanese forces or executed after capture.

In addition to large sabotage devices such as the limpet, SOE produced the tyreburster – a mini mine, activated by pressure, that was sufficiently powerful to blow the tyre of a wheeled vehicle. It also had an application as an anti-personnel weapon. Tyrebursters were camouflaged to permit their use in a variety of locations and were disguised as stones, rock fragments, mud, brick, coal, cork and animal excrement. In all, 185,813 camouflaged tyrebursters were produced up to the end of 1944 and a total of one and half million manufactured for SOE during the war.

Amongst the saboteurs who put them to good use was David Smiley. A regular army officer with a distinguished war record before joining SOE, he was twice sent into Albania where he served as a British Liaison Officer with the local guerrillas. Having laid an explosive charge on a bridge:

> 'We went onto the road and scattered a few tyre bursters (small explosive charges disguised to resemble mule droppings, which would blow a large hole in the tyre of any vehicle that ran over one) and made off to a position about two hundred yards away to watch. Within five minutes two vehicles had run over the tyre bursters and stopped on the bridge . . . with a flash and a tremendous explosion, the bridge went up, complete with the Germans on it.' [15]

SOE sabotage equipment ironically found an unusual use when it was put into service by members of the German Resistance in their attempts to kill Adolf Hitler. As early as the summer of 1942, Lieutenant-Colonel Freiherr von Gersdorff was instructed by his fellow conspirators to secure the best explosives and fuses. His enquiries led him to stores of British-manufactured material that had been captured in France, following Combined Operations raids on Dieppe and St Nazaire, or seized from Resistance groups. Trials left the Germans impressed with the performance of British plastic explosive and with Time Pencil

Fuzes and Lead Delays. The Clam was eventually selected as the most suitable charge, and on 7 March 1943 a bomb constructed from four Clams was placed aboard Hitler's aircraft at Smolensk airfield. The package had been disguised as two bottles of Cointreau liqueur and was given to an unsuspecting member of Hitler's staff. In the event, the device failed to detonate during the flight. When one of the conspirators later recovered it, he discovered that the fuse had malfunctioned due to the excessive cold resulting from flying at altitude. The Clams were to be used in a second attempt, shortly afterwards, in which von Gersdorff volunteered to act as a suicide bomber, blowing up the Führer and himself with explosives carried in the pockets of his uniform. He arranged to attend a function at which Hitler would be present and initiated the bomb's 10-minute fuse in anticipation of closing on his quarry. But Hitler unexpectedly cut short his visit and the attempt had to be aborted. However, this was by no means the last time SOE sabotage material was employed by the German Resistance. The bomb used by Count von Stauffenberg in the assassination attempt at the Wolf's Lair on 20 July 1944 consisted of 975 grams of British plastic explosive, two SOE detonators and a 30-minute delay fuse.[16] The explosion killed four members of Hitler's entourage, but the Führer sustained only minor injuries.

SOE's own plan to assassinate Hitler, Operation FOXLEY, envisaged the employment of a wide range of equipment. In spite of an impressive variety of schemes and methods of attack, ranging from bazookas and a sniper's rifle to poison and explosive, up-to-date intelligence was so poor that operational planning remained vague. In hindsight, the elaborate scheme appears significantly flawed. Not only were the planners unaware of the target's whereabouts, but the schemes ranged from the unworkable to the hopelessly impracticable.

Arguably SOE's most celebrated sabotage operation was Operation GUNNERSIDE, which achieved the destruction of German supplies of 'Heavy Water' manufactured at the Norsk Hydro plant at Rjukan in Norway. British Intelligence was aware of the use of 'Heavy Water' in retarding a nuclear reaction and were worried that this would assist German scientists in their experiments to produce an atomic bomb. The operational files reveal that one of the earlier editions of the Catalogue was used in the planning, and the list of sabotage material quotes the reference numbers of items required (Detonators H.21, Striker Boards F.48, etc.). The main demolition charges were made up specially for the operation, and were used to devastating effect when the team broke into the plant on 27–28 February 1943 and blew up the 'Heavy Water' production equipment and stocks. GUNNERSIDE was achieved with such surgical precision that the explosion was undetected by the guards, and all the saboteurs were able to make their escape without a shot being fired. It remains a (if not *the*) classic example of a *coup de main* feat of arms.

Although the standard sabotage equipment was the mainstay of SOE's operations, it would be inappropriate not to refer to the rather more esoteric devices produced by Stations IX, XII and XV, often in response to specific requests from the Country Sections.

Incendiary cigarettes were first requested by the Italian Section in April 1942. Research and development progressed well, and 130 'cigarettes' were supplied to the Section in August. Further orders followed and the quality of the device was regularly improved, with Egyptian and Turkish varieties made. By the end of 1944, 43,700 incendiary cigarettes had been manufactured and distributed.

The explosive bicycle pump was developed in 1943, trials being carried out at Station IX. By the end of 1944, 138 examples of this type of sophisticated booby trap had been manufactured, although there is no record of their use. Similarly, a torch was developed that could be used either as a grenade or as a booby trap. Experiments took place during 1943 and 50 examples were manufactured by the end of 1944, though again there is no record of their being used operationally.

The explosive rat has remained a source of fascination for all students of clandestine gadgetry. It was developed following a request from F Section early in 1941. One William Howard of Tottenham was persuaded to supply the required number of rodents, under the misconception that he was supplying London University for scientific experiments. One hundred of the devices were produced with the intention of them being planted by agents near boilers. It was assumed that a boilerman would throw the rat into the boiler, with the result that the fuse would ignite and the plastic explosive would be detonated. The files indicate that the first consignment sent to France was soon discovered by the Germans, who were singularly impressed by British ingenuity:

> 'The container was found by the enemy before any of the rats could be used for operational purposes, but their discovery had an extraordinary moral effect and the device was exhibited at all German Military Schools, a wide search being organized to find the "Hundreds of rats" which the enemy believed was distributed on the Continent. The trouble caused to them was a much greater success to us than if the rats had actually been used. It is obvious that in the latter case no evidence would have remained, and the enemy would not have discovered their existence.'[17]

The device does not, however, appear to have vanished entirely from SOE's armoury after this disappointing start, and the Camouflage Section's history[18] records that 65 explosive rats (along with 16 pieces of explosive coal, 4 explosive logs and 50 explosive fish-plates) were completed and dispatched to the German Section.

Weapons

Most of the firearms handled by SOE were standard military 'hardware' for the arming of resistance movements throughout the world. In the main this consisted of the delivery of tens of thousands of rifles, light machine guns and submachine guns to guerrilla and partisan groups, ranging from Poland to Burma. The organization also provided a wide range of pistols as personal-protection weapons for its agents, while SOE's scientists and technicians developed a small collection of specialized silenced weapons. Assassination formed a small but significant part of SOE's armoury, being used selectively to eliminate traitors and informants and to instil fear in enemy security forces. There is limited information surrounding the use of weapons such as the Silenced Sten, the Welrod and the Sleeve Gun. The Sten gun, a cheaply made and easily maintained submachine gun, was a standard weapon for resistance forces. In the autumn of 1942, the first silenced version was produced by Polish officers serving in the United Kingdom. Their design was improved and modified at Station IX and the first consignments were sent out to the field in June

1943, with improvements being carried out at Station VI, SOE's Arms Section at Bride Hall, Hertfordshire. Complementing the Silenced Sten was the Welrod, a simple but highly efficient silenced pistol designed by SOE's scientists and technicians. In October 1944, SOE in London warned its ANTRUM team operating near Alesund, in Norway, that a well-known collaborator, Ivar Grande, had moved into the area, and instructions were issued that he be liquidated. An experienced SOE operative, Ivar Naes, was chosen to carry out the task. His first plan was to kill his quarry with hand grenades, but the scheme was frustrated by a vigilant guard dog. It was then decided to shoot Grande with a Welrod as he left Gestapo headquarters, but intelligence was received that he wore body armour, which reduced the likelihood of killing him to an unacceptable degree. Finally, on 12 December 1944 two SOE operatives in a stolen car followed Grande as he bicycled home and killed him with a burst of fire from a Silenced Sten gun.[19]

In addition to specific targeting of individuals, SOE also planned and initiated a systematic liquidation offensive known as RATWEEK. Details are not fully known, but it is evident that supplies of Welrods and Silenced Stens formed one particular requirement for its implementation, with the heads of the Country Sections discussing their needs at a meeting as early as 10 June 1943. By the end of the year reports were being discussed at SOE Headquarters that suggested that RATWEEK was being implemented, notably in France and Belgium, where Nazi officials and collaborators had been eliminated.

Wing Commander F F E Yeo-Thomas, one of SOE's most highly decorated agents, envisaged a very personal use for silenced weapons after the war. Captured in Paris in March 1944 on his third mission, he endured dreadful suffering at the hands of his Nazi captors, managed to escape from Buchenwald concentration camp and eventually returned to Britain. He had barely begun his recovery when he requested permission to undertake Operation OUTHAUL, an attempt to trace former SS concentration camp guards hiding in the American Zone of Occupation of Germany. An alternative title for the operation was THUG – which, when considered in conjunction with the arsenal Yeo-Thomas intended taking with him (2 Silenced Stens, 2 Welrods, 2 carbines, 4 Colt pistols, locking knives and 4 pairs of handcuffs), gave a clear indication of the fate awaiting any Nazi he tracked down.[20]

It would appear that Yeo-Thomas had something of a penchant for AD/Z's wares, for he is also on record as having requested a Sleeve Gun for his last mission to France, Operation ASYMPTOTE. But there is no record of it being issued, and when he was captured he was found to be armed with only a Colt .32 automatic pistol, strapped to his thigh, and a tear-gas pen in his pocket.[21] It is doubtful that Yeo-Thomas would have been able to frustrate his attackers even if armed with a Sleeve Gun. There is, however, evidence to suggest that it was an efficient weapon. Major D H Everett, Head of User and Field Trials at Station IX, reported that he carried a concealed Sleeve Gun with him to the Mess one evening and fired a round into a sandbag that had been conveniently left on a chair. No-one in the Mess heard a thing.[22]

The Spigot Mortar appears amongst the largest weapons in the Catalogue, but few accounts are available in which its use is recorded. Devised by Major C V Clarke of Station XII, it was chosen as the main armament for the Brixham trawler *Maid Honor* when this vessel was selected for SOE's Operation POSTMASTER. The ship was to convey a small

The business end of a Sleeve Gun, photographed at Station IX. (Imperial War Museum, HU 56777)

team of men – drawn from the Small Scale Raiding Force (SSRF) – to West Africa, where they would 'cut out' Axis merchant shipping at anchor in the port of Santa Isabel, in the neutral Spanish colony of Fernando Po. Clarke himself installed the mortars on the *Maid Honor* and test-fired them during trials in Poole harbour. Thankfully the weapon was not required during the voyage south in the autumn of 1941, nor in the course of the comprehensively successful operation that was carried out on the night of 14 January 1942. The SOE files reveal that a Spigot Mortar was taken into the field on at least one occasion as part of the substantial armoury supplied to a team of Czechoslovak agents in order to carry out Operation ANTHROPOID – the liquidation of SS-Obergruppenführer Reinhard Heydrich, the Acting Reich Protector of Bohemia-Moravia. The operation was inspired by the Czechoslovak Government-in-Exile and, although the personnel selected to carry out the task were two Czechoslovak soldiers, Jan Kubis and Josef Gabcik, SOE was entrusted with training, equipping and transporting the assassins. Kubis and Gabcik were given very precise instruction by Majors Clarke and Woods at Station XII, where they rehearsed an attack upon a slow-moving car with a special blast grenade designed by the two SOE officers.[23] But there was a limit to the amount of preparation that the agents could be given, and it was recognized during the planning of the attack that they would have to seize any opportunity that presented itself. Consequently, they took a positive arsenal of weaponry with them, including:

2 Colt .38 Supers (with shoulder holsters)
4 Spare magazines
100 Rounds of ammunition
6 Percussion bombs with PE
2 Detonator magazines
2 Mills bombs (4 seconds)
1 Tree spigot mortar
1 Coil trip wire
2 Igniters
1 Spigot bomb
1 4-hour time delay for use with 2-lb PE charge
4 Electric detonators and 30-inch wire and battery
1 Sten gun
100 Rounds of ammunition for Sten gun
32 lbs PE
10 lbs Gelignite
2 yards Cordtex
4 Fog signals
3 Time pencils
1 Lethal hypodermic syringe

The assassins and their equipment were dropped by parachute during the night of 27–28 December 1941 and spent the next five months planning their attack. The range of weaponry at their disposal led them to consider mounting the operation against Heydrich's train or motor car and even the possibility of poisoning his food. In the event, the attempt was made in almost exactly the manner in which SOE's experts had instructed them. On the morning of 27 May 1942 Heydrich was driven to his office in Prague. He travelled in an open-topped limousine with only his chauffeur as bodyguard. As the car slowed at a hairpin bend, Kubis threw one of the bombs against the side of the car. To their consternation, the plan then came off the rails. Neither Heydrich nor his chauffeur appeared to have suffered any significant ill-effect from the blast and opened fire on their assailants. A second bomb and Gabcik's Sten gun had to be abandoned and the two would-be assassins fled, with first Kubis and then Gabcik pursued by the chauffeur. In the ensuing gunfight, Gabcik wounded the German in the leg and was able to make his escape. It appeared as if Operation ANTHROPOID had ended in abject failure, with Heydrich recovering in hospital from minor wounds while his SS men scoured Prague for his attackers. Thousands of Czechs were arrested and hundreds were later to be executed. In hiding, Kubis and Gabcik even considered giving themselves up to end the deadly retribution caused by their actions. In the event, they remained at large and eventually took refuge in a church along with several other SOE-trained agents for whom Prague had become too hot. Meanwhile, Heydrich's health suddenly deteriorated. He had contracted blood poisoning from bacteria carried by the horsehair of his car upholstery that had entered his wounds. Although he received the best medical care available, on 4 June he succumbed. Inexorably the Nazis closed in on the assassins and, following a betrayal, the church was besieged by SS troops. The battle raged for hours, until all of the Czechoslovak agents had either been killed in the exchange of fire or taken their suicide pills.

Wireless

SOE began its existence dependent upon SIS for its wireless communications and codes and ciphers. It later gained autonomy, and its workshops produced a range of wireless equipment that was of such quality that SIS frequently selected sets to be used in their own operations. SOE also established its own Special Training Schools, where its wireless operators learnt how to operate a variety of sets, not all of which are listed in the Catalogue.

In addition to its general application in air-to-ground and sea-to-land communications, the S-Phone proved increasingly useful in helping to check on the *bona fides* of SOE agents when it was suspected that they had been captured and were perhaps being forced to operate under duress. In March 1944, F Section was concerned that wireless messages from the ARCHDEACON circuit did not contain the checks arranged before the agents' departure. London sent a message to France stating that a senior officer would fly over in May to discuss the situation, using an S-Phone installed in an aircraft to talk to an agent on the ground. In fact, F Section's suspicions were fully justified, and it transpired that the Germans were running the circuit. To maintain the deception, the Nazis resolved to coerce captured British agents to carry out the dialogue under their direction. The first, Frank Pickersgill, who had been brought back to France from captivity in Germany, soon showed his mettle. He attacked his guards at the Gestapo headquarters in Paris, was shot during the fracas and was returned to prison. A second agent, John Starr, appeared at first to be more

Part of Station VIIA, SOE's wireless factory housed in the former Bontex Knitting Mills, Wembley, Middlesex. (Imperial War Museum, HU 56751)

cooperative, but as the aircraft was approaching the rendezvous he refused to follow instructions and a German officer was obliged to carry out the conversation. Hardly surprisingly, the SOE officer in the aircraft did not fail to recognize the German's accent and the deception was unmasked.[24] A rather more convivial use of the set was achieved by Richard Heslop during a supply drop that featured a conversation with the F Section staff officer Gerry Morel: 'He and I had a great chat, for his was the first English voice I had heard for six months.'[25] Another equally important use to which the S-Phone was put was the establishment of clandestine communication between Helsingør in German-occupied Denmark and Helsingborg in neutral Sweden.[26]

The Miniature Communications Receiver (M.C.R.1) and R.C.D. Receiver Type 31/1 were introduced when resistance forces needed to be issued instructions or informed of the course of the war but two-way communications were not required. The M.C.R.1 set was also known as the 'Biscuit', because it was packed in a metal box of similar dimensions to a Huntley & Palmer biscuit tin. The Jedburgh Set, Model 46/1, was developed for the three-man Jedburgh teams that were parachuted into France at the time of D-Day to help Resistance groups coordinate their activities with the needs of the Allied high command:

> 'At 45 lbs, it was not light by any standard, but it gave Jedburgh teams complete freedom of movement and total independence from external sources of power. Every Jedburgh team that went on operations went equipped with one – as well as a back-up B2 set – and while nobody enjoyed hearing the complaints of those assigned to cranking duties, all could sleep without worrying where the next "sched" could be arranged since, with the Jed-Set, the nearest clearing would do fine.'[27]

The Type A Mark III and Type B Mark II (or 'B2') sets were standard agent sets, though the Catalogue shows the packing for their delivery and not the usual suitcases in which they were camouflaged.

Surrounded by the 21st century's sophisticated communications, it is easy to forget that during the Second World War portable wireless sets required either mains or battery power. In the field a battery would require charging, and the Catalogue offers a selection of equipment – ranging from hand-powered to steam-driven generators – to be used for this purpose.

Geoffrey Barkham, an SOE agent operating on Crete in 1944, adjusts a battery charging machine. (Imperial War Museum, HU 56751)

Small boats

Although the *Sleeping Beauty* appears in the Catalogue as an SOE craft, there are other claims to its development – most notably that of 'Blondie' Hasler, the leader of Operation FRANKTON, the raid carried out by canoeist saboteurs on German shipping in Bordeaux. Another who is reported to have been involved in its development was Sir Malcolm Campbell. A motorized semi-submersible canoe, it was designed to be transported to a point close to its target by a larger vessel, or even dropped by a Lancaster bomber. The craft did not realize its potential and is perhaps most remembered for the role it was to have played in the disastrous Operation RIMAU. Fifteen *Sleeping Beauties* were sent out to Australia, where they were loaded aboard the minelaying submarine HMS *Porpoise* as part of the equipment to be used by a group of SOE saboteurs under the command of Lieutenant-Colonel Ivan Lyon. In contrast to Operation JAYWICK (Lyon's earlier highly successful raid on Singapore harbour), RIMAU was a catastrophe. The saboteurs commandeered a junk, but a firefight alerted the Japanese. The junk and *Sleeping Beauties* were scuttled, and Lyon and his men were either killed or executed after capture.

The *Welman* one-man submarine has received the unflattering description of 'ingenious but of dubious value'.[28] The forerunners of the Special Boat Service (SBS)

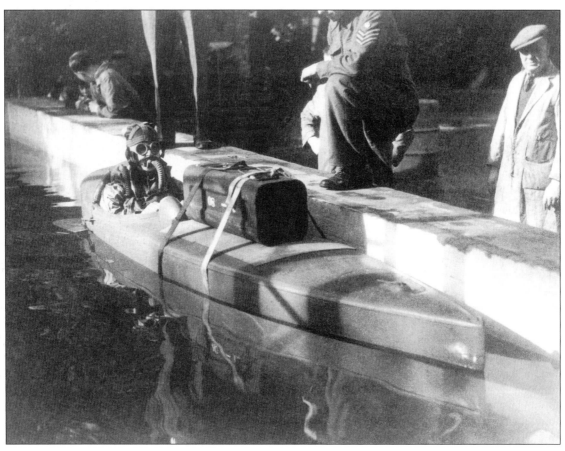

A Sleeping Beauty undergoing tests at Station IX's testing tank. The pilot appears to be wearing SOE's 'Amphibian' dual-purpose breathing apparatus and the parachutist's watersuit. (Imperial War Museum, HU 56775)

SOE staff load a Welman onto a trolley at Station IX. (Imperial War Museum, HU 56768)

flirted with the idea of adopting it, but a Combined Operations report stated:

> 'Eighty-five per cent of trained *Welman* operators conceive a dislike of going down in them. They say there is no way of getting out if anything goes wrong and if the fin drops off under water, no one knows which way up the *Welman* would arrive on the surface . . . the craft roll very badly . . .'[29]

It is believed that 19 hulls were built, but the *Welman* was used operationally only once, on an abortive raid in Norway. This was Operation GUIDANCE, carried out against the floating dock in Bergen in November 1943. The lead craft was spotted and hit by German fire, forcing it to be scuttled. The other three vessels in the attack party made their escape, but the lead craft was eventually raised from the seabed and the seaman made a prisoner of war.[30] It was intended that *Welman* submarines would be deployed in the Far East, and the first arrived in Australia in October 1944. However, it did not see action in that theatre, though training with it was undertaken at Garden Island, near Fremantle.

The *Welfreighter* was the largest of the submersible craft designed by SOE. It was constructed by Shelvoke & Dewry Ltd, a Letchworth-based company which in peacetime had manufactured municipal vehicles. With the exception of the engines, the entire craft was built in Hertfordshire with a maximum production level of one every seven days. 'Its user trial in the Irish Sea', one of SOE's scientists reflected, 'was abandoned when it was clear that it was unseaworthy except in very calm conditions.'[31] Like the *Welman*, the *Welfreighter* enjoyed an undistinguished war record that extended as far as Australia – where one of them 'turned up in Darwin towards the end of the war, too late to be of use.'[32]

Prototype of the Welfreighter undergoing trials at Laleham Reservoir, Staines, Middlesex.
(Imperial War Museum, HU 56786)

By the sixtieth anniversary of the foundation of SOE, most of its surviving files had been released into the Public Record Office; however, the details of Britain's post-war 'special operations' are sketchy and the archives remain closed. It has been reported in several published works that a number of former SOE personnel joined SIS after the Second World War.[33] Given the quality of the weapons and equipment designed and manufactured under SOE's auspices, it would be surprising and perhaps negligent if they had not remained available for government use. In the absence of official accounts, the ubiquitous David Smiley has provided a helpful insight into one aspect of post-war activity in his admission that, in the summer of 1949, he was seconded to SIS 'to run a training establishment for Albanians, who would be infiltrated into Albania'.[34] This attempt to resist the Communist regime was nurtured by several of SOE's old hands, and some three and a half years after the wartime organization's disbandment its ethos and equipment showed few signs of being outdated:

'We used the same B2 set that had been used by SOE in the war, but could not use batteries or charging engines as these would have been too heavy for man-packs. We therefore had to rely on a form of collapsible bicycle frame which a man had to pedal furiously to provide power during transmission. In the event it wasn't much good when used in Albania. Weapon training was carried out with pistols, Sten guns and grenades; minelaying and elementary demolition instruction was also given.'[35]

Notes to Introduction

1 Macrae, *Winston Churchill's Toyshop*, p. 12
2 Public Record Office, HS 7/49
3 Macrae, p. 88
4 Churchill, *The Second World War, Volume II: Their Finest Hour*, p. 148
5 Bruce Lockhart, *Diaries*, p. 366
6 *Handbook of Special Ammunition*
7 Public Record Office, HS 7/48
8 Ibid.
9 Heslop, *Xavier*, pp. 28–9
10 Hamilton Hill, *SOE Assignment*, p. 26
11 Manus, *Underwater Saboteur*, p. 179
12 Smiley, *Irregular Regular*, p. 145
13 Smiley, *Albanian Assignment*, p. 125
14 Goldsmith, *Accidental Agent*, p. 30
15 Smiley, *Albanian Assignment*, p. 126
16 This is the make-up of the second bomb, which was not used, but it is to be assumed that it would have been identical to the bomb used in the attempt itself.
17 Public Record Office, HS 7/49
18 Ibid.
19 Cruickshank, *SOE in Scandinavia*, pp. 18–19
20 Seaman, *Bravest of the Brave*, p. 211 and p. 243
21 Ibid., p. 136
22 Information supplied by Professor D H Everett
23 Peter Wilkinson, a senior SOE staff officer, wrote that another member of the Czechoslovak Section, Alfgar Hesketh Prichard, assisted Clarke in the design of the bomb. Wilkinson, *Foreign Fields*, p. 125
24 Foot, *SOE in France*, p. 333
25 Heslop, *Xavier*, p. 206
26 Cruickshank, *SOE in Scandinavia*, p. 17
27 Brown, *The Jedburghs: A Short History*, p. 8
28 Parker, *SBS*, p. 81
29 Ibid., p. 82
30 Cruickshank, *SOE in Scandinavia*, p. 120–1
31 Information supplied by Professor D H Everett
32 Powell, *War by Stealth*, p. 197
33 West, *Secret War* and Dorril, *MI6*
34 Smiley, *Irregular Regular*, p. 189
35 Ibid., p. 190

Select Bibliography

Brown, Arthur *The Jedburghs: A Short History*, privately printed, n.d.

Bruce Lockhart, Sir Robert *The Diaries of Sir Robert Bruce Lockhart, 1939–1965*, edited by Kenneth Young, Macmillan, London, 1980

Churchill, Winston S *The Second World War, Volume II: Their Finest Hour*, Cassell, London, 1949

Cruickshank, Charles *SOE in Scandinavia*, Oxford University Press, 1986

Dorril, Stephen *MI6*, Fourth Estate, London, 2000

Foot, M R D *SOE in France*, HMSO, London, 1966

Goldsmith, John *Accidental Agent*, Leo Cooper, London, 1971

Hamilton-Hill, Donald *SOE Assignment*, William Kimber, London, 1973

Heslop, Richard *Xavier*, Rupert Hart-Davis, London, 1970

Hoffmann, Peter *The History of the German Resistance 1933–1945*, Macdonald & Jane's, London, 1977

Hutchison, Sir James *That Drug Danger*, Standard Press, Montrose, 1977

Ladd, James *SBS, The Invisible Raiders*, Arms and Armour Press, London, 1983

Ladd, James and Melton, Keith *Clandestine Warfare*, Blandford Press, London, 1988

Lorain, Pierre *Secret Warfare*, Orbis, London, 1984

Macrae, Stuart *Winston Churchill's Toyshop*, The Roundwood Press, Warwick, 1971

Manus, Max *Underwater Saboteur*, William Kimber, London, 1953

Parker, John *SBS*, Headline, London, 1997

Powell, Alan *War by Stealth*, Melbourne University Press, 1996

Seaman, Mark (Introduction) *Operation Foxley: The British Plan to Kill Hitler*, Public Record Office, Kew, 1998

Seaman, Mark *Bravest of the Brave*, Michael O'Mara, London, 1997

Smiley, David *Albanian Assignment*, Sphere Books, London, 1984

Smiley, David *Irregular Regular*, Michael Russell, Norwich, 1994

West, Nigel *Secret War*, Hodder & Stoughton, London, 1992

Wilkinson, Peter *In Foreign Fields*, I B Tauris, London, 1997

●

Descriptive Catalogue

OF

Special Devices

AND

Supplies

●

COMPILED & ISSUED

BY

M.O.1. (S.P.)

THE WAR OFFICE.

1944.

INTRODUCTION

•

1. This Illustrated Catalogue contains descriptions of various stores produced by, or for, M.O.1. (S.P.). War Office. More detailed information in regard to the items set out in this Catalogue, can be obtained, if required, from M.O.1. (S.P.), War Office, or from our representatives in the theatre in which the information is required.

2. The illustrations are intended for identification purposes only.

3. This Catalogue has been prepared in loose leaf form to facilitate the insertion of new matter or amendments.

4. This Catalogue supersedes the Catalogue of Supplies, September, 1943.

Section I
INCENDIARY STORES

FLARES, GROUND, 15 MIN.

Catalogue No. C 206.

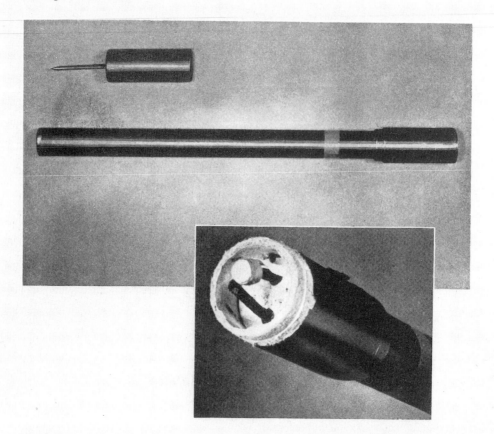

DESCRIPTION. The Flares are cylindrical in shape and painted black. They are available in three colours—red, white and green, which is shown by the band of tape round the Flare. They are supplied with a socket holder fitted with a spike which can be stuck in the ground. The Flare is provided with two Bickford Fuzes in the igniter head, one of which is fitted with a match head for direct ignition with striker board. The Flares have an average burning time of 15 mins.

METHOD OF USE.

1. Place in socket and stick into the ground.
2. Remove the top plate and metal lid.
3. Remove cardboard disc coated with striker composition.
4. For direct ignition, rub striker disc on match-headed Bickford Fuze.
5. To ignite with Time Pencils (Switch No. 10), cut clean ends on the two Bickford Fuzes and attach with adhesive tape.

DIMENSIONS. Length 27″ approx.
Length in holder, including spike 33″ approx.
Diameter 2″

WEIGHT. 2¾ lbs.

SHIPPING CLASSIFICATION.
Generic Title - - Flares, Ground.
Explosive Group - IX.
Storage and Stowage IV. A.S.P.

PACKING AND SPECIAL NOTES.
Red, Green or White Flares can be supplied. 12 in tin lined case.

PACKAGE DIMENSIONS. 31″ x 15″ x 10″

WEIGHT PACKED. 77 lbs.

34

INCENDIARIES, POCKET, TIME, MK. II. B
(P.R. 5's)

Catalogue No. C 2.

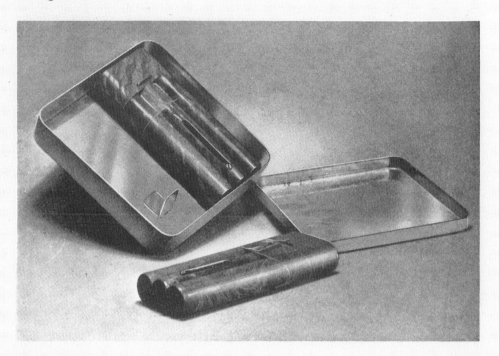

DESCRIPTION. This is the smallest device, incorporating its own delay, which is issued.

The case is divided into three cylindrical compartments, the centre one containing the Delay Mechanism similar to that of the Pencil Time Fuze (Switch No. 10) and two outer compartments containing incendiary composition.

The Incendiary is supplied with delays of $\frac{1}{4}$ hr., $\frac{1}{2}$ hr., 2 hrs., 6 hrs., 12 hrs., and 24 hrs. It burns with a hot flame for one minute and has a flare-like action.

METHOD OF USE.

1. Remove the cellophane.

2. Shake out wooden safety splint (N.B.—If it does not come out easily, never prise it out, but reject that incendiary).

3. Insert a coin in the slot and press down on the Copper Tube until the Ampoule, which is inside the Copper Tube, is crushed.

DIMENSIONS. $4\frac{1}{2}$" x $1\frac{3}{4}$" x $\frac{5}{8}$" **WEIGHT.** $3\frac{1}{2}$ ozs.

SHIPPING CLASSIFICATION.

Generic Title	- -	Bombs, Incendiary, D.A.P.
Explosive Group	-	XI.
Storage and Stowage	-	IV. O.A.S.

PACKING AND SPECIAL NOTES.

	DIMENSIONS.	WEIGHT.
2 Incendiaries are carried in one tin box, which is hermetically sealed in a transparent waterproof plastic envelope.	$4\frac{1}{16}$" x $5\frac{3}{16}$" x $\frac{7}{8}$".	$10\frac{1}{2}$ ozs.
100 Tins are packed in a commercial case (200 Incendiaries per case).	26" x 12" x 12".	84 lbs.

INCENDIARIES, 1¾ LB. MK. II
(FIREPOT)

Catalogue No. C 179.

DESCRIPTION. The Firepot consists of a short cylindrical case of magnesium primed with thermite and gunpowder. This priming is ignited from two quickmatch tails leading down from a small millboard container of S.R.252. This can be ignited either by Bickford Leads or by a match composition button. The Bickford has a delay of ten seconds followed by vigorous burning with showers of sparks lasting eight seconds, followed by slow burning of the magnesium case for ten to fifteen minutes.

METHOD OF USE. To prepare the bomb for use remove the tape which holds the lid in place and lift off the lid. In the centre of the bomb is a match head and two short lengths of safety fuze. For immediate use remove the striker board from the under side of the bomb by pulling off the tape and strike across the match head. The ends of the safety fuze are sealed and must be cut off before use.

DIMENSIONS. Height 2¼". Diameter 3¾".   **WEIGHT.** 1¾ lbs.

SHIPPING CLASSIFICATION.

Generic Title - -	Bombs, Incendiary, 1¾ lbs.	
Explosive Group -	XI.	
Storage and Stowage	IV. O.A.S.	

PACKING AND SPECIAL NOTES.

	DIMENSIONS.	**WEIGHT.**
36 per C. 207 Container.	18" x 13" x 11"	96 lbs.
18 per New Pack in Box H. 31 Mk. I E. have hermetically sealed tin liner.	20.5" x 9" x 10"	46 lbs.

INCENDIARY BLOCK, MK. I

Catalogue No. C 243a.

DESCRIPTION. The device consists of a nitrate and a wax block which are enclosed in a cellulose acetate case, making the whole completely waterproof. The Bickford Fuzes at one end of the Block are protected by a thin window and a tear-off strip. The nitrate face of the case is plain and the wax side has a raised longitudinal rib for identification purposes.

METHOD OF USE. The Block can be ignited either by striking the Copper Tube Igniters on a Striker Board, or by means of Time Pencils (Switch No. 10) attached to the Bickford Leads. The nitrate side of the Block must be placed in contact with the target.

DIMENSIONS. 5¼" x 2½" x 1¼"   **WEIGHT.** 12 ozs.

SHIPPING CLASSIFICATION.
Generic Title	Bomb Incendiary Cast Block.	
Explosive Group	XI.	
Storage and Stowage	IV.	O.A.S.

PACKING AND SPECIAL NOTES.
36 Incendiary Blocks and 36 Striker Boards packed in tin lined service case H.13 Mk. IV.E.

PACKAGE DIMENSIONS. 16" x 11" x 8".   **WEIGHT PACKED.** 40 lbs.

INCENDIARIES, THERMIT, 2½ LBS.
(THERMIT BOMBS)

Catalogue No. C 201.

DESCRIPTION.   The Bomb consists of a metal container filled with thermite, and is provided with two short lengths of Bickford Fuze fitted with Copper Tube Igniters. The Bomb can be ignited directly by means of a match striker surface, or by means of a delay device attached to the Bickford, e.g., the Pencil Time Fuze (Switch No. 10), after removal of the Copper Tube Igniters.

METHOD OF USE.   The Bomb is packed in a watertight tin with a screw-vac lid, the lid must be unscrewed to expose the Bickford Leads.

For particular work, the Bomb is most effective when placed vertically in position.

DIMENSIONS. Height 5″. Diameter 3″.   **WEIGHT.** 2½ lbs.

SHIPPING CLASSIFICATION. Generic Title - - Bombs, Incendiary, Thermit.
                                      Explosive Group - XI.
                                       Storage and Stowage IV.   O.A.S.

PACKING AND SPECIAL NOTES.
    36 Incendiaries are packed in Box C.179.

PACKAGE DIMENSIONS. 26″ x 13″ x 11″   **WEIGHT PACKED.** 116 lbs.

Section II
PREPARED CHARGES AND ANCILLARIES

HOLDFASTS, MAGNETIC

Catalogue No. K 177.

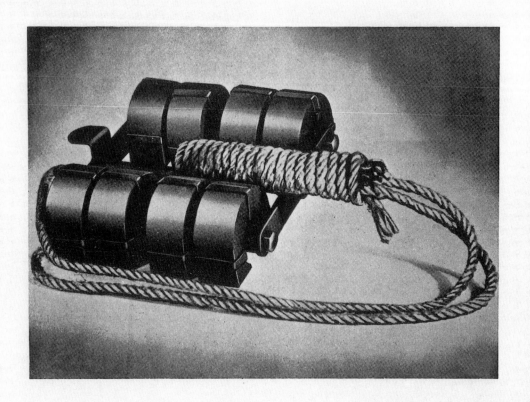

DESCRIPTION.   A brass frame, approximately 8½" x 5", each side fitted with four magnets. A cordage handle is attached to the centre of the frame.

METHOD OF USE.   In placing in position, to avoid noise, apply one edge first and ease over until all the Magnets are flat against the ship's side.

To release, tip over on one edge and pull free.

DIMENSIONS. Single - Length 9½". Width 6⅝". Depth 1¾".   **WEIGHT.** 7½ lbs.

PACKING AND SPECIAL NOTES.
In pairs on carrier. Stow away from Compasses.

PACKAGE DIMEMSIONS. 9½" x 8" x 3½"   **WEIGHT PACKED.** 17 lbs.

40

FUZE, ANTI-DISTURBANCE
(WATER-ARMED) MK. I. L

Catalogue No. B 230.

DESCRIPTION. This device is operated by the removal of a charge which has been set underwater. A delay action is fitted for the safety of the operator, consisting of a soluble pellet, and the fuze does not become alive until water has dissolved the pellet.

METHOD OF USE. An instance of its use is when it is embodied in a Limpet. The trigger in the base of the fuze rests upon the ship's side, and upon raising the fuze, the trigger is operated, and the charge is detonated. The anti-removal fuze is screwed into the threaded port of the under side of the Limpet. It will arm itself after approximately ten minutes and detonate the mine if it is subsequently moved away from the target.

DIMENSIONS. Length $2\frac{1}{2}''$
Diameter of Head $1\frac{7}{8}''$
Diameter of Base $1\frac{3}{16}''$

WEIGHT. $9\frac{5}{8}$ ozs.

SHIPPING CLASSIFICATION. Generic Title · · Fuzes with Bursters.
Explosive Group · VI.
Storage and Stowage III. O.A.S.

GRENADES, G.P.

Catalogue No. D 208.

DESCRIPTION. The Charge is fitted at one end with a threaded socket to take a No. 247 Fuze. The charge is enclosed in a metal case down the centre of which lies a copper tube sealed at one end with a wooden plug. To the plug is attached a spring and when the detonator is inserted into the open end of the metal sleeve this spring prevents the detonator from falling out and maintains it in the correct position in relation to the primers inside the charge.

METHOD OF USE.

(a) As a detonator charge the amount of explosive is sufficient to cut $\frac{3}{4}''$ M.S. plate. It can also be used to cut a railway line, by strapping two grenades, one metre apart, on to the web of the rail.

(b) For demolition purposes, its shape enables a number of charges to be built up into a large charge. The centre charge and the one furthest from the target should be initiated.

(c) As a grenade this charge is effective against unarmoured vehicles and as an anti-personnel grenade.

DIMENSIONS. $4\frac{3}{8}'' \times 1\frac{7}{8}'' \times 2\frac{1}{4}''$

WEIGHT. 1 lb.

SHIPPING CLASSIFICATION. Generic Title · · Grenades, Filled H.E.
Explosive Group · VII.
Storage and Stowage II. O.A.S.

PACKING AND SPECIAL NOTES.
50 Grenades per box each containing in addition five Fuzes No. 247 in metal cylinder and five No. 27 or No. 8 Detonators in Magazine Mk. II.

PACKAGE DIMENSIONS. $22'' \times 17'' \times 8''$

WEIGHT PACKED. 71 lbs.

FUZE, ANTI-DISTURBANCE
(WATER-ARMED) MK. I. L

GRENADES, G.P.

LIMPETS, RIGID, TYPE 6, MKS. I, IA, II

Catalogue No. D 101.

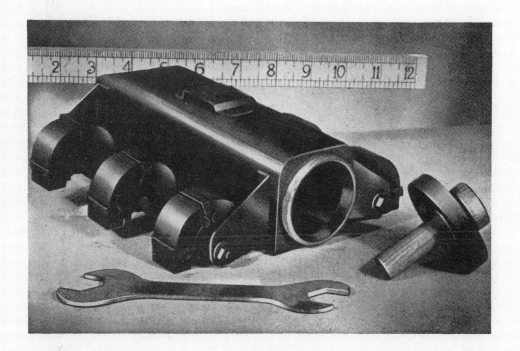

DESCRIPTION. The device consists of a rectangular brass container, lying across the centre of a frame, which supports the mountings of six Magnets. These Magnets are arranged in two rows, one at each side of the brass container, and each is mounted on a rubber bush to give it a little flexibility. One end of the container has a circular opening with a screw cap. Each end has a port, threaded to take an A.C. Delay Action Fuze.

The Mark I.A. Limpet is similar in all respects to the Mark I. except that it has a rubber washer under the filling cap.

The Mark II. Limpet is the Mark I.A. modified to take the Fuze, Anti-Disturbance (Water-Armed), Mark I.L.

METHOD OF USE. Remove the Rectifiers, assemble two A.C. Delay Action Fuzes and Bursters, and screw one assembly into each port. Fire the A.C. Delay Action Fuzes in the normal way.

DIMENSIONS. $9\frac{1}{2}''$ x $2\frac{3}{4}''$ x $1\frac{1}{2}''$ **WEIGHT.** Empty $7\frac{1}{2}$ lbs. Full 10 lbs.

SHIPPING CLASSIFICATION. Generic Title - - When filled—Charges, Demolition, Limpet "R"

Explosive Group - VII.

Storage and Stowage - III. (To be stowed away from Compasses).

PACKING AND SPECIAL NOTES.
Per pair on Carrier.

PACKAGE DIMENSIONS. $9\frac{1}{2}''$ x $5\frac{1}{2}''$ x 9'   **WEIGHT PACKED.** Empty $15\frac{1}{2}$ lbs. Full 20 lbs.

RODS, COLLAPSIBLE, PLACING, LIMPET
(PLACING RODS)

Catalogue No. D 198.

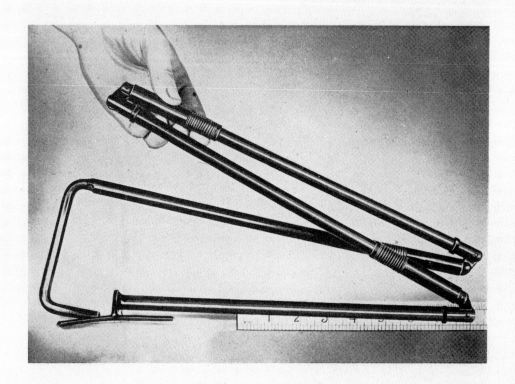

DESCRIPTION. This device consists of a rod which folds into four sections and is provided with a hooked handle at one end and a two-way bracket at the other; this bracket fits into a slot provided on the Limpet body.

METHOD OF USE. To open—pull the rod out into the extended position when it will automatically lock.

To fold—press the locking tube of each joint towards the handle of the rod when the link joint will be exposed and each of the four sections folded.

DIMENSIONS. Width 4¾". Length 15½" folded.   **WEIGHT.** 2 lbs.

PACKING AND SPECIAL NOTES.
   As required.

STANDARD CHARGE, 1½ LB.

Catalogue No. D 244.

DESCRIPTION. Contains 1½ pounds of P.E. and is provided with a central tubular primer of C.E. Pellets' in a cardboard tube, and is wrapped in rubberised fabric.

It may be cut into two or more lengths each of which will form a separate charge complete in itself.

METHOD OF USE. The charge may be initiated by inserting a detonator directly into the end of the tubular primer or a length of Cordtex may be threaded through the primer and the charge detonated by taping a detonator to the Cordtex.

DIMENSIONS. 6¼" x 2¼" x 1⅞".   **WEIGHT.** 1½ lbs.

SHIPPING CLASSIFICATION.
Generic Title - - Charges, Demolition.
Explosive Group - VII.
Storage and Stowage - III. O.A.S

PACKING AND SPECIAL NOTES.
P. 59 Cases. 25 in a Case.

PACKAGE DIMENSIONS. 19" x 8" x 8".   **WEIGHT PACKED.** 50 lbs.

Section III
INITIATING, DELAY ACTION AND BOOBY TRAP MECHANISMS

BURSTERS, DETONATOR, TYPE 6, MK. I & II

(TYPE 6 BURSTERS)

Catalogue No. E 207.

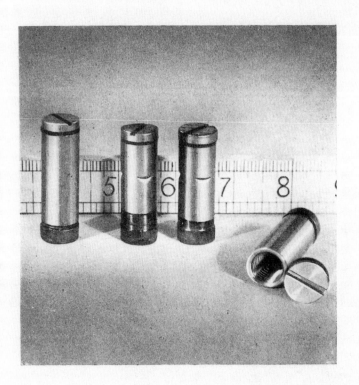

DESCRIPTION.   This Burster is designed to be waterproof, both in storage and when screwed on a Delay. It is more robust and more powerful than the 28A and should initiate all the explosives normally used for filling Limpets. It is normally issued in the same box as an A.C. Delay. The only external difference between the Mark I and Mark II Bursters is that the Mark I has three crimping marks in the middle of the body.

METHOD OF USE.   The waterproofing transit plug must first be removed by unscrewing it with the aid of a coin. The joint between the Burster and the Mark I A.C. Delay can be waterproofed with luting. Care must be taken if luting is used that none gets into the Burster on top of the Detonator or into the striker channel of the Delay, as this may hold up the striker and cause a failure.

In the case of a Mark IA A.C. Delay and a Mark II Burster used together, luting must NOT be used, as a rubber washer is provided for sealing purposes.

DIMENSIONS. ⅝" diam. x 2" long.   **WEIGHT.** 1¼ ozs.

SHIPPING CLASSIFICATION.
Generic Title	-	-	Detonator, Burster.
Explosive Group	-	-	X.
Storage and Stowage	-	III.	M.S.D.

PACKING AND SPECIAL NOTES.
Not packed separately. Two included in each mission pack and one in each air pack.

BOARDS, STRIKER

Catalogue No. F 48.

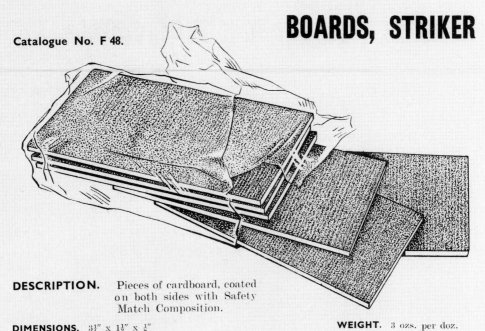

DESCRIPTION. Pieces of cardboard, coated on both sides with Safety Match Composition.

DIMENSIONS. $3\frac{1}{4}''$ x $1\frac{1}{2}''$ x $\frac{1}{8}''$ **WEIGHT.** 3 ozs. per doz.

PACKING AND SPECIAL NOTES.
6 Striker Boards wrapped in cellophane.
144 Striker Boards packed in hermetically sealed tin with tear-off strip.

PACKAGE DIMENSIONS. Tin - 5″ x 3″ x 4″   **WEIGHT PACKED.** 1.6 lbs. approx.

MATCHES, FUZEE, NON-FLAMING
(FUZEE, MATCHES)

Catalogue No. F 29.

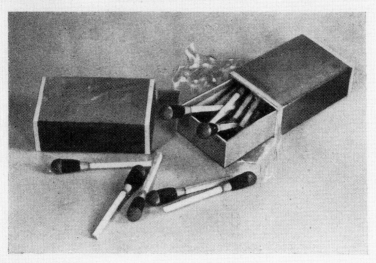

DESCRIPTION. They are slow-burning, non-flaming safety matches.

METHOD OF USE. They can be used with an ordinary match-box or with a striker board.

DIMENSIONS. $2\frac{1}{4}''$ x $1\frac{7}{16}''$ x $\frac{3}{4}''$.   **WEIGHT.** $\frac{3}{4}$ oz.

SHIPPING CLASSIFICATION.
Generic Title - - Fuzees, Safety.
Label - - - E.
Storage and Stowage - Dangerous Goods.

PACKING AND SPECIAL NOTES.
Each matchbox containing 20 Fuzees is wrapped in cellophane.
100 Boxes are packed and hermetically sealed in each of the two tin liners of Case H.30, Mk. IE. which therefore holds 200 boxes in all.

PACKAGE DIMENSIONS. Case H.30, Mk. IE. 16″ x $10\frac{1}{4}''$ x $8\frac{1}{2}''$ **WEIGHT PACKED.** 20 lbs. approx.

CABLE, ELECTRIC, DURATWINFLEX

Catalogue No. F 158b.

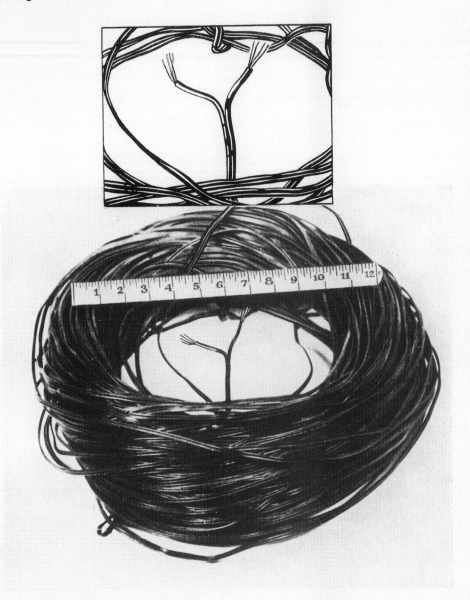

DESCRIPTION.   The insulating medium of Duratwinflex is resistant to petrol and oil, as well as water.

Resistance is 4·72 ohms per 100 yards double.

Gauge 4/26.

WEIGHT. 5.42 lbs. per 100 yds.

PACKING AND SPECIAL NOTES.
As required.

CAPS, PERCUSSION WITH HOLDERS AND SPRING SNOUTS
(CAPS, SPRING SNOUT)

Catalogue No. F 204.

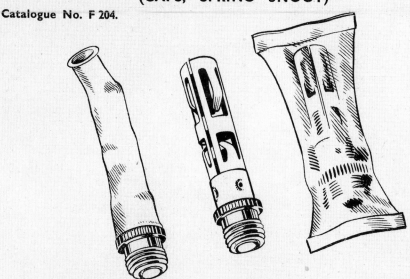

DESCRIPTION. The device consists of a brass adaptor with a percussion cap securely held in one end. A Spring Snout is attached to the other end of the adaptor by means of a crimping ring. Either a No. 8 Detonator or a length of Fuze, Bickford or Instantaneous, can be inserted into the Spring Snout.

METHOD OF USE. A length of Fuze or a No. 8 Detonator is fitted into the Spring Snout. The adaptor is then screwed into the switch.

DIMENSIONS. $1\frac{3}{8}''$ long.   **WEIGHT.** 2 ozs. approx.

SHIPPING CLASSIFICATION.
Generic Title - - Caps, Percussion with Spring Snouts.
Explosive Group - VI.
Storage and Stowage I. · O.A.S.

PACKING AND SPECIAL NOTES.
Each article is sealed in a waterproof sheath.
70 articles so covered are packed in a tin box with taped lid.

PACKAGE DIMENSIONS. $3\frac{5}{8}'' \times 4'' \times 2''$ **WEIGHT PACKED.** 1 lb. 5 ozs.

SWITCH NO. 4 (TYPE 6 PULL SWITCH)
Catalogue No. B 105.

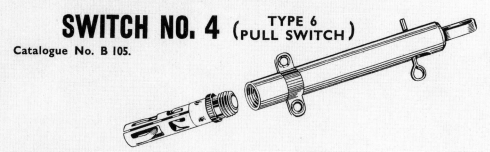

DESCRIPTION. This is a simple mechanism having a Spring Snout at one end to receive the Safety Fuze and at the other end a metal loop which can be pulled. A safety pin prevents the striker inside the device from coming down on to the cap in the base.

METHOD OF USE. To operate the igniter remove the safety pin and pull on the loop. A pull of more than 6 lbs. will operate the device.

DIMENSIONS. $3\frac{7}{8}''$ long x $\frac{7}{16}''$ x $\frac{1}{2}''$ diam.   **WEIGHT.** $1\frac{1}{4}$ ozs.

SHIPPING CLASSIFICATION.
Generic Title - - Igniters, Mechanism, Pull.
Explosive Group - VI.
Storage and Stowage I. O.A.S.

PACKING AND SPECIAL NOTES.

	DIMENSIONS.	WEIGHT.
2 Switches per carton - - -	$3\frac{3}{4}'' \times 2'' \times \frac{5}{8}''$	3 ozs.
5 Cartons per tin - - -	$3\frac{13}{16}'' \times 3\frac{9}{16}'' \times 2\frac{1}{16}''$	$1\frac{3}{4}$ lbs.
20 Tins per case - - -	$20'' \times 9\frac{1}{2}'' \times 5\frac{3}{4}''$	33 lbs.

FUZES, DELAY ACTION, A.C., MK. 1A (A.C. DELAYS)

Catalogue No. A 100.

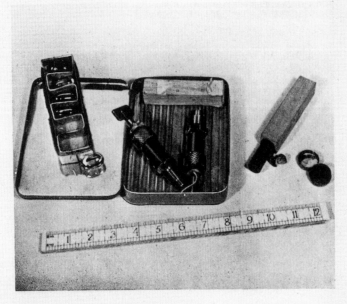

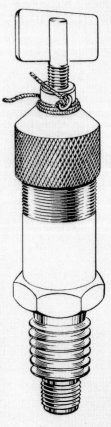

DESCRIPTION.

This Delay has a small cylindrical body, on one end of which is a thumb screw, and on the other are threads by which a Type 6 Burster may be fitted to the Delay, and the Delay as a whole fitted to a Type 6 Limpet. The body contains an ampoule filled with a liquid which dissolves celluloid, and a spring loaded striker mechanism; the striker being retained by a celluloid washer. Six timings between 4½ hours and 5½ days are available and are indicated by the colour of the liquid in the ampoule. When the thumb screw is fully home the ampoule is broken and the liquid will soften the celluloid until the washer no longer retains the striker, which fires the burster.

METHOD OF USE.

(1) Unscrew the tail half of the body and insert an ampoule of the correct timing. Replace the tail.

(2) Screw the Fuze into the previously prepared Limpet port.

(3) Remove the safety pin and crush the ampoule by screwing up the thumb screw of the fuze to its full extent.

DIMENSIONS. 4¾" long x 1" diameter.   **WEIGHT.** 6¼ ozs.

SHIPPING CLASSIFICATION.
Generic Title - - - Detonator, Burster, A.C.
Explosive Group - X.
Label - - - B.
Storage and Stowage III. M.S.D.

PACKING AND SPECIAL NOTES.

	DIMENSIONS.	WEIGHT.
OPERATIONAL. One Fuze (each containing a red ampoule) per tin complete with carton of five ampoules and one Burster in wooden holder.	5⅜" x 3¾" x 1⁵⁄₁₆"	1¼ lbs.
SHIPPING AND STORAGE. Two Fuzes and two Bursters per tin without ampoules, 250 Fuzes per case.	37" x 18" x 12"	216 lbs.

TIMINGS. A full table giving delays at various temperatures is given in the tin. The timings given below are for 15°C.

Red, 4½ hrs.   Orange, 7½ hrs.   Yellow, 15 hrs.
Green, 26 hrs.   Blue, 42 hrs.   Violet, 5½ days.

IGNITERS, SAFETY FUZE, COPPER TUBE
(COPPER TUBE IGNITERS)

Catalogue No. F 49.

DESCRIPTION. A small copper tube, closed at one end with safety match composition.

METHOD OF USE. It can be carried ready crimped on to the desired length of fuze, and is ignited by striking the composition on a safety match box or striker board.

DIMENSIONS. Length ⅝" x ¼" Diameter. **WEIGHT.** 3 ozs. 25 wrapped.

SHIPPING CLASSIFICATION.
Generic Title	-	Igniters, Fuze.
Explosive Group	-	VI.
Storage and Stowage	-	I. O.A.S.

PACKING AND SPECIAL NOTES.

	DIMENSIONS.	WEIGHT.
25 Igniters per tin.	2½" x ¾"	1½ ozs.

New packing for a small per cent.

10 Igniters in Detonator Magazine Mark II	1" x 2⅛"	1 oz.
200 or more Magazines in Case, Wood, Packing or as required.		

IGNITERS, FUZE, FOG SIGNAL, MK. 1A
IGNITERS, FUZE, FOG SIGNAL, MK. 1A DUMMY

Catalogue No. B 8.   B 8d.   (FOG SIGNALS)

DESCRIPTION. The Igniter is mounted on a spring clip so that it can quickly be slipped on the line, where it is held firmly in position. A spring adaptor projects from one side, into which a detonator can be pushed.

Inside the Igniter there are three percussion caps. When pressure is applied to the top, these caps are fired and ignite a wad of quick match, the flash from which initiates the detonator.

METHOD OF USE. The Igniters should be used in pairs, each about one metre away from the explosive charges, with the spring adaptors pointing outwards from the track. Push the open end of a detonator into each spring adaptor.

N.B. If the spring adaptors lie on the inside of the rail, they will be cut off by the flange of the locomotive wheel and the charge will be rendered useless.

(For Dimensions, etc., see foot of next page).

IGNITERS, FUZE, FOG SIGNAL, MK. IA
IGNITERS, FUZE, FOG SIGNAL, MK. IA
DUMMY

Catalogue No. B 8. B 8d.   (FOG SIGNALS)

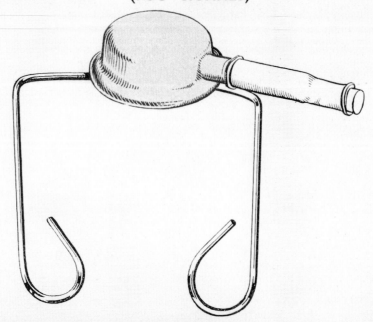

DIMENSIONS. 4″ x 3½″ x $\frac{9}{16}$″ including clip which folds flat.   **WEIGHT.** 1½ ozs.

SHIPPING CLASSIFICATION. (Refers to B.8. only).

Generic Title -	Igniters, Fuze, Fog Signal.
Explosive Group -	VI.
Storage and Stowage -	O.A.S.(C)

PACKING AND SPECIAL NOTES.

	DIMENSIONS.	WEIGHT.
4 Igniters in 1 vacuum tin.	4⅝″ x 3⅞″ x 1½″	9½ ozs.
588 Igniters (147) tins per case.	31″ x 18″ x 14″	112 lbs.

SWITCH NO. 5
(TYPE 6 PRESSURE SWITCH)

Catalogue No. B 106.

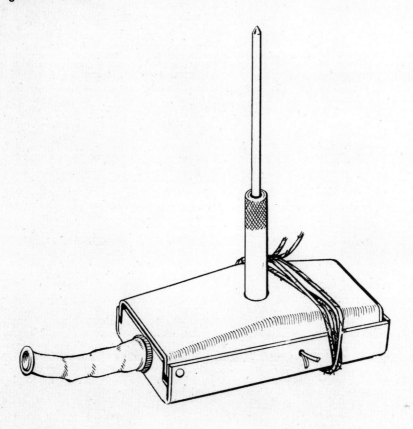

DESCRIPTION. This store is a flat oblong mechanism with an adjustable Extension Rod screwed into the top of the lid. When pressure of 50 lbs. or more is applied to the rod or the top of the box, a Trip mechanism releases a striker which in turn detonates a percussion cap which is screwed into the end of the box. A very small movement operates the switch.

METHOD OF USE. When used on a railway, the body of the switch is set up on the ballast, with which it is afterwards covered, the extension rod being adjusted under the rail. Depression of the rail, when a train passes, operates the switch. It is not so positive in operation as the Fog Signal and should therefore only be used if absolutely necessary. Before concealing the switch do not forget to remove the Safety Pin.

DIMENSIONS. $3\frac{7}{8}''$ long x $1\frac{5}{8}''$ x $\frac{3}{4}''$ diam.   **WEIGHT.** $5\frac{1}{2}$ ozs.
   (with extension socket removed 2" across safety pin)

SHIPPING CLASSIFICATION.   Generic Title   -   -   Igniters, Mechanism, Pull.
                               Explosive Group   -   VI.
                               Storage and Stowage   I.   O.A.S.

PACKING AND SPECIAL NOTES.   **DIMENSIONS.**   **WEIGHT.**

				DIMENSIONS.	WEIGHT.
2 Switches per carton	-	-	-	$3\frac{7}{8}''$ x $3\frac{3}{8}''$ x 1"	12 ozs.
5 Cartons per tin	-	-	-	$5\frac{1}{4}''$ x $4\frac{1}{16}''$ x $3\frac{5}{8}''$	4 lbs.
20 Tins per case	-	-	-	$22\frac{1}{2}''$ x $11\frac{1}{2}''$ x $8\frac{1}{4}''$	84 lbs.

SWITCH NO. 6.
(TYPE 6 RELEASE SWITCH)

Catalogue No. B 107.

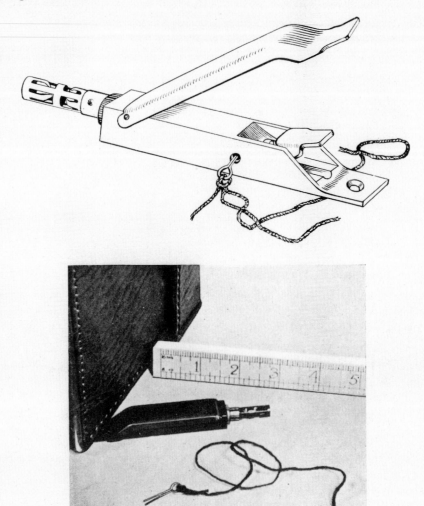

DESCRIPTION. This device is a small rectangular box with hinged lid, the other end of which forms a flat tail. As long as this tail is held down the switch is safe. When released the hinged cover rises and the switch fires.

METHOD OF USE. The weight placed on the tail should exceed 5 lbs. as if it is insufficient the safety pin will not come out easily. Do not forget to remove the Safety Pin. Place the Switch underneath anything which is likely to be lifted up by the enemy.

DIMENSIONS. $4\frac{1}{2}''$ x $\frac{5}{8}''$ x $\frac{7}{16}''$ diam.   **WEIGHT.** 3 ozs.
(1″ across safety pin)

SHIPPING CLASSIFICATION.

Generic Title - -	Igniters, Mechanism, Release.	
Explosive Group -	VI.	
Storage and Stowage	I. O.A.S.	

PACKING AND SPECIAL NOTES.

		DIMENSIONS.	WEIGHT.
2 Switches per carton	- -	$3\frac{3}{4}''$ x $2\frac{3}{8}''$ x $\frac{7}{8}''$	6 ozs.
5 Cartons per tin -	- -	$4\frac{5}{16}''$ x $3\frac{1}{16}''$ x $2\frac{7}{16}''$	$2\frac{1}{2}$ lbs.
10 Tins per case -	- -	$22''$ x $10\frac{1}{2}''$ x $6\frac{1}{4}''$	60 lbs.

SWITCH NO. 10
(TIME PENCILS)

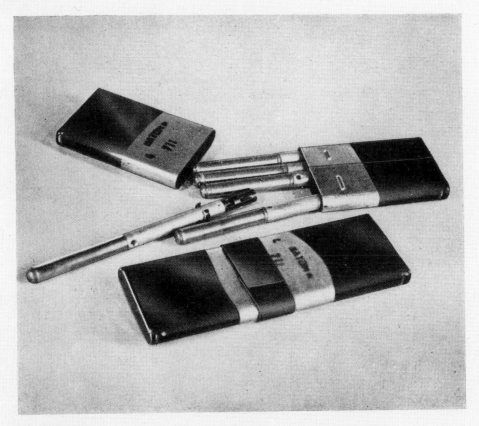

DESCRIPTION. This is a delay action fuze shaped liked a pencil. One end consists of a copper tube, the other end is a spring snout which will take a No. 8 Detonator or a length of Bickford. Timings vary between 10 minutes and 24 hours and are indicated by colours shown on the safety strip of the switch. The copper tube can be crushed by hand and this breaks a glass ampoule inside containing a corrosive liquid. This liquid attacks a steel wire restraining a spring loaded striker. When the corrosion is complete the striker is released to fire a cap which ignites a safety fuze or detonator.

METHOD OF USE.

(1) Insert the detonator or safety fuze in the spring snout.

(2) Crush the ampoule containing the liquid, by squeezing the copper tube.

(3) Shake the pencil to ensure that the liquid is in good contact with the steel wire.

(4) Remove the safety strip.

DIMENSIONS. 5¼" long x ⅜" diameter.   **WEIGHT.** 0.65 ozs.

SHIPPING CLASSIFICATION.
Generic Title - - Igniter, Fuze.
Explosive Group - - VI.
Storage and Stowage - I. O.A.S.

PACKING AND SPECIAL NOTES.	**DIMENSIONS.**	**WEIGHT.**
5 Switches per tin	5 5⁄16″ x 1 7⁄8″ x 7⁄16″	5 ozs.
150 Tins per case	16¼″ x 13″ x 7¾″	62 lbs.

TIMINGS. The period of delay for the switch is indicated by the colour of the Safety Strip. The timings given below are for 15°C. but at higher temperatures the delays are considerably shortened.

Black, 10 mins.   Red, ½ hr.   White, 2 hrs.
Green, 5½ hrs.   Yellow, 12 hrs.   Blue, 24 hrs.

57

TYREBURSTER

DESCRIPTION.   It consists of an outer case of thin tinned steel in two overlapping and loosely fitted halves, containing a ring of H.E., in the centre of which is a special pressure switch. A minimum load of 150 lbs. on the case causes the two halves to telescope and the mechanism to operate and set off the charge.

METHOD OF USE.   The Tyreburster is placed on the road or in ground where vehicles are likely to move. On soft ground a stone or other hard body should be placed under the Tyreburster. If this is not done the device may be pushed into the ground by the vehicle without exploding.

DIMENSIONS. Diam. 5 cms. Thickness 2 cms.   **WEIGHT.** 4 ozs.

SHIPPING CLASSIFICATION. Generic Title   -   Destructors Contact.

　　　　　　　　　　　　　　　　　Explosive Group   -   VI.

　　　　　　　　　　　　　　　　　Storage and Stowage   O.A.S.

PACKING AND SPECIAL NOTES.

　　Camouflaged and packed as required.

　　Camouflaged Bursters representing a wide variety of rocks are already in production.

WIRE TRAP, ·014"

DESCRIPTION. ·014" diameter black, tempered steel wire which is almost invisible and, provided that it has not been kinked, will stand a steady pull of 30 lbs. It is wound on wooden spools in 50 yd. lengths.

DIMENSIONS. 50 yds. spool. $2\frac{5}{8}$" diam. x $\frac{1}{2}$" thick.   **WEIGHT.** $2\frac{1}{4}$ ozs.

PACKING AND SPECIAL NOTES.

800 spools per case.

It has been estimated that a number of reels have only 30 to 40 yds. instead of the specified 50 yds.

PACKAGE DIMENSIONS. 30" x 22" x 13"   **WEIGHT PACKED.** 164 lbs.

WIRE TRIP, ·032"

Catalogue No. B 36.

DESCRIPTION. ·032" diameter black, tempered steel wire which is almost invisible and provided, that it has not been kinked, will stand a steady pull of 150 lbs. It is wound on wooden spools in 25 yd. lengths.

METHOD OF USE.

(1) As a Trip Wire. Stretch the wire across the site, choosing a place where it will be hidden by grass etc., and fix to a firm support at either end, about 4" above the ground.

(2) In place of Booby Trap Wire.

DIMENSIONS. 25 yds. spool. $3\frac{1}{2}$" diam. x $\frac{1}{2}$" thick.   **WEIGHT.** $4\frac{3}{4}$ ozs.

PACKING AND SPECIAL NOTES.

400 spools per case.

It is worth noting that a large proportion of the reels have less than the specified lengths—in some cases the reels have only 20 to 22 yds.

PACKAGE DIMENSIONS. 30" x 22" x 13"   **WEIGHT PACKED.** 160 lbs.

Section IV
TOOLS AND ANCILLARY EQUIPMENT

CUTTERS, WIRE, TYPE 6

Catalogue No. G 165.

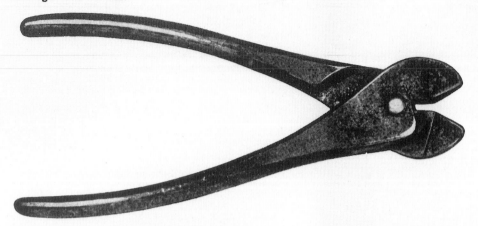

DESCRIPTION. This Wire Cutter is capable of cutting Dannert wire when used with one hand. The Jaws are flared out, so that they may be easily engaged in the dark. There is a hole at the end of one handle, for the attachment of a Lanyard.

METHOD OF USE. Pull the Wire as far into the Jaws of the cutter as possible, and clip sharply, gripping as near to the ends of the handles as possible in order to get the maximum leverage.

N.B.—A sharp action will cut the wire much more easily than steady pressure.

DIMENSIONS. $8\frac{1}{2}'' \times 1\frac{3}{4}'' \times \frac{3}{4}''$ **WEIGHT.** 1 lb.

PACKING AND SPECIAL NOTES.
    As required.
    Can be supplied with insulated handles as a special order.

FROGS, CUTTERS, WIRE, TYPE 6

Catalogue No. G 166.

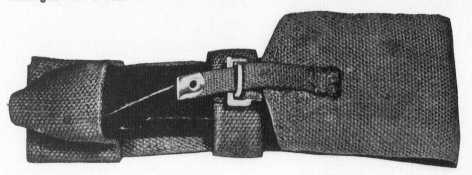

DESCRIPTION. The Frog is made of khaki webbing, and has a quick-opening type of fastening and a loop at the back for wearing on the belt.

DIMENSIONS. $9\frac{1}{2}'' \times 3'' \times 1\frac{1}{4}''$.   **WEIGHT.** $3\frac{1}{2}$ ozs.

PACKING AND SPECIAL NOTES.
    As required.

KNIVES, DAGGER JACK, D.B.

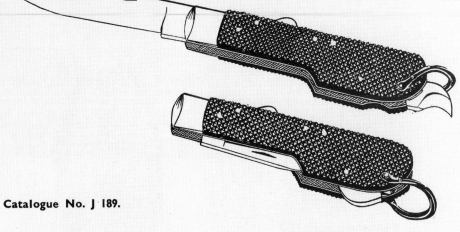

Catalogue No. J 189.

DESCRIPTION. A folding knife, similar to the Knife Dagger Jack, Plain (Item No. 137), but with an additional Tyre-Slashing Blade.

The large blade is dagger-shaped, sharpened along one side for the whole of its length and along the other for one-third. The second blade is small and hook-shaped, and is specially designed to cut the rubber of a tyre.

DIMENSIONS. 5" x 1" **WEIGHT.** 4 oz.

PACKING AND SPECIAL NOTES.
As required with tyrecutter.

KNIVES, DAGGER JACK, SINGLE BLADE

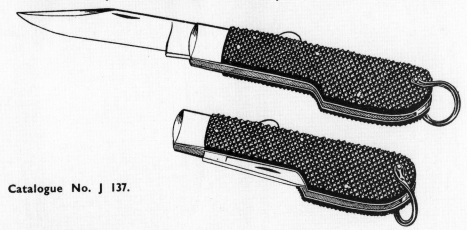

Catalogue No. J 137.

DESCRIPTION. A folding knife fitted with a locking device to prevent the blade from closing. The blade is dagger-shaped, sharpened along one side for the whole of its length and along the other for one-third. The knife is provided with a Shackle.

DIMENSIONS.
Length	- -	$4\frac{5}{8}''$
Width	- -	1"
Thickness	- -	$\frac{1}{2}''$

WEIGHT. $3\frac{1}{2}$ ozs.

PACKING AND SPECIAL NOTES.
As required.

PLIERS, INSULATED

Catalogue Nos. G 73.
G 73a.

PLIERS, PLAIN

DESCRIPTION.   A pair of strong Pliers which can be provided with plastic covered handles, giving insulation up to 400 volts, if required.

DIMENSIONS.

$8\frac{1}{2}''$ x $2\frac{1}{2}''$ x $\frac{7}{8}''$ (Insulated).

$7''$ x $2''$ x $\frac{3}{4}''$ (Plain).

WEIGHT.

1 lb.

$\frac{3}{4}$ lb.

PACKING AND SPECIAL NOTES.

As required. Insulation up to 400 volts.

JEMMIES

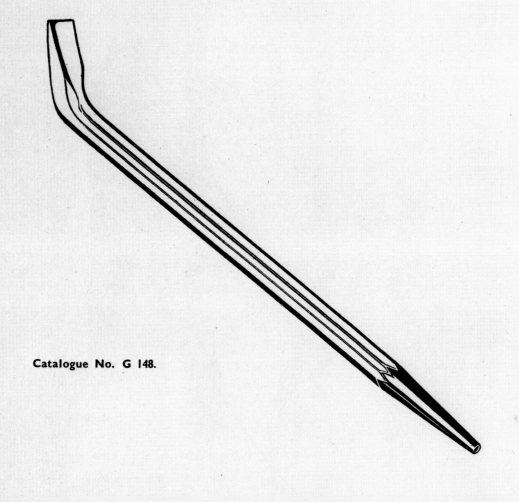

Catalogue No. G 148.

DESCRIPTION.   A burglar's Jemmy made of Tungsten Steel, with one chisel end. When this chisel end is used as a lever, it will withstand the weight of a fourteen stone man.

DIMENSIONS.   **WEIGHT.**
Length 14″ x Diameter ⅝″   14 ozs.

PACKING AND SPECIAL NOTES.
As required.

SPADE, LIGHTWEIGHT

Catalogue No. G 74.

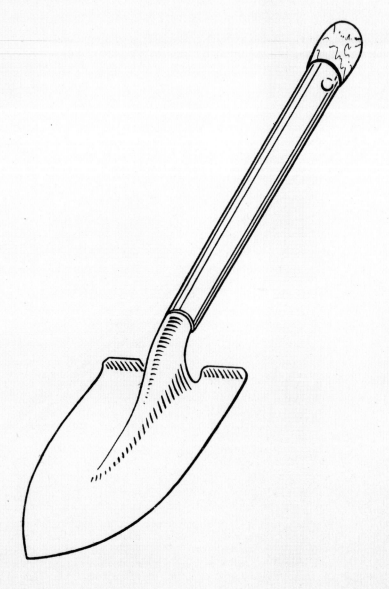

DESCRIPTION.   A small, short-handled Spade with a heart-shaped Blade the edge of which is sharpened, the top of the Blade is turned over giving a good bearing surface for the foot.

DIMENSIONS.

Blade	-	9″ long x 6¼″ wide.
Handle	-	21½″ long x 1¼″ diam.
Overall	-	29″ long x 6¼″ wide.

WEIGHT.

2 lbs.

PACKING AND SPECIAL NOTES.
   As required.

SCREWDRIVERS, PLAIN, SMALL

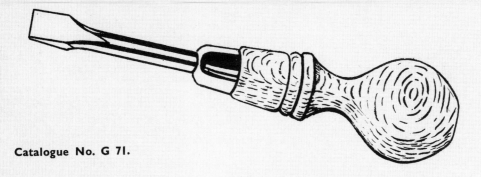

Catalogue No. G 71.

DESCRIPTION.   A strong Screwdriver with a blade two inches long by quarter inch wide and a wooden handle.

DIMENSIONS. 5″ x 1¼″ x 1″   **WEIGHT.** 1½ ozs.

PACKING AND SPECIAL NOTES.
  As required.

TOOLS, CRIMPING, TYPE 6

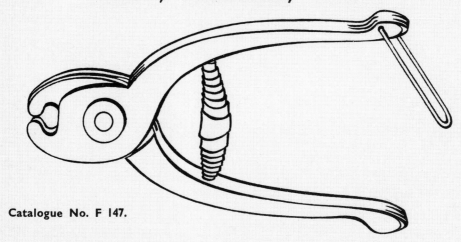

Catalogue No. F 147.

DESCRIPTION.   The Crimping Tool is fitted with double Jaws to give a double, waterproof crimp—No. 8 A.S.A. or No. 27 Detonator. A Spring between the handles just below the pivot, facilitates opening, and a Catch across the ends of the handles keeps the tool closed when not in use.

DIMENSIONS. 5⅞″ x 1¾″ x ½″   **WEIGHT.** 5½ ozs.

PACKING AND SPECIAL NOTES.
  As required.

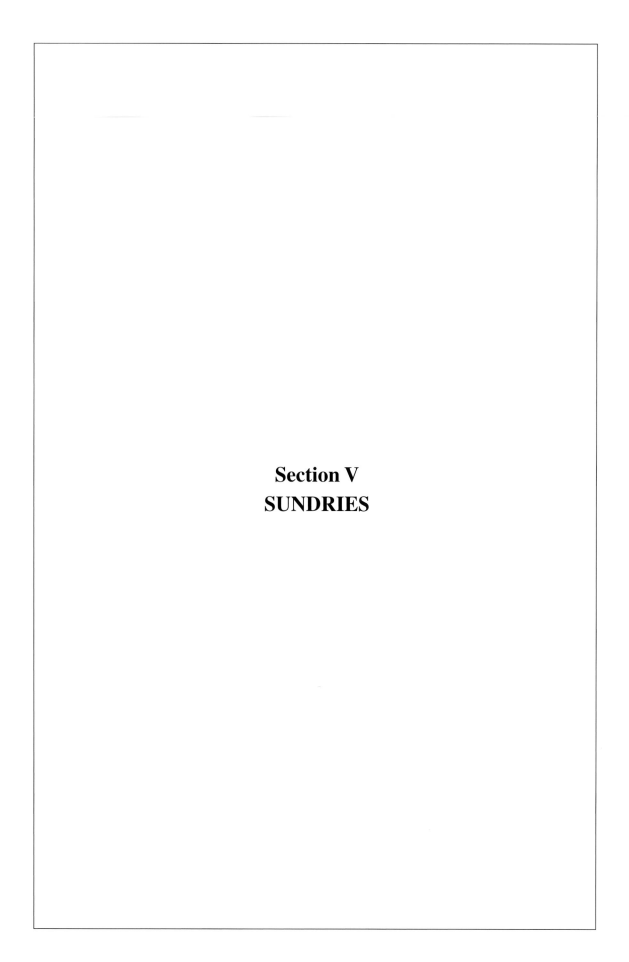

Section V
SUNDRIES

BAGS, MAIL, CANVAS

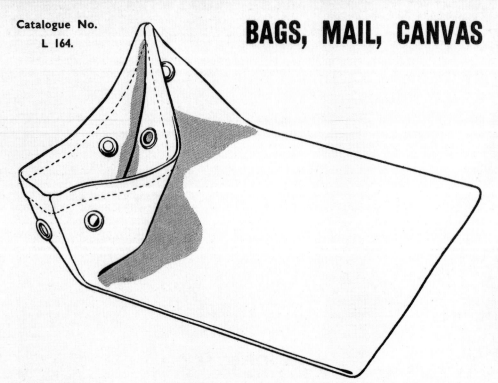

DESCRIPTION. Heavy white canvas mailbags, with brass Eyelets round the top.

DIMENSIONS.	WEIGHT.	DIMENSIONS.	WEIGHT.
Size 1—13″ x 12″	4½ ozs.	Size 6—32″ x 22″	17 ozs.
,, 2—17″ x 13″	7 ,,	,, 7—34″ x 24″	18½ ,,
,, 3—20″ x 14″	8 ,,	,, 8—40″ x 36″	1 lb. 14 ozs.
,, 4—26″ x 18″	12 ,,	,, 9—48″ x 36″	2¼ lb.
,, 5—28″ x 20″	15 ,,	,, 10—54″ x 40″	2¾ ,,

PACKING AND SPECIAL NOTES. As required.

BAGS, PAPER, DAMP - PROOF

Catalogue No. L 176.

DESCRIPTION.

A large paper Bag on a rectangular base, made of strong creosoted paper. These Bags are only intended for splash proofing stores and should not be regarded as either waterproof or completely dampproof.

METHOD OF USE.

(1) Open out the Bag, which is normally supplied flat.
(2) After packing, roll over the top, press flat, and seal with Adhesive Tape.

DIMENSIONS. 10½″ x 9″ x 6″   **WEIGHT.** 3½ ozs.

PACKING AND SPECIAL NOTES. Folded flat.

BALLOONS, LONG

Catalogue No. F 51.

DESCRIPTION. A strong rubber balloon which can be used for waterproofing a Switch No. 10 when a short under water delay is required. It can also be used for rain and weather-proofing during operations in the tropics.

DIMENSIONS. 7½″ x 1¼″ flat. **WEIGHT.** 1 oz. per 10.

PACKING AND SPECIAL NOTES.
  As required.

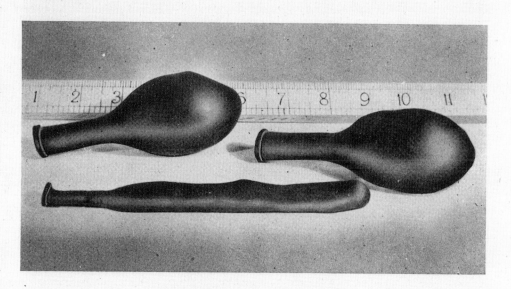

BALLOONS, ROUND

Catalogue No. F 50.

DESCRIPTION. A strong rubber balloon used for waterproofing Igniters, Safety Fuze, Copper Tube Igniters, or Switches No. 5.

DIMENSIONS. 4″ x 2¼″. **WEIGHT.** 1 oz. per 14.

PACKING AND SPECIAL NOTES.
  As required.

DIPSANIL V

Catalogue No. N 297.

DESCRIPTION. A wax emulsion which is used to waterproof ordinary cotton, woollen, silk or artificial silk garments.

METHOD OF USE. The garment is first thoroughly washed in soap and hot water and well rinsed; it is then squeezed well in a mixture of Dipsanil V and warm water, and finally dried thoroughly.

PACKING AND SPECIAL NOTES.
  Dipsanil V can be supplied on request in quantities as required.

71

DISCS, LUMINOUS, BAND
DISCS, LUMINOUS, SINGLE

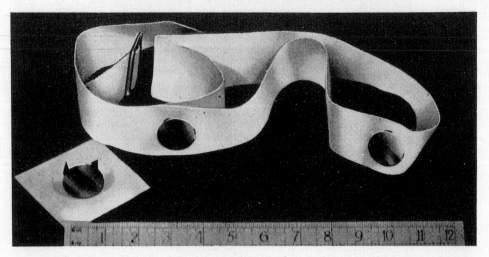

DESCRIPTION. The Luminous Band consists of white twill webbing. Unless otherwise requested, three Discs, Luminous, are attached symmetrically. The Band is fitted with a three prong buckle for attachment to containers.

The 1¼" Discs are made of 26 gauge sheet iron coated with radioactive luminous paint. They are provided with four prongs which serve as a means of attachment to canvas bands or other articles.

DIMENSIONS.
Band, 4' 3" long x 2" wide.
Disc, 1¼" diam.

WEIGHT.
approx. 2 ozs.
·16 oz. each.

PACKING AND SPECIAL NOTES.
Supplied and packed as required.

TAPE, ADHESIVE, KHAKI ¾"

Catalogue No. H 31.

DESCRIPTION.

A fifteen yard roll of ¾" wide strong, khaki adhesive tape.

It is used for making up explosive or incendiary charges, binding cordtex to detonators, etc., binding charges to their targets, or for making watertight closures for containers.

DIMENSIONS.
15 yard roll. Width ¾". Diam. 3¼".

WEIGHT.
2½ ozs.

PACKING AND SPECIAL NOTES.
14 rolls per carton.
Also special waterproof pack—200 coils in a commercial tin-lined case. All air extracted and filled with inert gas for tropical storage.

DRIERS, SIZE 2

Catalogue No. H 219.

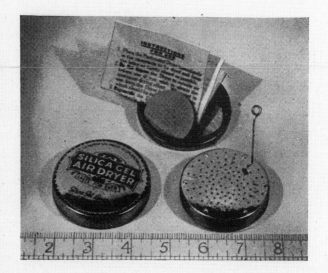

DESCRIPTION. These consist of an outer airtight tin, approximately $2\frac{1}{2}''$ in diameter, and an inner sealed container containing dried silica gel.

The airtight seal of the outer container is formed by the tight fit of the lid and not by cement or tape.

The inner container is made of aluminium alloy and is perforated on the top and bottom surfaces with small holes to allow passage of air through silica gel.

METHOD OF USE. The inner container is taken out of the airtight tin and one is used for every five cubic feet of air requiring to be kept dry.

DIMENSIONS. Thickness $\frac{3}{4}''$. Diameter $2\frac{1}{2}''$.   **WEIGHT.** 55—65 grammes.

PACKING AND SPECIAL NOTES. As required.

FABRIC, RUBBERISED

Catalogue No. D 112.

DESCRIPTION.

The Fabric is composed of single-ply cotton cloth, rubberised on one side. It is fairly strong, but can be torn, and is not completely waterproof.

DIMENSIONS. 60″ wide.

WEIGHT. $11\frac{1}{4}$ ozs. per sq. yd.

PACKING AND SPECIAL NOTES.
100 yds. fabric (approximately) per bale.

PACKAGE DIMENSIONS.
72″ x 10″

WEIGHT. 107 lbs.

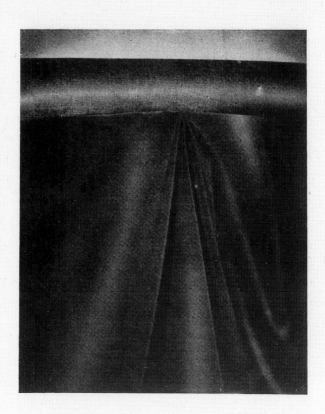

GLOVES, RUBBER, INSULATED, PAIRS

Catalogue No. H 151.

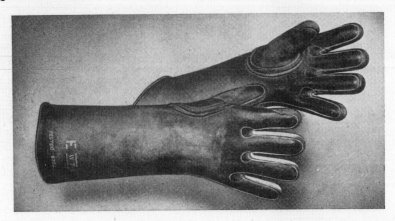

DESCRIPTION.   A pair of heavy, Insulated Rubber Gloves with thirteen-inch gauntlets.

DIMENSIONS. Length 16⅛". Width 7".   **WEIGHT.** 2 lbs. 6 ozs.

PACKING AND SPECIAL NOTES. As required. 13" gauntlets. The life of a pair of these gloves is not more than six months, depending on storage conditions, and should be returned for re-testing at the end of this time.

MAGAZINES, DETONATOR, MK. II.

Catalogue No. H 21.

DESCRIPTION.

Cylindrical plastic container with a screw cap which makes a waterproof seal when screwed down on a plastic washer.

The magazine holds five No. 27 or No. 8 Detonators which are inserted open end down on the felt pad in the bottom of the magazine.

The magazines can also be issued filled with Copper Tube Igniters.

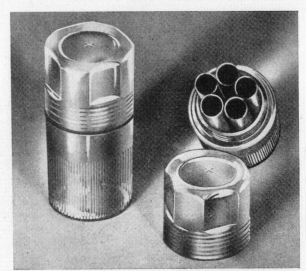

DIMENSIONS. 2¼" long x 1" diam.   **WEIGHT.** ½ oz. empty.

SHIPPING CLASSIFICATION. Generic Title   -   -   Magazines, Detonators.
                            Explosive Group   -   X.
                            Storage and Stowage   III.   M.S.D.

PACKING AND SPECIAL NOTES.
    The above Shipping Classification only applies when Magazines are sent out with Detonators. 130 filled magazines are packed in a stout wooden box. All spaces being filled with sawdust.

PACKAGE DIMENSIONS.   **WEIGHT PACKED.**
    Various sized boxes may be used. Usual   Box W.3 Mk. IV holding 130 Magazines loaded
case for detonators is Box W.3 Mk. IV,   with detonators weighs 11 lbs.
16·3" x 6·125" x 7·4"

MAGNETS

Catalogue No. D 108.

DESCRIPTION. These high power magnets are in the form of a horse-shoe and give a minimum direct pull on a clean steel plate of between 25 and 30 lbs. The North Pole is marked either with a dimple or a polished line on the outside leg of the magnet.

DIMENSIONS. 2¼" x 1⅞" x 1"   **WEIGHT.** 1 lb. 3 ozs.

PACKING AND SPECIAL NOTES. 120 in a case. To be stowed away from compasses.

PACKAGE DIMENSIONS. 20" x 12" x 6"   **WEIGHT PACKED.** 69 lbs.

PLASTICINE, CERISE

Catalogue No. H 171.

DESCRIPTION. Cerise-coloured modelling paste, approximately equivalent in weight and plasticity to Plastic Explosive.

No water is required, but a little vaseline may be used to soften the paste if necessary.

DIMENSIONS. 9¾" x 2" x 1"   **WEIGHT.** Stick 1 lb.

PACKING AND SPECIAL NOTES. As required.

SOLUTION, BOSTIK

Catalogue No. D 113.

DESCRIPTION.

A thick, black, sticky substance to which rubber and certain other materials, such as wood, cotton fabric and leather will adhere.

It dries quickly, taking about ten minutes to set on fabric and up to an hour on other materials. It can be removed by benzene or any rubber solvent, of the quickest being carbon tetrachloride.

DIMENSIONS. $4\frac{1}{2}''$ long x $\frac{3}{4}''$ diam. **WEIGHT.** $1\frac{1}{2}$ ozs. per tube.

SHIPPING CLASSIFICATION. Generic Title - - Bostik Solution.
Label - - B
Storage and Stowage - Dangerous Goods. Flash point under 73°

PACKING AND SPECIAL NOTES. 36 tubes per tin.

PACKAGE DIMENSIONS. 9'' x 5'' x 4'' **WEIGHT PACKED.** $4\frac{1}{2}$ lbs.

VASELINE TUBES

Catalogue No. H 32.

DESCRIPTION.

Standard petroleum jelly in a plain tube.

———

DIMENSIONS.
$4\frac{1}{4}''$ long. 1'' diam.

WEIGHT. $2\frac{1}{2}$ ozs.

PACKING AND SPECIAL NOTES. 6 Tubes per tin. May be issued in tins on account of shortage of tubes.

PACKAGE DIMENSIONS.
$6\frac{1}{2}''$ x $4\frac{7}{8}''$ x $1\frac{1}{4}''$

WEIGHT PACKED.
$17\frac{1}{4}$ ozs.

PAPER, SOLUBLE, FOOLSCAP

Catalogue No. H 70.

DESCRIPTION.

Sheets of white paper, which can be written on in pencil, typescript or ink, or used in a duplicator if each sheet is carefully blotted; it is practically non-inflammable.

When the paper is placed in water, it rapidly disintegrates into a semi-soluble slime; the disintegration is accelerated by vigorous stirring.

It can be eaten without harmful effects, but has a disagreeable taste.

———

DIMENSIONS. $13\frac{1}{4}''$ x 8'' **WEIGHT.** $5\frac{1}{4}$ lbs. per packet of 500 sheets.

PACKING AND SPECIAL NOTES. 50 sheets in tin box, hermetically soldered with tear-off strip.

ROPE, ALPINE
Catalogue No. K 167.

DESCRIPTION.

A fine manilla Rope, also containing either sisal or cord, having a breaking strain of 22 cwt.

For use as a knotted climbing rope or for making up into rope ladders.

DIMENSIONS. Circumference 1½″

WEIGHT. 7¾ lbs. per 100 ft.

PACKING AND SPECIAL NOTES.
As required.

Usually supplied in 120 ft. lengths.

ROPE, LADDERS
Catalogue No. K 168.

DESCRIPTION. Rope Ladders or Knotted Climbing Ropes are made to any desired specification. The Rope can be of any thickness, but Rope, Alpine (Item No. 167) is recommended.

A Standard Rope Ladder 9″ wide has 19 rungs, each 9″ apart and is fitted with a Grapnel.

DIMENSIONS. 16½″ long.   **WEIGHT.** 11½ lbs.

PACKING AND SPECIAL NOTES. As required.

PAPER, NITRATED
Catalogue No. N 298.

DESCRIPTION. This paper is similar to and as strong as air mail paper, the sheets having a red edge. It may be used for writing, printing, typing or duplicating and can be destroyed by fire faster than similar ordinary paper and is normal in appearance. Although it absorbs ink freely, the writing will still remain legible.

METHOD OF USE. To destroy it, apply flame or spark to a point on the paper; this may be done through a small hole in the envelope or wrapper.

DIMENSIONS. Single sheet 10″ x 7½″

SHIPPING CLASSIFICATION.
Generic Title	-	Nitrocellulose.
Explosive Group	-	III.
Storage and Stowage	II.	M.S.B.

PACKING AND SPECIAL NOTES. As required. Do not file with ordinary paper. The paper should be stored under reasonably dry conditions with not more than 20 sheets in one pack. Limited supplies available.

TORCH, BATTERIES (LARGE)

Catalogue No. H 146.

DESCRIPTION.
Ever-Ready No. 1829 in a plain wrapper. The burning time is about 5 hours.

DIMENSIONS.
$4\frac{3}{4}''$ long x $1\frac{1}{4}''$ diam.

WEIGHT. $6\frac{1}{4}$ ozs.

PACKING AND SPECIAL NOTES. 4 doz. batteries packed in 2 lots of 2 doz. in soldered tin containers of Box 30, Mk. I.E.

TORCH, BATTERIES (SMALL)

Catalogue No. H 145.

DESCRIPTION.
Every-Ready No. 1839 in plain wrapper. The burning time is about $2\frac{1}{2}$ hrs.

DIMENSIONS.
$3\frac{3}{4}''$ long x $1''$ diam.

WEIGHT. 3 oz.

PACKING AND SPECIAL NOTES. 1 gross batteries packed in 2 lots of 2 doz. in soldered tin containers of Box 30, Mk. IE.

TORCH, BULBS

Catalogue No. H 144.

DESCRIPTION.   A standard 3·5 volt spotlight Bulb.

DIMENSIONS. $1''$ long x $\frac{1}{2}''$ diam.   **WEIGHT.** ·032 oz.

PACKING AND SPECIAL NOTES.
As required.

TORCHES, SMALL

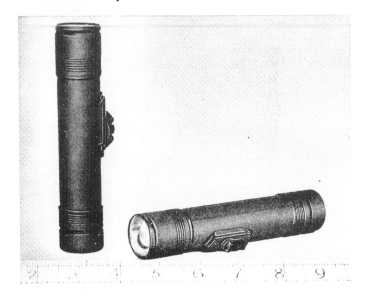

Catalogue No.
H. 139.

DESCRIPTION.   A modified No. 1163 Ever-Ready Torch,

The bottom End Cap contains a spare bulb, and the Torch has a matt black finish.

DIMENSIONS. Length 6″. Diam. 1″. Glass Diam. 1½″   **WEIGHT.** 3 ozs.

PACKING AND SPECIAL NOTES. As required. Bottom end cap has spare bulb.

TORCHES, LARGE

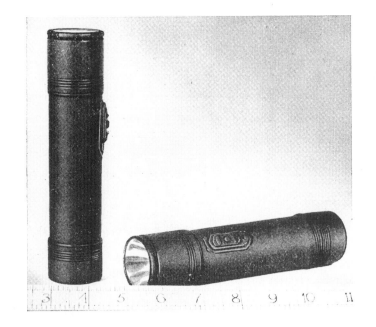

Catalogue No.
H 140.

DESCRIPTION.   A modified No. 2268 Every-Ready Torch.

The bottom End Cap contains a spare bulb, and the torch has a matt black finish.

DIMENSIONS. Length 7″. Diam. 1½″. Glass 1¾″.   **WEIGHT.** 4½ ozs.

PACKING AND SPECIAL NOTES. As required. Bottom end cap has spare bulb.

TORCH, FILTERS, LARGE

Catalogue No. H 141.

DESCRIPTION. Supplied in Red, Yellow, Green or Blue. These Filters slip on over the head of the Torch, Large (Item No. 140) and are held in place by two tongues which grip the Torch.

For signalling purposes.

DIMENSIONS. 1⅝" x 1¹/₁₆"   **WEIGHT.** ¾ oz.

PACKING AND SPECIAL NOTES. As required.

TORCH, FILTERS, ULTRA VIOLET

Catalogue No. H 68.

DESCRIPTION. This Filter slips on over the head of the Torch, Large (Item No. 140) and is held in place by two tongues which grip the Torch.

For reading messages or maps, in a darkened room written in fluorescent ink.

DIMENSIONS. Diam. 1⅝". Depth ¹¹/₁₆".   **WEIGHT.** ¾ oz.

PACKING AND SPECIAL NOTES. As required. To fit Torches, Large (H 140).

WINDERS, FUZE

Catalogue No. H 45.

DESCRIPTION. The apparatus consists of two parts; the Winder and the Spindle, which is affixed to a plate drilled for screwing on to a table.

The Winder is adapted for standard 24-foot lengths of Safety Fuze; the finished coil measures approximately 4" diam. x 1½" thick. The Winder should not however, be used for Detonator Fuze, as the tight coils tend to break up the continuity of the filling.

DIMENSIONS. Set up Length 13¾". Width 4½". Height 5".   **WEIGHT.** 3½ lbs.

PACKING AND SPECIAL NOTES. In box.

PACKAGE DIMENSIONS. 9" x 4½" x 6"   **WEIGHT PACKED.** 3½ lbs.

WINDOWS, SPLINTERPROOF, FRAMED

Catalogue No. H 169.

DESCRIPTION.

A heavy metal Frame fitted with a $2\frac{1}{2}''$ thick Triplex Window, $11''$ wide x $5''$ high. Windows, Splinterproof, Spare, are spare Triplex Windows.

Two or more can be built into a sandbag redoubt to form an observation post.

METHOD OF USE.

When assembling the Window, it is important to remember that the thin laminations of glass should be to the outside, and the thick laminations to the inside of the observation post.

DIMENSIONS.
Frame— $24''$ x $23''$ x $15''$ erected.
$24''$ x $15''$ x $4\frac{1}{2}''$ dismantled.
Window—$11''$ x $5''$ x $2\frac{1}{2}''$

WEIGHT.
Frame 76 lbs.
Window $12\frac{1}{4}$ lbs.

PACKING AND SPECIAL NOTES. 2 Frames and 2 Windows per case. As required.

PACKAGE DIMENSIONS. $38''$ x $18''$ x $13''$ **WEIGHT PACKED.** 181 lbs.

WINDOWS, SPLINTERPROOF, SPARE

Catalogue No. H 170.

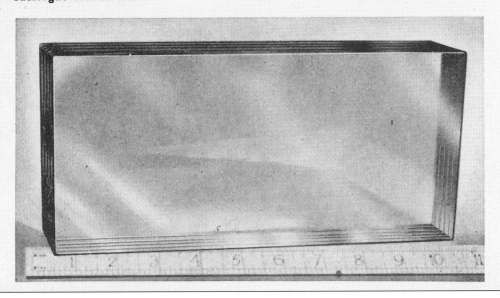

Section VI
ARMS AND EQUIPMENT

GUN, STEN, SILENCED, MK. II

Catalogue No. M 211.

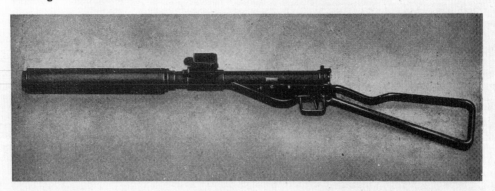

DESCRIPTION. The Sten Silencer is a cylinder fitted with a bursting chamber and a series of metal baffles. It is detachable from the gun for packing and can be used with a standard production model Sten.

The Silencer can be fitted to any standard Sten Gun, reducing the velocity to about 980 feet per second, and removing the muzzle flash. This gives an automatic weapon which can be used without attracting much attention. The noise is unrecognisable as a small arms shot at 200 yards distance from the firer, where only the faintest click is heard.

It may be used at ranges from 0 to 50 yards in the dark, or up to 75 yards in daylight, enabling single shots to be fired whilst the firer and direction of shots remain undetected.

METHOD OF USE. The Silencer SHOULD ONLY BE USED ON THE GUN WITH WHICH IT IS ISSUED and no alteration is to be made to the gun, as the Silencer is tested and matched to its gun before issue.

DIMENSIONS. Overall length of Silencer $12\frac{3}{4}''$. **WEIGHT.** Complete with barrel 1 lb. 14 ozs.
Diameter $1\frac{5}{8}''$.
Gun complete with Silencer $37\frac{1}{4}''$.
PACKING AND SPECIAL NOTES. As required. The Sten can be fitted with luminous night sights for special operations.

RAIN COWL, GUN, SPIGOT, TREE TYPE

Catalogue No. N 255.

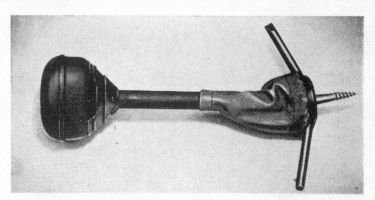

DESCRIPTION. The Rain Cowl is made in canvas. A steel wire through one end, is supplied for attaching it to a Tree Spigot.

METHOD OF USE. After a Tree Spigot (B. 116) has been sighted, the Rain Cowl is slipped over the Spigot and sprung between the clamping and seating plates so that any rain will run down on the back of the former. The press stud is then undone allowing the bomb tail to be slipped over the Spigot and pushed home. The Bomb Tail is then covered by the Rain Cowl which is attached by closing the press studs.

DIMENSIONS. $9'' \times 7'' \times 5''$.
PACKING AND SPECIAL NOTES. One Rain Cowl is packed in each C.207 container.

WELROD, MK. II.A ('32)

Catalogue No. M 213.

DESCRIPTION. The Welrod is a firearm designed for silence. It is a compact tube weapon to be used in a two-handed grip, one hand gripping the magazine which acts as a pistol grip, and the other hand gripping the barrel of the silencer in a convenient forward position. The trigger action is similar to a colt automatic. Due to the high efficiency of the baffled silencer, a shot fired at 50 yards is not recognisable as a shot from a firearm.

The safety-catch is situated at the rear of the magazine housing, and is hand controlled. The sights are fixed and are sufficiently accurate to give 3 in. groups at up to 10 yards range. The recommended operational range is 8 yards.

METHOD OF USE. The magazine may be charged with one to five cartridges. The charged magazine is inserted into the housing, and the action is cocked by turning the breech operating handle in an anti-clockwise direction, and drawing the bolt to the rear. It is closed by driving the bolt home and turning the breech operating handle in a clockwise direction until it fully engages the stop.

DIMENSIONS. Mk. IIA. Overall length, 12¼".
9 mm. Overall length, 14⅜".

WEIGHT. 35 ozs.
3 lbs. 4 ozs.

PACKING AND SPECIAL NOTES.
As required.
Night sights on both types are a standard fitting.

BOMB, SPIGOT, GUN, 3 LBS. H.E., MK. I

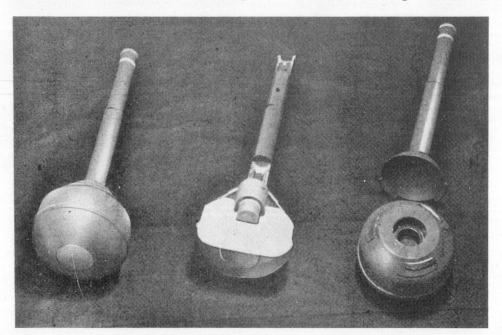

GUN, SPIGOT, IN FIRING POSITION

SHOT, PRACTICE, GUN, SPIGOT

BOMB, SPIGOT, GUN, 3 LBS. H.E., MK. I
BOMB, DRILL, MK. I, GUN, SPIGOT
SHOT, PRACTICE, GUN, SPIGOT

Catalogue No. B 119.
    „   „   B 119e.
    „   „   B 119d.

DESCRIPTION. The Service Bomb 3 lbs. H.E. for the Tree Spigot (B.116) is the live round that is fired at the enemy.

It consists of a head with a thin front that collapses when it strikes a target placing the explosive in intimate contact with it and a hollow tubular tail that fits on the Tree Spigot. Before firing, a fuze (B.222) is fitted into the bomb head and the tail attached to it. It has a silencing arrangement in the tail to eliminate the noise of discharge on firing,

The Bomb, Drill, (B119e) is similar to the live one except that it is inert filled, and has a distinguishing "D."

The Practice Shot (B119d) is supplied for firing practice on a range, and consists of a solid steel bomb head, bored to take a special screwed bomb tail which can be reloaded. It is painted white in order that it can be easily recognisable.

METHOD OF USE. Remove the lever lid from the bomb tail by catching it on the chisel point of the Tree Spigot. Place the bomb on the cocked Spigot. It is then quite ready for firing. The tail already carries a cartridge. Care should be taken not to damage the front of the bomb which is very thin and liable to dent.

The Practice Shot is fired in the same manner as the Service Bomb, but a cartridge and wad must be inserted into the tail tube before each shot.

DIMENSIONS.
    H.E. and Drill $5\frac{7}{16}''$ diam.
                    1' 4'' length
    Practice, Head 3'' diam. x $2\frac{3}{4}''$
           Tail $1\frac{1}{2}''$ diam. x $10\frac{1}{2}''$
    Total length $11\frac{1}{4}''$

WEIGHT.
5 lbs. $5\frac{1}{2}$ ozs. without the fuze.

5 lbs. $14\frac{1}{2}$ ozs.

SHIPPING CLASSIFICATION.
    Generic Title - - Bombs, Spigot, Gun
    Explosive Group - VIII
    Storage and Stowage - II. O.A.S.

PACKING AND SPECIAL NOTES.
Normally packed three in C.207 container with remainder of Tree Spigot equipment.
Otherwise heads and tails packed separately in special transit case.

PACKAGE DIMENSIONS.
    Heads only - 21'' x $13\frac{1}{2}''$ x 11''
    Tail only - - $36\frac{1}{2}''$ x $13\frac{1}{2}''$ x $16\frac{1}{4}''$
    C.207 - - 1' $3\frac{7}{8}''$

CONTAINER, GUN, SPIGOT, TREE TYPE

Catalogue No. N 257.

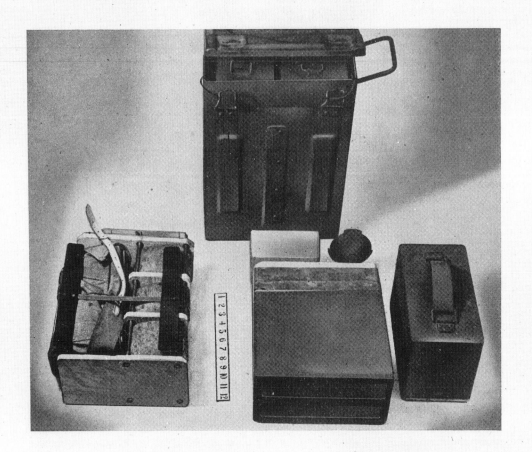

DESCRIPTION.   The C.207 Container consists of an outer steel container with two cells inside.

The two inside cells are soldered up to ensure that the stores are not damaged by moisture. The kit is made up so that the operator has all that is required for using the Tree Spigot in the field.

METHOD OF USE.   The stores should be kept in the Container as long as possible to protect them from climatic effects.

In tropical countries the stores should be kept in a cool place.

DIMENSIONS.

C.207 Container	-	$18\frac{1}{2}''$ x 13'' x $11\frac{1}{2}''$.
Each Cell	-	11'' x $5\frac{1}{2}''$ x $4\frac{1}{2}''$.

WEIGHT.

18 lbs. (empty).
6 lbs.

PACKING AND SPECIAL NOTES.

The C.207 Container is a complete unit in itself and is ready for the field.

PACKAGE DIMENSIONS.

C.207 Container	-	$18\frac{1}{2}''$ x 13'' x $11\frac{1}{2}''$.
Each Cell	-	11'' x $5\frac{1}{2}''$ x $4\frac{1}{2}''$.

WEIGHT PACKED.

63 lbs. (full).
A Cell $20\frac{1}{2}$ lbs.
B Cell $24\frac{1}{2}$ lbs.

FUZE, GRAZE, BOMB, GUN, SPIGOT
FUZE, GRAZE, BOMB, GUN, SPIGOT
(DEMONSTRATION)
FUZE, GRAZE, BOMB, GUN, SPIGOT, DUMMY

Catalogue Nos. B 222, B 222b, B 222a.

DESCRIPTION. This is the Fuze for the Service Bomb, 3 lb. H.E. (B. 119). The Fuze is perfectly safe against dropping from heights up to twenty feet. It is roughly cylindrical in shape with a reduced front and can only be inserted into the bomb in one way.

The Demonstration Fuze is a sectional working model of the Fuze and is intended for demonstration purposes only.

The Dummy Fuze is identified by having a large "D" painted on top.

METHOD OF USE.

Remove the head from the tail in the Service Bomb, Gun, Tree Spigot, insert the Fuze and reclamp the head to tail. There is no safety pin as the Fuze is armed by set-back when the shot is fired.

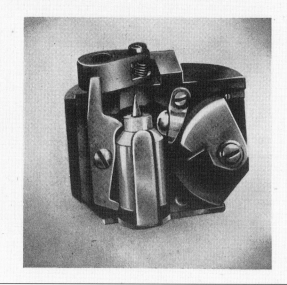

DIMENSIONS. Separately : Length 2½"
Width 1¾"
Depth 1¼".

WEIGHT. 6½ ozs.

SHIPPING CLASSIFICATION.
Generic Title - - Fuzes for Bombs.
Explosive Group - VI.
Storage and Stowage I. O.A.S. (C)

PACKING AND SPECIAL NOTES.
Fuzes are packed in tins of three, and are protected with cardboard rings.

PACKAGE DIMENSIONS.
Length 8⅝" x Width 2" x Depth 2"

WEIGHT PACKED. 1 lb. 8 ozs.

FUZE, TIME, TREE SPIGOT

Catalogue No. B 118.

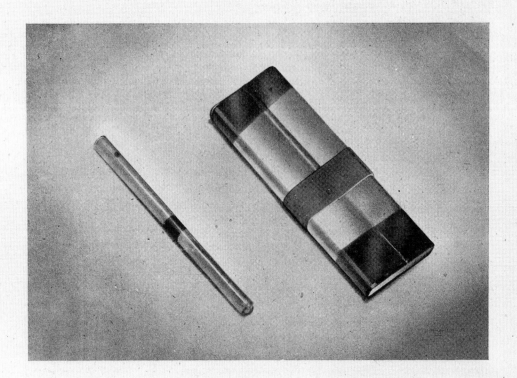

DESCRIPTION. This is a delay mechanism similar to Switch No. 10. except that there is no spring snout or cap.

METHOD OF USE. The device is used to replace normal striker mechanism.

PACKING AND SPECIAL NOTES.

One tin of Fuzes (5 assorted timings) is put with each C.207 Container for carriage with the rucksack.

If desired "Black" (ten minute) Fuzes, Time, Tree Spigot can be supplied for training purposes.

GUN, SPIGOT, TREE TYPE

Catalogue No. B 116.

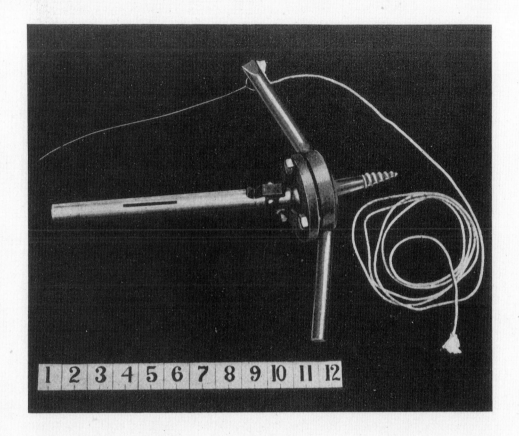

DESCRIPTION. The Gun, Spigot, Tree Type, is a device which projects a bomb charged with 3 lbs. of 808 explosive. It can be screwed into wood or brickwork and is aimed with a special sight.

METHOD OF USE. The Gun is screwed into a tree after all the loose bark has been removed. Two handles are provided to assist in doing this and a chisel edge at the end of one of the handles helps to remove the bark. The Spigot is then cocked by removing the Spigot Piece and compressing the Striker Spring with the striker until it can be held back by a lanyard or Trip Wire. The Spigot is ultimately fired by withdrawing the lanyard or trip wire. For delay firing, a Fuze, Time, Tree, Spigot can be inserted open end first into the Spigot end. After the Spigot end is replaced the bomb is placed on the Spigot which is then ready for firing.

DIMENSIONS. Length 14″. Width 11″. Depth 3¼″.   **WEIGHT.** 5 lbs.

PACKING AND SPECIAL NOTES.
Normally packed one in C.207 with remainder of equipment.
They can be supplied separately for training or other purposes.

CARTRIDGES, GUN, SPIGOT
WADS,   „   „

Catalogue No. B 120.
„   „   B 120a.

DESCRIPTION.   The Cartridge for the Gun, Spigot, Tree Type, is similar in appearance to a shot-gun cartridge but is a blank.

A cartridge is required for the Shot, Practice, but not however for the Service Bomb, as one is already supplied in the tail of the latter.

The Wad (B.120a) is a small silencing arrangement used in conjunction with the Cartridge in this apparatus. (Each Wad can only be used once). It is therefore necessary to indent for the same number of Wads as Cartridges.

METHOD OF USE.   See SHOT, PRACTICE, GUN, TREE SPIGOT TYPE.

DIMENSIONS.   **WEIGHT.**

Cartridge separately :   Length $1\frac{13}{16}''$.
                             Width $\frac{7}{8}''$ diam.   0·5 oz.
                             Depth $\frac{7}{8}''$ diam.

           Wad : $\frac{3}{8}''$ x .8″ diam. $\frac{1}{3}$ oz.

SHIPPING CLASSIFICATION. Generic Title   -   -   Cartridges, Small Arms, Blank.
                                     Explosive Group   -   VI.
                                     Storage and Stowage   I.   O.A.S. (C)

PACKING AND SPECIAL NOTES.
The Cartridges are packed in cardboard boxes 25 to each box.
Wads are supplied 250 to the cardboard box.

PACKAGE DIMENSIONS.   **WEIGHT PACKED.**
           $4\frac{3}{8}''$ x $4\frac{3}{8}''$ x 2″.   1 lb.

RUCKSACK, GUN SPIGOT, TREE TYPE

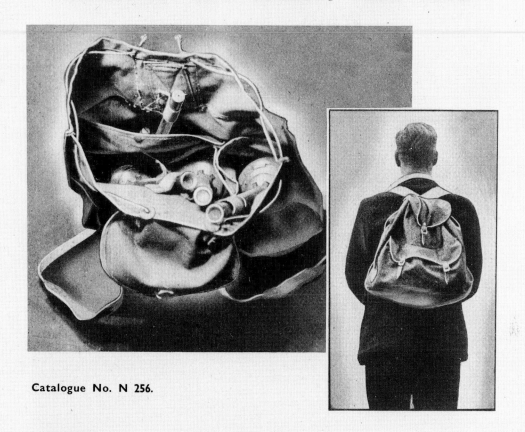

Catalogue No. N 256.

DESCRIPTION. The Rucksack for the Tree Spigot is designed to appear like any other rucksack, but it is fitted up inside to contain in the main pocket—one Tree Spigot (B.116) and three Service Bombs, three pounds H.E. already fuzed. In the front pocket—one Tree Spigot Sight, one tin of Fuzes, Time, Tree Spigot, two coils of Trip Wire, Lanyard, and one Rain Cowl.

A special frame is provided to distribute the load over the wearer's back so that the discomfort of carrying a knobbly and weighty load is cut to a minimum.

METHOD OF USE. Remove the stores from the C.207 Container. Remove the cardboard tubes from the Tree Spigot handles and screw one on the Tree Spigot screw to protect the rucksack. Fit the spring steel frame to the back of the rucksack. Fill the rucksack with the remainer of the contents of the C.207 Container as shown in the photographs. The operator will find that the best way to put on and remove the rucksack is to place it on a table at a convenient height, or hold the rucksack up against a wall or bank between his back and the wall while he puts his arms through the straps.

DIMENSIONS.
18" x 17" x 6"

PACKING AND SPECIAL NOTES.
The Rucksack is packed in the C.207 container.

PACKAGE DIMENSIONS.
18" x 17" x 6"

WEIGHT.
approx. 3 lbs.

WEIGHT PACKED.
approx. 29 lbs.

SIGHTS, GUN, SPIGOT

Catalogue No.
B 117.

DESCRIPTION. The sight, which is used with Gun, Spigot, Tree Type (B. 116) is similar to the view finder of a camera. It is provided with cross wires on a ground glass screen for aiming, and a range scale on the side, which has to be set at the correct range.

METHOD OF USE. After cocking the Gun, place the Sight on the Spigot and free the ball and socket joint by loosening the clamp screw; point the Spigot in the desired direction, then clamp up the ball and socket joint. Remove the Sight and the Spigot is then left aiming in the correct direction.

DIMENSIONS. Length 4½". Width 2¼". Depth 4¾."   **WEIGHT.** 1 lb. 8 ozs.

PACKING AND SPECIAL NOTES.

The Sights are packed in a special cardboard box which protects them should they be dropped.

One Sight is supplied with each C.207 container with the remainder of the equipment. They are also supplied separately for training purposes when required.

For training it is not necessary to have one sight for each Tree Spigot as the same sight can be used to sight any number of Tree Spigots. Therefore do not ask for one sight for each Tree Spigot unless necessary,

PACKAGE DIMENSIONS.   **WEIGHT PACKED.**
Length 6" x Width 5¼" x Depth 3⅜".   2 lbs. 1 oz.

Section VII
"AD HOC" DEVICES

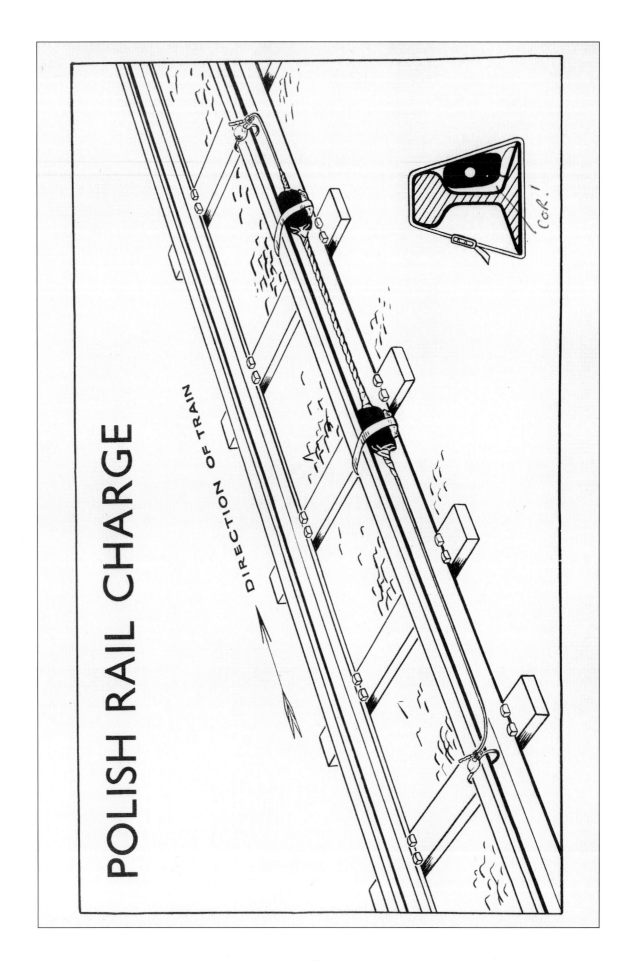

RAIL CHARGE, POLISH

Catalogue No. N 250.

DESCRIPTION. As French Rail Charge (D.248) but designed for single track railway.

The charge consists of two ¾-lb. units each comprised of three separately wrapped sticks of P.E., the centre one being primed at each end with a one ounce C.E. Primer. These charges are attached to a special cordtex lead, and so spaced along it that there is between them one metre of double cordtex, and at each end a one metre single cordtex tail. Each of these units is enclosed in a rubberised fabric sleeve, to which is sewn a webbing strap for fixing to the rail. The whole is packed in a rubberised fabric bag along with a tin containing two fog signals and two No. 8 detonators, these latter being enclosed in a wooden block.

METHOD OF USE. Detonators are inserted into the two fog signal initiators, and are then taped to each of the single cordtex tails, three or four inches from the end. The charge is then strapped to the railway line with one fog signal at each end.

The locomotive, no matter from which side it approaches, crushes one of the fog signals, which in turn initiates the detonator and the charge. The charge normally removes about one metre of rail.

DIMENSIONS. 7¾″ x 5″ x 4½″   **WEIGHT.** 2 lbs. 9 ozs.

SHIPPING CLASSIFICATION. Generic Title - - Charges, Demolition.
                              Explosive Group - VII.
                              Storage and Stowage III.   O.A.S.

PACKING AND SPECIAL NOTES.
As required.

RAIL CHARGE, FRENCH

Catalogue No. D 248.

DESCRIPTION. The charge consists of two ¾-lb. units each comprised of three separately wrapped sticks of P.E., the centre one being primed at each end with a one ounce C.E. Primer. These charges are attached to a double cordtex lead, and so spaced along it that there is one metre between them, a thirty-two centimetres double tail at one end and at the other end a double tail, of which one strand is one metre and the other one metre fifteen centimetres long. Each of these units is enclosed in a rubberised fabric sleeve to which is sewn a webbing strap for fixing to the rail. The whole is packed in a rubberised fabric bag along with a tin containing two fog signals and two No. 8 detonators, these latter being enclosed in a wooden block.

METHOD OF USE. Detonators are inserted into the two fog signal initiators, and are then taped to each of the long double cordtex tails, three or four inches from the end. The charge is then strapped to the railway line, the fog signals at the end from which the train will approach.

The locomotive crushes the fog signals, which fire, and in turn initiate the detonators and charge. The charge normally removes about one metre of rail.

DIMENSIONS. 7¾″ x 5″ x 4½″.   **WEIGHT.** 2 lbs. 10 ozs.

SHIPPING CLASSIFICATION. Generic Title - - Charges, Demolition.
                              Explosive Group - VII.
                              Storage and Stowage III.   O.A.S.

PACKING AND SPECIAL NOTES.
As required.

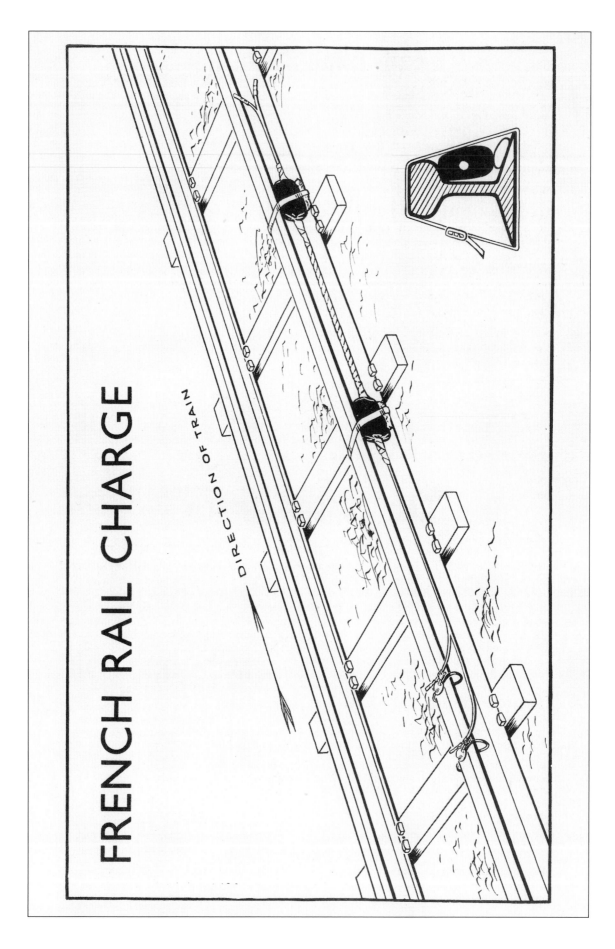

HAVERSACKS, GUERILLA

Catalogue No. N 253.

DESCRIPTION.

Webbing Haversack, can be worn on the back or slung at the side. It has two loops for a belt for support, when worn at the side.

It carries one Sten Gun, and has pockets for seven loaded magazines, four hand grenades and detonators. There is also room for any personal equipment.

DIMENSIONS. $14'' \times 3\frac{3}{4}''$

PACKING AND SPECIAL NOTES.
As required.

PACKS, QUICK RELEASE

Catalogue No. J 224.

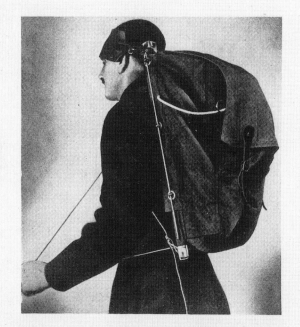

DESCRIPTION. The Pack comprises two main assembles; the Cradle and the Bag or Pack. The cradle is a wooden frame curved to fit the back, to which is attached a head strap, the shoulder straps and the Quick Release Buckle.

The Pack consists of a large Bag having two pockets, which will hold approximately one hundred pounds in weight. The Pack is attached to the Cradle by eye-screws supplied on the right and left hand sides of the Cradle Frame.

METHOD OF USE. The operator must grasp the release cord firmly in his left hand at the lowest point and exert a sharp downward pull, at the same time jerking off the head band.

DIMENSIONS. 24" deep. 18" wide. 3" thick.　　　**WEIGHT.** 6 lbs. (average).

PACKING AND SPECIAL NOTES. As required.

SPIKES, ATTACHMENT
(LONG AND SHORT HANDLES)

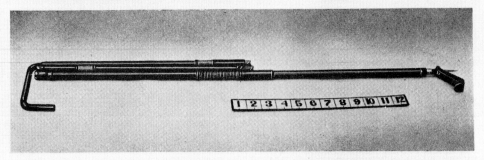

Spike, Attachment (Long Handle)

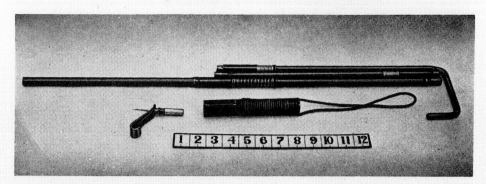

Spike, Attachment (Long and Short Handles)

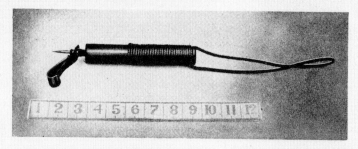

Spike, Attachment (Short Handle)

DESCRIPTION. This is a Spike which can be driven into a wooden ship or structure so that an explosive charge can be hung from it. The device consists of a small cylindrical body from which a snap hook is loosely hung. The handle is bound with cord to prevent slipping and a loop is provided to facilitate handling.

METHOD OF USE. The device is fitted into the handle and a sharp blow at approximately 45° is aimed at the spot selected for fixing the charge. The handle is withdrawn and the charge, previously provided with a cord loop, is hung on the hook.

Where absolute silence makes the aforementioned method undesirable, the following alternative is used. A 20 s.w.g. copper shear wire is passed through holes provided in the handle. The Spike is then pushed into the wood. When the pressure exerted on the handle is approximately 40 lbs. the wire is sheared, giving a "hammer-blow" effect which drives the Spike fully home.

A modified limpet placing rod can be used instead of the standard handle where it is desired to place the charge below the surface of the water.

DIMENSIONS.   **WEIGHT.**
Body   -   - $2\frac{1}{8}''$ x $\frac{3}{8}''$.   1 lb.
Steel Spike - $\frac{1}{8}''$ dia. x $1''$ long.   1 oz.

100

STANDARD CHARGE, 3 LBS.

Catalogue No. D 245.

DESCRIPTION. The charge contains three pounds of P.E. and is provided with a central tubular primer of C.E. Pellets in a cardboard tube. It is wrapped in rubberised fabric.

It may be cut into two or more lengths, each of which will form a separate charge complete in itself.

METHOD OF USE. The charge may be initiated by inserting a detonator directly into the end of the tubular primer or a length of cordtex may be threaded through the primer and the charge detonated by taping a detonator to the cordtex.

DIMENSIONS. Length 10½". Height 2¼". Width 2¼" **WEIGHT.** 3 lbs.

SHIPPING CLASSIFICATION.
Generic Title - - Charges, Demolition.
Explosive Group - VII.
Storage and Stowage - III. O.A.S.

PACKING AND SPECIAL NOTES. As required.

STANDARD CHARGE, 1½ LB., SPLIT
STANDARD CHARGE, 3 LB., SPLIT

Catalogue Nos. N 251.
N 252.

DESCRIPTION. The charges contain P.E. and are provided with a one ounce C.E. Primer and double cordtex tail at each end. The explosive is made up into two equal blocks, each separately wrapped in rubberised fabric, but bound together by a wrapping of adhesive tape to form a single charge. On removing the wrapping of tape, the two portions of the charge may be pulled apart and will slide on the cordtex leads which pass right through the charge. A loop in each length of cordtex (one at each end) permits the charge being opened up a limited distance. It is not recommended that this should exceed six inches. The cordtex tails are normally three feet long at one end and eighteen inches long at the other.

METHOD OF USE. The charge is initiated by means of a detonator in the usual way. It is recommended that where a single charge is being used that the two tails should be brought together and the detonator taped to the junction.

DIMENSIONS.

1½ lb. charge - 6½" x 1⅞" x 2¼"
(actual charge exclusive of tails)
3 lb. charge - 10½" x 2¼" x 2¼"
(actual charge exclusive of tails)

WEIGHT.

1 lb. 12½ ozs.

3 lbs. 5 ozs.

SHIPPING CLASSIFICATION.
Generic Title - - Charges, Demolition.
Explosive Group - VII.
Storage and Stowage III. O.A.S

PACKING AND SPECIAL NOTES. As required.

STANDARD CHARGE, 3 LBS.

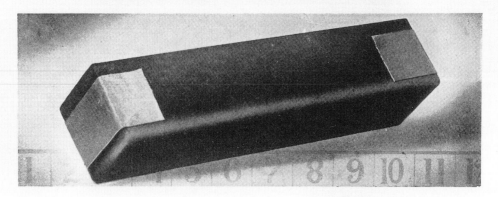

STANDARD CHARGE, 1½ LB., SPLIT

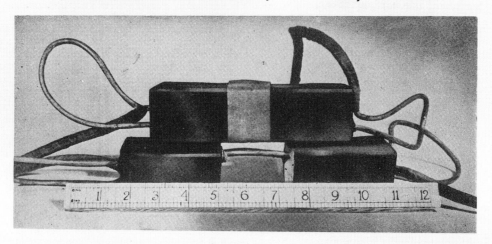

STANDARD CHARGE, 3 LB., SPLIT

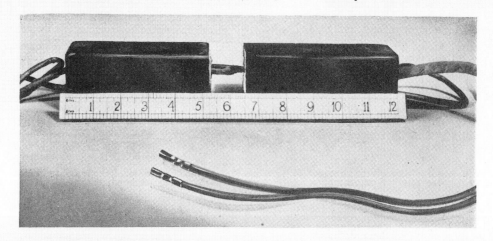

SLEEVE GUN

DESCRIPTION. Like the Sleeve Gun Mk. I the Mk. II is a short length, silent, murder weapon, firing 0·32 inch ammunition. It is a single shot weapon designed for carriage in the sleeve with the trigger near the muzzle to aid unobtrusive firing when the gun is slid from the sleeve into the hand. The gun is intended for use in contact with the target, but may be used at ranges up to about three yards; the silencing element cannot be removed for replacement since the gun is not intended for prolonged use.

The gun is fitted at the rear end with a ring to which the carrying lanyard can be attached.

In appearance the main difference between the Sleeve Gun Mks. I and II, is in the cocking tube of the Mk. I, which runs parallel to the main cylinder of the gun for its whole length; the depth of the weapon is thus near to its maximum value of $1\frac{3}{4}$ inches throughout the length of the gun. The Mk. II has no cocking tube and the only considerable protuberance from the main cylinder is the trigger; except for the foremost inch of the gun, the depth is therefore little more than the cylinder diameter of $1\frac{1}{4}$ inches. As a result, the Mk. II is a slimmer weapon than the Mk. I and much neater in appearance.

METHOD OF USE. The gun is carried up the sleeve until required, it is then slid into the hand and the muzzle pressed against the victim, at the same time operating the trigger with the thumb. After use, the gun returns to its position up the sleeve and all evidence such as the empty case is retained in the gun.

DIMENSIONS. Overall length $8\frac{3}{4}''$. Diam. $1\frac{1}{4}''$.   **WEIGHT.** 26 ozs.

Section VIII
UNDER WATER EQUIPMENT

AMPHIBIAN, BREATHING APPARATUS

Catalogue No. N 258.

DESCRIPTION. This breathing apparatus consists of an oxygen bottle containing one and a half hours supply; also there is an automatic reducing device which ensures a flow of 1·5 to 2·0 litres per minute. The cannister of protosorb or carbon dioxide absorbent is connected to the breathing bag and purifies the exhaled air; a by-pass valve is also supplied if the flow does not prove sufficient.

METHOD OF USE. The main valve is turned on and a few puffs given on the by-pass, then the breathing bag is about two-thirds full. The mouthpiece is inserted, lungs emptied and valve opened. Breathing should be quite normal. If the breathing seems to be cut short, use the by-pass quite freely, in short quick puffs.

When the exhaust valve is beneath the surface, it must be opened.

WEIGHT. In air, 28¾ lbs. In water, 7½ lbs.

SHIPPING CLASSIFICATION.

Generic Title · · Amphibian dual purpose breathing apparatus.

PACKING AND SPECIAL NOTES.

It should always be stowed dry and if possible, with a full cylinder of oxygen and empty protosorb canister, fitted as if for use.

It is most important to check all the valves, washers, etc., and the valves should be greased occasionally.

WEIGHT PACKED. 28¾ lbs.

CONTAINERS, DEEP WATER, QUICK OPENING, MK. I & II

Catalogue No. L 175.

MK. I.   MK. 2.

DESCRIPTION. The Container is made of steel, and has a quick-release lid inset into one end and a carrying handle on the other.

The Container can be opened or closed in a few seconds.

A load of sixty pounds of stores is required to give the Container a negative buoyancy, and it is watertight to a depth of fifteen fathoms. Its capacity is approximately 1·2 cubic feet.

In the Mark I Container, the base is convex and the carrying handle projects beyond it. In the Mark II, the base is concave and the carrying handle is inside the concavity, so that the Container can stand firmly on its base.

METHOD OF USE. The lid is opened and closed by screwing the bar, unlocking the fixing bar underneath.

Care must be taken to see that the rubber ring lies flat in its groove and the bar is screwed down as tightly as possible, otherwise the Container will not be watertight.

DIMENSIONS. Length 25¾". Diameter 12¼".   **WEIGHT.** 50 lbs.

PACKING AND SPECIAL NOTES. Loose.

Usually made up with "A" and "B" Moorings, but can be supplied separately if required.

The Mk. II will supersede the Mk. I when supplies of the latter are exhausted.

POUCHES, SWIMMING, INNER CASE
POUCHES, SWIMMING, OUTER CASE

Catalogue Nos. J 173.   J 172.

DESCRIPTION.   The Inner Case is a rubberised fabric bag, the top of which can be rolled over and sealed with adhesive tape.

The Outer Case is provided with tapes for tying over the shoulders and round the chest.

DIMENSIONS.

Inner Case—Length 15".   Width 6¾".

Outer Case—Length 12".   Width 6¾".

WEIGHT.

1¼ ozs.

3 ozs.

PACKING AND SPECIAL NOTES. As required.

TACKLE, MOORING, TYPES 'A' & 'B'

Catalogue No. K 194.

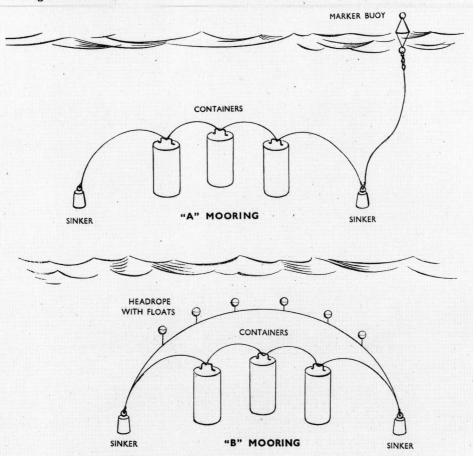

MARKER BUOY

CONTAINERS

SINKER   **"A" MOORING**   SINKER

HEADROPE WITH FLOATS

CONTAINERS

SINKER   **"B" MOORING**   SINKER

DESCRIPTION. The Moorings are made up from the components mentioned under K 194 and K 195.

They are designed for the concealing of stores in estuaries, fjords, etc., where it is possible to have access to them from a small boat. There are two main types:—

Mooring, Type "A." This is marked by a buoy, in which case the double conical mooring buoy is supplied. It is suggested, however, that whenever possible this should be replaced by a marking buoy normally used in the locality.

Mooring, Type "B." This is designed for places where a marking buoy would be liable to lead to suspicion. In this case the moorings are supplied with a head rope which floats at half the depth and is attached to the two ends of the mooring.

Each type is made up with any number of containers required, but normally not more than five are used.

METHOD OF USE. The moorings are prepared before being used, and they are carefully stacked in the boat so that they can be paid out over the back without the ropes becoming entangled. They are deposited from the boat at the spot selected.

PACKING AND SPECIAL NOTES.

As required.

Demands should state whether "A" or "B" Type required.

TACKLE, MOORING, BUOY, FLOATING

Catalogue No. N 259.

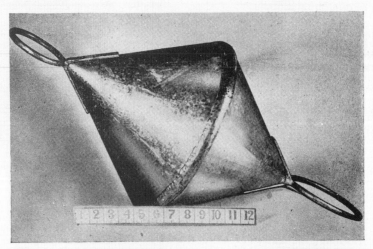

DESCRIPTION. The above is a marker buoy used in the "A" Type Mooring to mark the spot where the moorings are located, and to enable them to be raised from the bottom.

TACKLE, MOORING, GRAPNELS

Catalogue No. K 195.

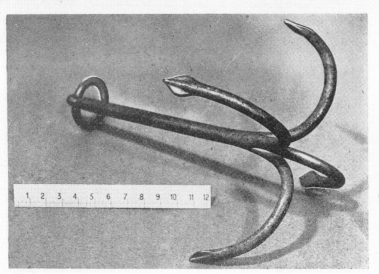

DESCRIPTION. Three or four pronged grapnels of the ordinary type for dragging up underwater ropes, etc.

METHOD OF USE. The "B" Type Mooring have to be laid in such a position that the head rope intersects a given line at right angles, the line being fixed by two points on the seashore or by one point and a compass bearing. The sweeping is carried out by moving along the line in a boat with the grapnel trailing from the back of the boat, just along the bottom of the sea.

DIMENSIONS. Length 22". Width 15".   **WEIGHT.** 9 lbs.
PACKING AND SPECIAL NOTES. As required.

110

TACKLE, MOORING, FLOATS, HOLLOW, STEEL

Catalogue No. K 194c.

DESCRIPTION.
The above consists of a hollow steel float provided with a two-inch ring for attaching them to the rope and they are used in conjunction with moorings.

METHOD OF USE.
The floats are attached to the head rope by passing the bight of the rope through the ring which loops it over the float and then pulls the rope tight as shown in the photograph. The floats are attached to the rope at four fathoms intervals.

Allowance must be made for shortening of the rope when the floats are attached.

PACKING AND SPECIAL NOTES.
They are usually made up with "A" and "B" Moorings but can be supplied separately.

TACKLE, MOORING, SINKERS, DAN BUOY
(56 LBS.)

Catalogue No. K 194e.

DESCRIPTION.
The Sinkers, Dan Buoy, 56 lbs. are used in conjunction with the underwater moorings to sink the end of the ropes to the bottom of the sea.

METHOD OF USE.
The Sinkers are used at both ends of the "A" and "B" Moorings and with the anchor buoy in the "A" Type Mooring. They are attached to the ropes by means of D Shackles (K 194d).

WEIGHT. 56 lbs.

PACKING AND SPECIAL NOTES.
They are usually made up with "A" and "B" Moorings but can be supplied separately.

TACKLE, MOORING, CORDAGE, TARRED, 1½"
" " SHACKLES, D-SCREW
" " SWIVEL, GALVANISED
" " THIMBLES

Catalogue Nos. K 194a.   K 194d.
            N 260.   K 194b.

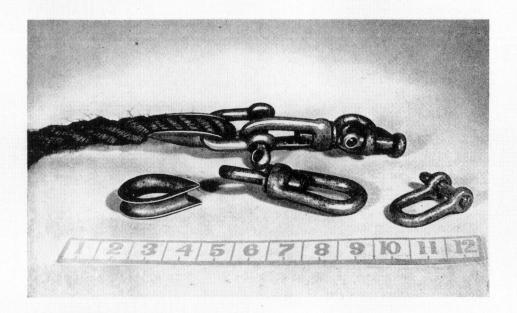

DESCRIPTION.   The following stores are accessories of Tackle, Moorings, Types "A" and "B" (K.194).

Cordage, Tarred (K.194a) is made up to suit individual requirements.

The Shackle (K.194d) has a lock which can be opened and closed and used with the eye splice if required.

The two ends of the Galvanised Swivel (N.260) are free to spin one in relation to the other and is provided for all corded joints.

The Thimble (K.194b) is used with an eye splice in order to prevent the rope fraying when the splice passes through the metal part of the "D" Shackle (K.194d).

PACKING AND SPECIAL NOTES.

These stores are usually made up with types "A" and "B" Moorings, but can be supplied separately.

Section IX
MEDICAL DRUGS AND FOOD

BANDAGE KIT

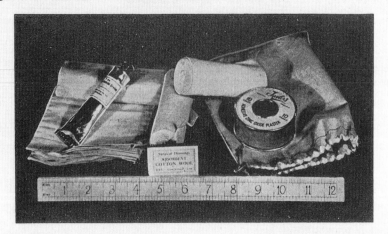

DESCRIPTION. A kit containing bandages, cotton wool, adhesive plaster and antiseptic ointment; packed in a rubberised bag. Suitable for one or two men.

DIMENSIONS. 8″ x 6″ x 3″

FIELD MEDICAL KIT

Catalogue Nos. N 268 unit A.I   N 270 unit B.I   N 272 unit B.III
              N 269 „   A.II   N 271   „   B.II

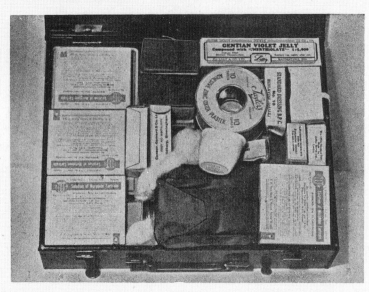

DESCRIPTION. A compact Medical and First Aid Kit suitable for units of ten men and upwards; intended primarily for use in temperate climates. It consists of five units, each packed in a metal case:—

Units A.I and A.II together—supply First Aid Dressings and Medical Comforts suitable for use by laymen.

Units B.I and B.II together—supply a supplementary selection of simple surgical instruments and drugs (including intravenous anæsthetic) suitable for use by medically qualified men.

Unit B.III—supplies vaccines, syringes and intravenous anæsthetic suitable for use by medically qualified men.

DIMENSIONS. Each unit 10½″ x 8½″ x 2½″   **WEIGHT.** A.I 6 lb. 4 oz.   B.I 5 lb. 14 oz.   B.III 5 lb.
                                           A.II 6 lb.   B.II 5 lb. 4 oz.

GLOVES, RUBBER, SURGICAL

Catalogue No. H 210.

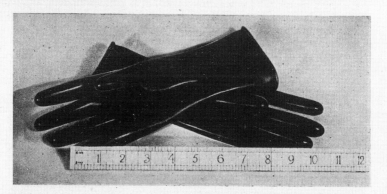

DESCRIPTION. A general purpose rubber glove made of para rubber, useful for handling nitro-glycerine explosive and 808.

METHOD OF USE. To put on, turn the glove inside out and sprinkle some French Chalk over it, the hand will then slip in easily. Alternatively, wash the hands and put the gloves on while the hands are still soapy. To remove, begin at the wrist and turn inside out. Do not attempt to take them off by pulling with fingers.

DIMENSIONS. Size 8.
Size 8½. **WEIGHT.** 1 oz. per pair.

SHIPPING CLASSIFICATION. Generic Title   -   Gloves, Rubber, Surgical
PACKING AND SPECIAL NOTES. As required.

TABLETS, AIR SICK

Catalogue No. N 280.

DESCRIPTION. Compound tablets (R.A.F. formulæ) which will reduce the incidence of air-sickness by about 50%. Success cannot be guaranteed in any individual case.

METHOD OF USE. Take four tablets half an hour before take-off. Do not exceed this dose. It is essential that the drug should be taken <u>before</u> nausea is felt.

DIMENSIONS. $\frac{1}{4}"$ x $\frac{1}{8}"$
PACKING AND SPECIAL NOTES. No standard pack.

TABLETS, SEA SICK

Catalogue No. N 279.

DESCRIPTION. Tablets of the most efficient drug known for this purpose; it will reduce the incidence of sea-sickness by about 50%. Success in any individual case cannot be guaranteed.

METHOD OF USE. Take two tablets one hour before the expected time of onset of sickness, followed by one tablet at the end of each six hours up to a maximum of 48 hours. This dosage must not be exceeded. It is essential that the drug should be taken <u>before</u> nausea is felt.

DIMENSIONS. $\frac{1}{8}"$ diam. x $\frac{1}{16}"$
PACKING AND SPECIAL NOTES. No standard pack.

INDIVIDUAL RATIONS (EUROPEAN)

Catalogue Nos. N 285—Biscuit and Chocolate.   N 283—Dehydrated Mutton.
N 286—Biscuit and Dried Fruit.   N 287—Kreyberg III.
N 282—Dehydrated Beef.   N 288—Margarine one man—day.
N 284—Dehydrated Beef and Sage.

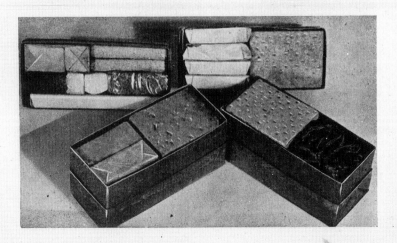

DESCRIPTION. Standardised compact rations for use in temperate climates. Packed in one man-meal units in taped waxed cartons. A variety of contents is available from which a suitable choice may be made, depending on the needs and tastes of the user. These rations represent the maximum attainable degree of lightness and compactness.

METHOD OF USE. All components can, if necessary, be eaten without cooking, except the blocked coffee. The dehydrated meat and potato are, however, best cooked; this is done in 10 to 15 minutes, by crumbling them into water and bringing it to the boil.

DIMENSIONS.   **WEIGHT.**

Cartons   5" x 2¼" x 2⅛" external   approximately 10½ ozs.
Margarine   2⅝" diam. x 1¼" external   approximately 3½ ozs.

TABLETS, WATER PURIFYING

Catalogue No. N 281.

DESCRIPTION. Tablets for dissolving in infected fresh water so as to make it safe to drink.

METHOD OF USE. The tablets are effective only in fresh clear water; muddy or thick water must be cleared by filtration.

Add one tablet to one litre (1¾ pints) of water; shake well for a few minutes; stand for half an hour before drinking.

DIMENSIONS. $\frac{7}{32}$" diam. x $\frac{3}{32}$"

PACKING AND SPECIAL NOTES. No standard pack.

Section X
MAN AND SUPPLIES DROPPING EQUIPMENT

BANDAGES, ANKLE, PAIRS

Catalogue No. N 262.

DESCRIPTION.

Standard unmarked surgical elastic crepe bandage for supporting the ankles.

WEIGHT. 2 ozs. approx.

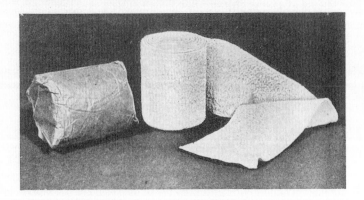

BOOTS, CANVAS, ANTI - MUD

Catalogue No. J 223.

DESCRIPTION.

These overboots are made of canvas and have tying cord at ankle, instep and top. The old type is fitted with sorbo rubber heel and sole, but the new issue has a leather sole. Made in one size only, which is sufficiently large to fit over any normal boot. No markings.

PACKING AND SPECIAL NOTES.

As required.

WEIGHT. 2½ lbs. per pair.

BRIEF CASES

Catalogue No. N 264.

DESCRIPTION.

These cases are made of real or imitation leather in various shades of brown or black, fitted with a lock and in some cases two leather straps.

They bear no trade names or other markings. Cases have been camouflaged to represent age and normal wear.

DIMENSIONS. 11" x 16"

WEIGHT. 2 lbs.

FLASKS, SPIRIT

Catalogue No. N 263.

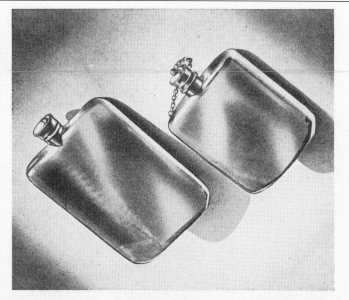

DESCRIPTION.

White metal flasks with cork lined screw stoppers. These flasks are made in two sizes—four ounce and eight ounce. Shaped to fit in a hip pocket. They bear no markings.

DIMENSIONS.

4 oz. - 3" x 4½" x 7/10"
8 oz. - 4" x 6" x 7/10"

WEIGHT. 9 ozs.
¾ lb.

PARACHUTIST EQUIPMENT

Catalogue Nos. G 75a.
G 75b.
G 75c.
G 75d.

| WEB, SPADES, 48", BELT |
| WEB, „ 52", BELT |
| WEB, „ LEG STRAPS |
| WEB, „ TOOL CARRIERS |

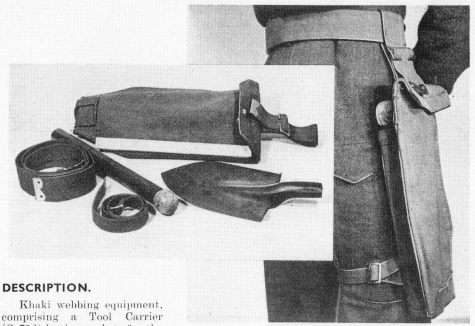

DESCRIPTION.

Khaki webbing equipment, comprising a Tool Carrier (G 75d) having pockets for the Blade and Handle of the Spade, Parachutist (G 75). The carrier is worn on the hip, strapped to the waist by means of the Belt (G 75a or b) and to the thigh by means of the Leg Strap (G 75c).

DIMENSIONS. Belt (G 75a) 48" x 2"
Belt (G 75b) 52" x 2"
Leg Strap (G 75c) 29" x 1"
Tool Carrier (G 75d) 15" x 12"

TOTAL WEIGHT.
1 lb. 7 ozs.

PACKING AND SPECIAL NOTES. As required.

PARACHUTIST EQUIPMENT, PADS, SPINE
PARACHUTIST EQUIPMENT, PADS, HEEL

Catalogue Nos. N 261a, N 261b.

PARACHUTIST EQUIPMENT, PADS, KNEE

Catalogue No. N 261c.

DESCRIPTION. SPINE PAD—A sheet of sorbo rubber, one inch thick. It is fitted round its edges with canvas; this was formerly used to enable the pad to be stitched into the parachutist suit, but it is not now used as the pad fits into a pocket in the back of the suit, giving protection to the wearer's spine on landing.

HEEL PADS—Small shaped pads of sorbo rubber to fit into the heel of wearer's shoes or boots, tapered from $\frac{1}{2}$ inch maximum thickness.

KNEE PADS—Stocking type material, fitted with a khaki cloth edging at its two sides. A leather boot lace quick release device is provided, and the front of the pad is stuffed with kapok.

No markings on any of these pads.

DIMENSIONS.		WEIGHT.
Spine Pad	- 9″ x 12″ x 1″	1 lb.
Heel Pad	- 2¾″ x 4″ x ½″	4 ozs. per pair.
Knee Pad	- Length 9″	1¼ lbs. per pair.

PARACHUTIST, SPADES, MK. II (A)

Catalogue No. G 75.

DESCRIPTION. A collapsible Spade consisting of a heart shaped Blade with a tapered shank, and a short tubular metal Handle into which the shank fits. The edge of the Blade is sharpened, and the top is turned over to give a good bearing surface for the foot.

METHOD OF USE. The spade is primarily intended for burying Parachutes, but can also be used as an Entrenching Tool.

DIMENSIONS. Blade 12½". Handle 14" x 1½". Assembled overall 25¼" x 6". **TOTAL WEIGHT.** 2 lbs.

PACKING AND SPECIAL NOTES. As required.

PARACHUTIST, WATERSUIT, MK. V

Catalogue No. N 265.

DESCRIPTION.

The suit consists of a large overall of waterproof material of ample dimensions, terminating in rubber soles. It has a circular hole at the top made of rubber fabric through which the wearer enters the suit. Rubber wrist bands are provided to prevent ingress of water at the wrists. A skeleton head harness of stout webbing about 1½ inches wide, fitted with a metal buckle, is worn with the suit to ensure a tight fit to the face opening and is put on last. A small external pocket is fitted to each sleeve, the one on the left for a knife, and on the right for a compass.

The wrists are re-inforced with strong elastic latex type rubber as is the heel and foot.

The suit is made in one size only but permits the wearing of ample clothing underneath.

WEIGHT. 5½ lbs.

HARNESS, WIRE, PANNIERS
Catalogue Nos. 15C/247 (Type A). 15C/248 (Type B). 15C/249 (Type C).

HARNESS TYPE (with Pannier and Pack).

DESCRIPTION. These Harness Types are to specific sizes to fit Types A, B and C Panniers respectively, but the design conforms to the basic design for all types of packages irrespective of size which conform to the square or rectangular shape of the Panniers. The Harness consists essentially of four strops, two positioned vertically and centrally on each side of the package, the other two being positioned horizontally at given points around the package. The strops are stitched together at their intersections, and one vertical strop is provided with two rings, triangular positioned, so that the rings are equidistant from the centre of the intersection of the vertical strops, and are positioned approximately six to eight inches below the top corners of the package on opposed sides when the Harness is fitted. The strops are secured by means of double circular rings attached to one extremity of each strop, the other extremity mating with these rings when the Harness is fitted, so that the Harness can be adjusted very tightly to the package. Harnesses of this type are made up to conform to the external dimensions of their respective packages.

METHOD OF USE. The Harnesses are fitted to their respective Panniers, as shown in the photograph, and tightened by hand to fit as snugly as possible, ensuring that the triangular rings are equidistant from the upper corner of the Pannier or package. Harnesses of this type are generally fitted with the packs adjustable already described, the snap hooks of which mate with the triangular rings of the Harness. Certain types for use with packs embodying single point suspension are provided with a snap hook which is positioned at the centre of the top of the package, the intersection of two main vertical strops passing through the slot of the snap hook.

WEIGHT. All approx. 2 lbs. each.

PACKING AND SPECIAL NOTES.

Harness webbing should not come in contact with sea water. If a tin lined case is not used, waterproof material must be wrapped around the webbing to prevent damage, and the box in which it is shipped lined with similar material.

CANOPIES AND PACKS, ADJUSTABLE

(16' 6" — 20' — 24' — 28' — 32')

Catalogue Nos.	15 /83/8 81/151/150	Jacob material.
„	„ 15C/83/8 81/151/150	Khaki material.
„	„ 15C/16 /161/160/159/158	Portland stone material.
„	„ 15C/31.	20' rough type, white.
„	„ 15C/156/155/154/153/152	White material.

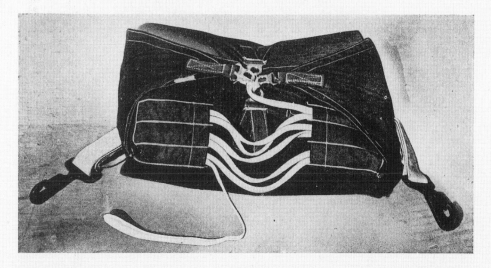

DESCRIPTION. These parachutes and packs are basically of similar design. The dimensions refer to the diameters of the respective canopies, and the pack covers are scaled up from the smallest dimension to the largest to accommodate the ascending scale of sizes. The pack cover is of conventional design, being secured by means of a breaking cord through which the loop at one end of the silk, nylon or celanese cord static line is passed, release being made by the breakage of the final tie. The essential point of the design is that the snap hooks, one of which is positioned at each end of the pack, can be adjusted by means of a strop provided so that the distance between them can be varied through a large range. This strop also ensures continuity between the snap hooks, and the adjustment provided permits the use of a pack of given size on packages or containers of varied dimensions, so that the pack is virtually universal in application.

METHOD OF USE. These packs are used universally on special packages, the adjustment provided on the attachments permitting their employment on containers no matter what may be the relative positions of the triangular rings with which the pack snap hooks mate. The governing factor in the choice of pack size, is the gross weight of the package, the scale being arranged to ensure a standard rate of descent, irrespective of package weight or dimensions.

DIMENSIONS.

			WEIGHT.	
16' 6" Parachute	15½" x 9½" x 6".			7 lbs. 8 ozs.
20'	„	16" x 11" x 6".		9 lbs. 14 ozs.
24'	„	17" x 12¼" x 7".		12 lbs. 15 ozs.
28'	„	19½" x 12½" x 8".		15 lbs. 12 ozs
32'	„	19½" x 12½" x 9½".		18 lbs. 7 ozs.

PACKING AND SPECIAL NOTES. These parachutes are packed in tin lined cases in order to prevent damage by sea water. Various sizes of parachutes should be packed in individual cases so that if loss occurs by enemy action, it may be possible to salvage at least one of them, thus enabling the unit to carry on operations.

PACKAGE DIMENSIONS. Three types of tin lined cases are used to ship parachutes.

Inside Dimensions.	Weight Empty.
3' x 2' x 2'.	1 cwt.
3' 8" x 2' 4" x 2' 10".	1 cwt. 3 qrs. 18 lbs.
3' 8" x 3' 8" x 2' 2".	1 cwt. 2 qrs. 13 lbs.

"C" & "H" CONTAINERS, PARACHUTES, JACOB, WHITE, KHAKI

Catalogue Nos. 15C/63, 15C/118, 15C 206.

DESCRIPTION. OLD TYPE (still in use)—15C/63, pack and parachute in material camouflaged to Jacob design ; 15C/118, parachute in khaki material. The latter differs only in colour and not in design.

NEW TYPE—15C/206, pack and parachute, of simplified construction and modified internal suspension, are both in khaki material. External appearance is similar to the old type, and general packing details apply to both.

Both types are two-point suspension packs, carrying two snap hooks externally at diametrically opposed points, each snap hook positioned to mate with the D-rings provided on the "C" type container, and with the slotted portion of the securing rod on the "H" type container. The packs are secured and released by means of a spring pin attached to a double silk, nylon or celanese cord. The major difference between the old and new types is in the internal suspension connections. With the old type, the rigging lines are connected directly to the snap hooks, whilst in the new type, the lines are connected to a centrally disposed loop of a webbing strop the extremities of which are attached to a snap hook.

METHOD OF USE. These parachute packs are constructed to fit the bucket provided in the ends of the containers, the snap hooks mating with the suspension fittings embodied on the containers. Embodiment on the containers only involves the fitting of the pack into the stowage and the connection of the snap hooks to their respective fittings. The static line is attached to the appropriate strong point on the aircraft after the containers are loaded on to the bomb racks.

DIMENSIONS.

10" x 15" diameter

WEIGHT.

16 lbs.

PACKING AND SPECIAL NOTES.

These parachutes are packed in tin lined cases in order to prevent damage by sea water.

PACKAGE DIMENSIONS.

Three types of tin lined cases are used to ship parachutes.

Inside Dimensions.

3' x 2' x 2'

3' 8" x 2' 4" x 2' 10"

3' 8" x 3' 8" x 2' 2"

Weight Empty.

1 cwt.

1 cwt. 3 qrs. 18 lbs.

1 cwt. 2 qrs. 13 lbs.

CONTAINERS, "C" TYPE, CELL

Catalogue No. 15C/2. Jacob.
     „   „ 15C/8. White.

"C" TYPE CELL SMALL   **"C" TYPE CELL LARGE**

DESCRIPTION.   The large cells are those fitted to standard Type "C" containers, and the small cells are those used in the obsolete small Type "C" container (twelve inches diameter). The cells are in fact metal drums with flat lids which are secured by means of quick release catches into the top of the cells, and bed into a rubber ring embodied around the housing. These lids are provided with two hinged handles for transportation purposes, in each type.

METHOD OF USE.

These cells are dropped singly by parachute and are usually packed with small fire-arms and/or small arms ammunition. They are provided with a standard package harness made to the cylindrical dimensions, and are not covered. A hairlok disc is embodied on each end, and the harness is made to fit the cell complete with hairlok discs, a standard parachute in adjustable pack being embodied. In some cases, single point suspension is used, in which case a small snap hook is embodied centrally at the top of the cell harness, the main vertical straps passing through the slot in the snap hook at their point of intersection. The single D-ring of this type of parachute pack mates with this snap hook.

DIMENSIONS. Large Cell - 15" diam. x 19" high.   **WEIGHT.** 16 lbs.
               Small Cell - 12" diam. x 19" high.   14 lbs.

PACKING AND SPECIAL NOTES. Must be preserved from contact with sea water.

CURLED KORAN FIBRE

Catalogue Nos. 32B/733. 60" needled on canvas.

32B/734. 40" needled on canvas.

32B/NIV. loose.

DESCRIPTION.   Curled Koran Fibre is a proprietary name for curled coir fibre which has the appearance of coarse curled hair of a bright brown colour. The items listed as "needled on canvas" are made up by stitching a layer of intertwined coir fibre, at intervals, to sheets of hessian. In this form the Koran Fibre can be wrapped around stores in the form of a parcel, and can thus be readily used in conjunction with panniers and other parachute packages. Loose Koran Fibre is obtained in bales, and comprises the fibre only. Koran Fibre combines shock-absorbent qualities with extreme lightness, so that several thicknesses can be used without undue weight to procure adequate absorption of shock.

METHOD OF USE. Koran Fibre needled on canvas is used in conjunction with panniers, and also as a subsidiary shock-absorbent wrapping for packages in conjunction with Hairlok where the force of impact is less likely to prove injurious to the store. Loose Koran Fibre can be used for internal packing in cells, containers or packages, and makes an extremely useful filling where stores do not occupy the whole container space.

DIMENSIONS.

Sheets - 40" and 60" wide.
1" thick.

WEIGHT.

4½ ozs. per square foot.

PACKING AND SPECIAL NOTES.

Wrapped in grease-proof paper to prevent damage by sea water, the whole being enclosed in hessian canvas. Quantity per bale depends largely upon stowage space, but the words "NOT TO BE OVERSTOWED" must be painted on the bale. This prevents other cargo being stowed upon the bales which might compress the store and damage its shock-absorbent properties.

CONTAINERS, "C" TYPE

Catalogue No. 15C/65. Jacob.

"   "   15C/120. White.

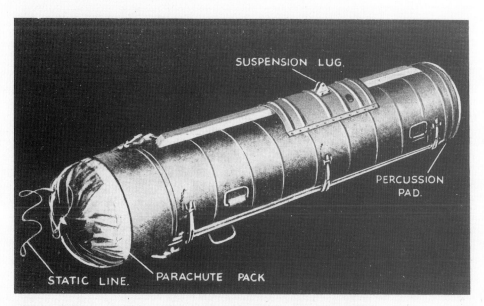

CONTAINER READY FOR ATTACHMENT TO AIRCRAFT

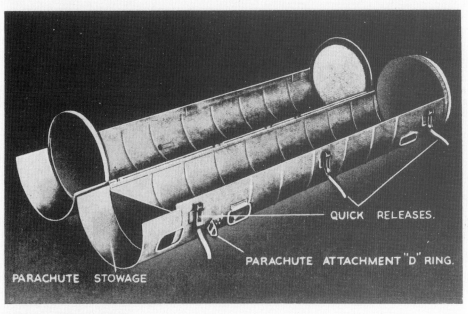

CONTAINER OPEN

CONTAINERS, "C" TYPE

Catalogue No. 15C/65.   Jacob.

    „   15C/120.   White.

DESCRIPTION.   The container body is in longitudinal halves of semi-circular sections which are hinged together along one side by five hinges. Each half is made in sheet metal with circumferential strengthening swages at intervals along the length and two internal longitudinal reinforcing bars. At one-third and two-third circumferential positions along the container, two sets of lugs are rivetted to the inside of the container for the positioning of the three identical internal cells which are normally embodied, and into which the stores are stowed. The container can be used for stores of longer dimensions, without the cells. One end of the container body is open, but a metal bulkhead is fitted in each half, a short distance from the end, and these bulkheads form a compartment for the stowage of the parachute pack. Each half compartment embodies an aperture through which passes the corresponding parachute pack snap-hook which is attached to a D-ring fixed to the outside of the container body at the appropriate position. At the other end of the container a circular metal end is fitted in each half and on the old type a circular sorbo percussion pad is glued to the outside of the external metal disc. In some new types this is replaced by a metal percussion head similar to that used for the " H " type container.

When closed the two halves of the container are held together by three quick release catches, each unit comprising a catch-hook and a locking holder rivetted to the top half of the container, and a quick release lever rivetted in a corresponding position on the bottom half of the container. The quick release lever is locked in the closed position by means of an anchored split pin. Carrying and opening handles are positioned at each end on the outside of each half, and the container should always be carried by these handles.

The complete container, when assembled as illustrated in Fig. 1 can be fitted to the 500 lb. and universal bomb carriers, for which purpose it is provided with a single lug for direct attachment to the release unit.

METHOD OF USE.   Stores are stowed in the internal cells, or if of dimensions longer than the length of the cell, may be stowed in the container body with suitable packing. The cells are positioned by the internal lugs and by wooden discs which mate with these lugs, and should be provided with webbing strops around their circumference for ease of withdrawal and carriage. After the cells are installed the two halves of the container body are hinged together and locked in this condition by the locking catches, care being taken to lock the release levers with the pins provided.

DIMENSIONS.
    Internal 56" long x 14"
    Overall 5' 8" x 15" dia.

WEIGHT.
    96 lbs.

PACKING AND SPECIAL NOTES.
    Must be preserved from contact with sea water.

PARACHUTIST, SUITS (STRIPTEASE SUITS)

Catalogue No. 22C/733 (Size 1). 22C/734 (Size 2)
22C/735 (Size 3). 22C/736 (Size 4).

GLOVES, GAUNTLET

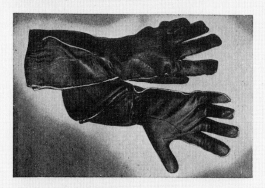

GLOVES, LININGS, SILK

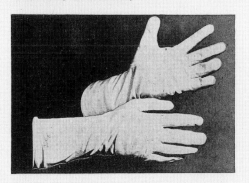

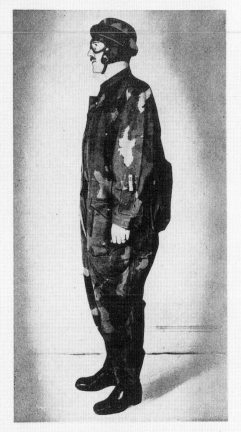

DESCRIPTION. These are made of either white or camouflaged canvas in four sizes. A zip fastener on each side is fitted for rapid exit from the suit, and these fasteners can be operated in either direction. A fly zip is also provided. On the left hip, is an external pocket for pistol and on the inside is a felt lined pocket designed to fit the spade, parachutist. Slightly to the rear of this pocket is a long narrow pocket for the spade handle.

At the lower outside edge of the left sleeve is a pocket for dagger or fighting knife and under each armpit, also outside, is a further pocket large enough to hold a second pistol, or emergency rations, etc. One large and one smaller pocket is fitted inside on the right.

A large pocket is provided to receive the spine pad, if used. This pocket is large enough to hold a brief case. At the neck is a leather strap to which is attached the helmet. All pockets have press stud fasteners.

The suits are large enough to permit of the wearing of two greatcoats if desired.

Flying Gauntlets with silk linings and Waistcoats, life saving, can also be used with these suits if required, in which case the standard R.A.F. pattern is provided.

DIMENSIONS.		WEIGHT
Size 1	- Up to 5 ft. 4 ins.	
,, 2	- From 5 ft. 4 ins. to 5 ft. 8 ins.	
,, 3	- From 5 ft. 8 ins. to 5 ft. 11 ins.	4½ lbs.
,, 4	- From 5 ft. 11 ins. to 6 ft. 4 ins.	

PARACHUTISTS, HELMETS

Catalogue No. 22C/965 (Size 1). 22C/966 (Size 2). 22C/967 (Size 3). 22C/968 (Size 4).

DESCRIPTION. Made of similar material to the suits, parachutist and in the same colours. There are four sizes all fitted with mica goggles fastened to the back of the helmet. These goggles are trimmed with plush at the edges.

An adjustable soft leather chin strap is provided, and a strap at the base connects with that in the neck of the striptease suit.

The sides are extended to form ear flaps. Round the crown and over the skull, from front to rear, are ribs of padding to give protection to the wearer.

Press stud fittings are provided for oxygen mask and inter-communication microphone. **WEIGHT** 8 ozs.

SHEETS, RUBBERISED, HAIR (HAIRLOK)
Catalogue No. 32C/190.

HAIRLOK BOX

DETAIL SHOWING TEXTURE

STANDARD HAIRLOK SHEET

DESCRIPTION. Shock absorbent material composed of hair, bound with Latex rubber and moulded to the size required. Grey in colour, the nature of its composition being obvious from its appearance. The material can be cut with a sharp knife.

Experiment has proved that this material represents the most efficient shock absorbing medium for use with packages, whatever the type, as it results in shock absorption without undue rebound.

METHOD OF USE. The sheets are used for the assembly of sectional shock absorbent boxes for the accommodation of stores to be dropped by parachute when such stores are of too fragile a nature for inclusion in standard metal containers or panniers. The sheets are cut into sections of the size required to form the sectional box, conforming to the cubic capacity necessary to accommodate the stores. Sections of the sheets are also used as the shock absorbent base for other types of packages.

DIMENSIONS.
6' x 3' x 2" sheets

WEIGHT.
15 lbs. approx.

PACKING AND SPECIAL NOTES.
Packed in bales of ten sheets, wrapped in grease-proof paper to prevent damage by sea water, the whole being enclosed in hessian canvas. As this material is shock absorbent, and in order to prevent other cargo being stowed upon its surface, thus causing it to lose its properties, the words " NOT TO BE OVERSTOWED " are painted on the package.

PACKAGE DIMENSIONS.
Bales of ten sheets—6' x 3' x 1' 11"

WEIGHT PACKED.
Weight of bale—1 cwt. 2 qrs. 22 lbs.

CONTAINERS, "H" TYPE

Catalogue No. 15C/170.

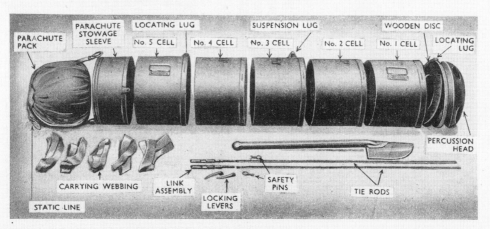

LAYOUT OF CONTAINER COMPONENTS

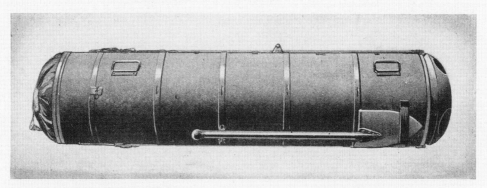

CONTAINER READY FOR ATTACHMENT TO AIRCRAFT

CONTAINERS, "H" TYPE, SPADES

Catalogue No. 15C/229.

DESCRIPTION. The blade of the spade is of metal, into which fits a short wooden handle which terminates in a knob for additional ease in handling. See Figs. 1 and 2 Containers, "H" Type.

METHOD OF USE. The spade is fitted to the clip and bracket provided for that purpose on the Container "H" Type, to which it is locked by a safety pin passing through the bracket. Detachment is easy, and the spade is for use in digging a hole for the burial of the unwanted components of the container, the parachute and any other redundant equipment.

DIMENSIONS. Length 3' 1". Greatest width 8". **WEIGHT.** 3 lbs.

PACKING AND SPECIAL NOTES. Must be preserved from contact with sea water.

CONTAINERS, "H" TYPE

Catalogue No. 15C/170.

DESCRIPTION. The container consists essentially of seven main items; the five small supply cells, in which the stores are stowed, the percussion head (15C/212), and the bucket for the stowage of the parachute pack.

These items when assembled are secured together by means of two tie rods which mate with link assemblies provided with eyebolts for the reception of the parachute pack snap-hooks; the tie rods and links being locked together by means of locking levers which embody internally threaded sleeves which mate with the threaded portions of the rods and links. The levers are locked by means of safety pins. The tie rods and links pass through lugs close to the extremities of the container and serve to lock the cells together, each cell bedding into a housing embodied around the lid of the adjacent cell. The threaded portions of the tie rods and the links each carry two flats, as also do the internally threaded portions of the locking lever sleeves. When the container is fully assembled, the female and male portions of the threads mate together, but when the locking lever is raised, the flats in the female and male portions register and the tie rod and the locking lever can then be parted for instantaneous breaking down of the assembled cells. Each cell has a tapering line painted on its side, and when assembled, this line should appear as a straight line tapering in width towards the percussion head end. Incorrect order of assembly will be indicated by irregularities in this line. Clips and brackets are provided for the reception of the spade if required, the spade being secured in position by means of a safety pin passing through holes in the bracket.

The complete container, when assembled as illustrated, can be fitted to the 500 lb. and the universal bomb carriers, for which purpose it is provided with a single lug for direct attachment to the release unit of the bomb carrier.

METHOD OF USE. Stores are stowed in the respective cells, and the detachable lids secured prior to assembly of the cells. Each cell is then bedded completely and accurately in the housing of the adjacent cell with the sleeve or bucket end standing on the floor, the sets of carrying webbing being inserted where appropriate. After each cell has been correctly fitted, the percussion head is placed in position, and the whole locked by means of the tie rods and locking levers, care being taken to lock the portions as appropriate with safety pins. The parachute pack is fitted into the bucket and the snap hooks attached to their respective eyebolts in the links.

DIMENSIONS.
A, B, D and E cells each 14½" x 9½" deep.
C cell 14" x 8".
Overall 5' 6" x 15" diam.

WEIGHT

86 lbs.

PACKING AND SPECIAL NOTES.
Must be preserved from contact with sea water.

PANNIERS, WIRE

Catalogue Nos.
15C/233 (Type A)
15C/234 (Type AZ)
15C/235 (Type B)
15C/243 (Type BZ)
15C/236 (Type C)
15C/244 (Type CZ)

DESCRIPTION. These panniers are made up on a frame of spring steel wire, to which a lattice work of mild steel wire is fitted, the whole being covered with khaki canvas duck. The pannier consists of two portions, the base and the top or lid, which are identical in design, but the lid is dimensioned so that it fits snugly over the base and thus forms a fully enclosed box. The sides of both the base and lid are hinged, so that the panniers may be transported and stored in a collapsed condition. When the panniers are assembled for use, the hinged sides are secured by means of a staple and double hasp, which is locked in position with a spring wire safety pin and are simply collapsed by the removal of this locking pin and staple for ease of unloading.

The types differ only in dimensions, a different basic type letter being given to panniers of these different sizes. The suffix " Z " indicates that the basic type has a wire coil spring shock absorbing panel fitted to the bottom side of the base, certain stores being approved for dropping with this type of shock absorption in lieu of a sheet of hairlok. The harness types A, B and C, already described, fit the panniers type A, B and C respectively, and as the AZ and any other " Z " type differ only in internal shock absorbing devices, the harness for the basic type also fits the sub-type " Z."

METHOD OF USE. These panniers are used in conjunction with the harnesses and the adjustable packs already described. Cases containing stores, or individual items of stores are stowed in the base of the pannier, the bottom side being lined either with the wire, coil, spring panel or with a panel of hairlok, the remainder being lined with one or two layers of Koran fibre needled on canvas.

Attachment of the parachute is made so that this bottom side makes initial contact with the ground upon alighting.

DIMENSIONS.			WEIGHT.	
A Type	-	22″ x 16″ x 16″		21 lbs.
AZ Type	-	22″ x 16″ x 16″		23 lbs.
B Type	-	24″ x 18″ x 20″		25 lbs.
C Type	-	29″ x 18″ x 13″		21 lbs.

PACKING AND SPECIAL NOTES. The Panniers are collapsible and can be shipped in wooden cases, which must be weather-proof to avoid rust.

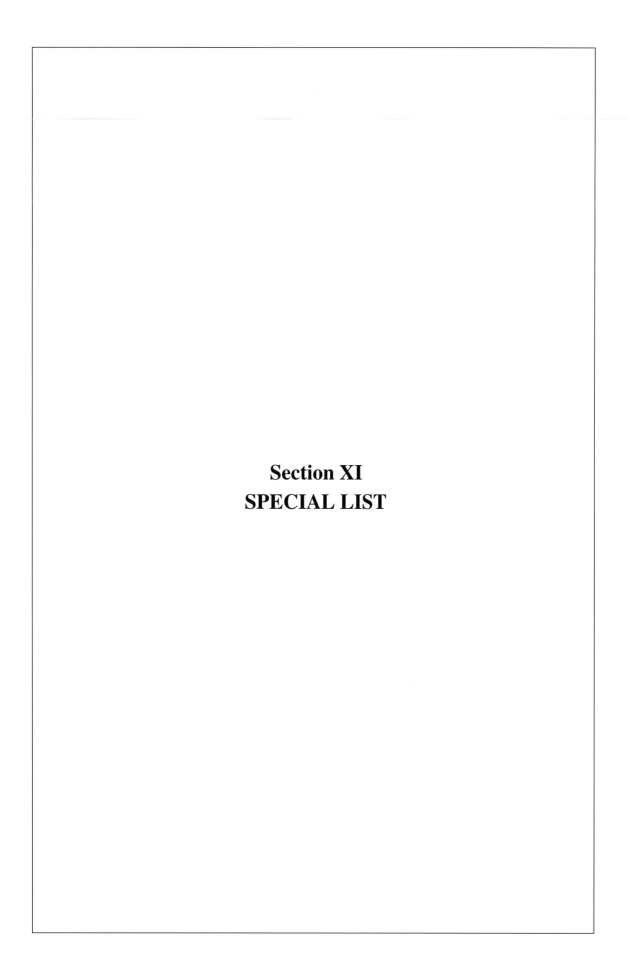

Section XI
SPECIAL LIST

ABRASIVE POWDER

Catalogue No. HS 77c.

DESCRIPTION.

A fine carborundum powder, which is grey in colour and crystalline in substance.

METHOD OF USE.

Mix with the lubricating oil, or throw in dry if parts are exposed.

DIMENSIONS.

Height $2\frac{3}{8}''$.   Width $2\frac{1}{4}''$.
Thickness $1\frac{1}{4}''$.

WEIGHT. 3 oz. per tin.

PACKING AND SPECIAL NOTES.

As required.

DRAGS, DOG

Catalogue No. HS 226.

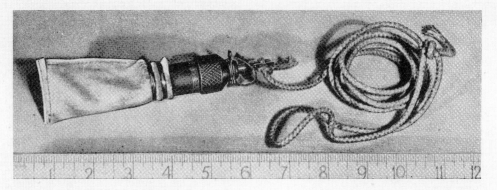

DESCRIPTION.   A bag made of cloth in two layers and containing two shrapnel bullets, is attached to the lower end of a brass tube by wires twisted round the bag over two grooves in the tube. In the upper part of the tube is an ampoule containing powerfully smelling substances dissolved in oil. Screwed on to the upper end of the tube is a cap containing a screwed plunger attached by a butterfly nut. When this nut is screwed down, the plunger descends and crushes the ampoule, releasing its contents into the bag. A safety pin is provided in the stem of the plunger. A cord is attached to the butterfly nut and wound round the drag. The drag is contained in a metal case to protect it from damage and from moisture.

METHOD OF USE. The greatest care must be taken not to foul one's own fingers or clothes with the drag after the ampoule has been broken, and similarly the greatest care must be taken not to step on to any part of the drag trail.

The drag trail should be at least a mile long and should end on hard roads or hard ground at an angle to the direction finally taken.

DIMENSIONS. Length $4\frac{5}{8}''$. Diameter $1''$.   **WEIGHT.** 7 ozs.

PACKING AND SPECIAL NOTES.
Packed separately in circular tins.

PACKAGE DIMENSIONS. Tin $6'' \times 1\frac{1}{2}''$ diameter.   **WEIGHT PACKED.** 8 ozs.

FACE CREAM

Catalogue No.
NS 299.

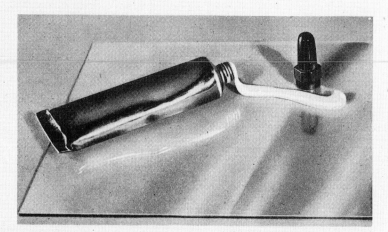

DESCRIPTION. Face Cream is the code name for a material which can be used for frosting glass, and which has been made up to resemble a cosmetic preparation ; that is, it is in the form of a perfumed cream.

METHOD OF USE. For large areas of glass, as on a windscreen, the material should be applied **very liberally,** using, for example, a complete Pigmentan Tube for about ten square decimetres. On clean glass, frosting will take place in about five minutes, but longer time may be necessary on dirty glass. It is safe to spread the cream out with the fingers, provided they are washed shortly afterwards. If applied to other parts of the body mild blistering may occur if contact is prolonged. For sabotaging optical instruments only small quantities are required. For writing on glass the collapsible tube is very suitable and a thin line of cream may easily be extruded in the form of letters.

PACKING AND SPECIAL NOTES.
    (a) In small collapsible tubes camouflaged as Pigmentan—the popular German suntan cream which is understood to have been widely used all over the Continent before the war.
    (b) In large collapsible tubes as shaving cream with suitable inscriptions in different languages.

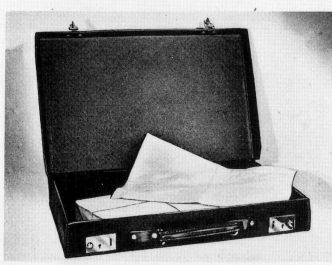

INCENDIARY ATTACHE CASE

Catalogue No.
NS 301.

DESCRIPTION. The external appearance is that of an ordinary case. One camouflaged parcel inside the case contains a thermit charge, battery, and an arming switch. The electric wiring is concealed under the lining of the case. Two quilts of potassium nitrate are provided to assist in combustion of documents. The locks are converted to act as switches and control the firing of the charge.

METHOD OF USE. The arming switch is set to "ON" position. To close and open the case safely the knob of the right-hand lock must be pressed and held to the right. If this is not done the charge will fire when left-hand knob is moved.

SHIPPING CLASSIFICATION. Explosive Group - XI.
                       Storage and Stowage   IV.   O.A.S.
PACKING AND SPECIAL NOTES. Instructions for use are provided with each case.

KNIVES, THUMB

Catalogue No. JS 188.

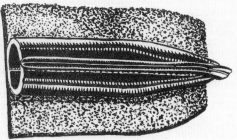

DESCRIPTION. A very small, dagger-shaped knife, sharpened for the full length of the blade along one edge, and for three-quarters of the length along the other; the remaining quarter is flattened to give a grip for the thumb. The hilt is only one inch long, and the Knife can easily be concealed in the hand.

The Knife is provided with a leather sheath, with flaps which can be sewn to the clothing.

DIMENSIONS. In sheath 4" x 2". Knife $3\frac{1}{4}$" x $\frac{3}{4}$".   **WEIGHT.** $\frac{3}{4}$ oz.

PACKING AND SPECIAL NOTES. As required.

MONEY BELT, CALICO

Catalogue No. NS 306.

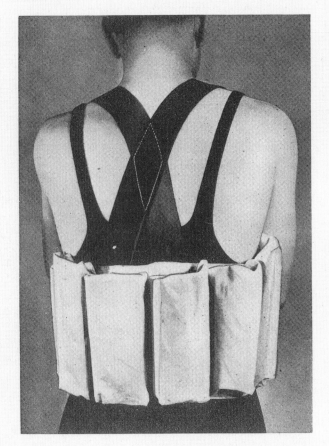

DESCRIPTION.

Type 1.	Three pockets size	$9\frac{3}{4}$" x $5\frac{1}{2}$" x $1\frac{3}{4}$"
„ 2.	Three pockets size	$9\frac{3}{4}$" x $5\frac{1}{2}$" x 1"
„ 3.	Three pockets size	10" x 5" x 1"
„ 4.	Six pockets size	$3\frac{1}{4}$" x 7" x $1\frac{1}{2}$"
„ 5.	Four pockets size	$7\frac{3}{4}$" x $4\frac{3}{4}$" x $1\frac{1}{4}$"

All with three 2" buckle fastenings and shoulder straps.

PACKING AND SPECIAL NOTES.

As required. This is not a standard store, but these can be made up to meet special demands.

Catalogue No.
NS 305.

MONEY BELT, SUEDE

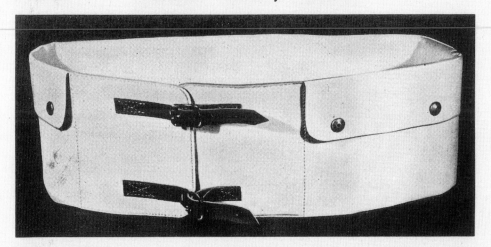

DESCRIPTION.

Type 1. 6" deep. Length of pockets vary according to waist measurements. Three pockets with zip fasteners.

Type 2. 4½" deep. Length of pockets vary according to waist measurements. Three pockets with press-button fastenings.

PACKING AND SPECIAL NOTES.

As required.

This is not a special store, but belts are made up to personal dimensions, etc., when requested.

MUCUNA
(ITCHING POWDER)

Catalogue No.
NS 300.

DESCRIPTION. This powder is composed of minute seed hairs which owing to their peculiar structure cause considerable itching when applied to the skin.

METHOD OF USE. The greatest effect is produced by applying the powder to the inside of underclothing.

PACKING AND SPECIAL NOTES.

As required.

This material is supplied in foot powder tins for the purpose of camouflage.

INCENDIARY BRIEFCASE (SINGLE LOCK)

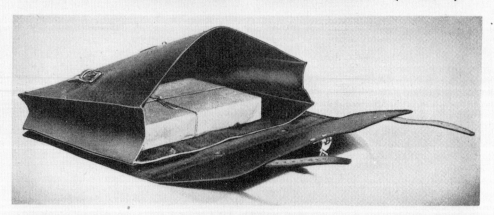

DESCRIPTION. The external appearance is that of an ordinary Briefcase. A camouflaged parcel inside the case contains a thermit charge, battery and arming switch. The electric wiring is concealed in the lining of the case. One quilt of potassium nitrate is provided to assist in combustion of documents. The lock is converted to act as a switch. Another switch, under a patch of rexine inside the case, takes the place of the right hand lock on double lock types.

METHOD OF USE. The arming switch is set to "ON" position. To close and open the case safely, the switch under the patch of rexine must be depressed to its full extent and held thus while the outer lock is manipulated. If this is not done the charge will fire when the external lock is moved.

SHIPPING CLASSIFICATION. Explosive Group - XI.
Storage and Stowage IV. O.A.S

PACKING AND SPECIAL NOTES. Instructions for use are provided with each case.

INCENDIARY CIGARETTES

DESCRIPTION. This device consists of a small incendiary pellet placed inside any type of cigarette. The incendiary pellet is nearer one end of the cigarette than the other and can easily be located by touch.

When ignited the pellet gives a hot flame for about five seconds.

If the cigarette is lit at the end near the pellet the delay will be about two minutes. If lit at the other end the delay will be about three or four minutes. At each end of the pellet there is match composition and the flame produced lasts for about three to five secs.

METHOD OF USE. To obtain the best results it should not be buried more than one inch in the kindling, preferably placed near the surface, thereby assuring a good supply of oxygen.

SHIPPING CLASSIFICATION. Explosive Group - XI.
Storage and Stowage IV. O.A.S.

PACKING AND SPECIAL NOTES.
As required. It is not intended to make this a standard store, but numbers can easily be made to meet special demands.

INCENDIARY SUITCASE

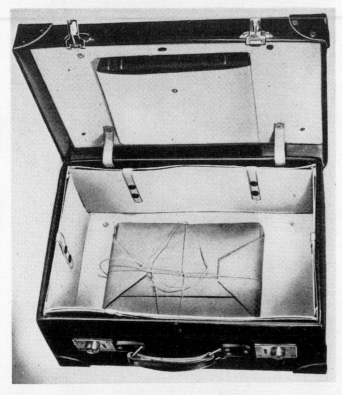

DESCRIPTION. External appearance is that of an ordinary suitcase. Internally there are two camouflaged thermit charges, one in the lid, the other in the bottom of the case. The electric battery and wiring are concealed under the camouflage and lining of the case. Five quilts of potassium nitrate are provided to assist combustion of documents. The locks are converted to act as switches and control the firing of the charges.

METHOD OF USE. The arming switch incorporated in the lower thermit unit is set to the " ON " position. To close and open the case safely the knob of the right-hand lock must be pressed and held to the right. If this is not done the charges will fire when the left-hand knob is moved.

SHIPPING CLASSIFICATION.
Explosive Group — XI.
Storage and Stowage IV. O.A.S.

PACKING AND SPECIAL NOTES.
Full instructions for use are provided with each case.

INKS, SECRET

Catalogue No. HS 69.

DESCRIPTION. Application for these inks should be made through the usual channels, giving details of the country in which the ink is to be used, or alternatively the countries through which correspondence is likely to pass if the ink is being used for external use. Method of camouflage required should also be stated.

A suitable ink cannot be provided unless the aforementioned information is granted.

POLAROID, SQUARES

Catalogue No. HS 67.

DESCRIPTION.
Four-inch squares of Polaroid, which resembles transparent celluloid of a pale, greeny-yellow colour.

METHOD OF USE. When two sheets of Polaroid are placed between the eye of the observer and a source of light, they can be turned in parallel planes in relation to each other so that they either allow practically all the light to pass through them or else stop it altogether. This is due to the fact that Polaroid has a crystalline structure; when the crystals lie at right angles to each other, no light can pass.

DIMENSIONS. $4'' \times 4'' \times \frac{1}{16}''$.   **WEIGHT.** $\frac{1}{4}$ oz.

PACKING AND SPECIAL NOTES. As required. In short supply.

Catalogue Nos.
HS 180.
HS 181.
HS 182.

TORCHES, FRENCH
TORCHES, FRENCH, BATTERIES
TORCHES, FRENCH, BULBS

DESCRIPTION.
The Torch, Battery and Bulb are exact replicas of a French make. The Torch is of the box type, and has a carrying loop.

DIMENSIONS.

Torches—Length $4\frac{3}{16}''$, Width $2\frac{11}{16}''$, Depth $1\frac{3}{8}''$.

Batteries—Length $2\frac{9}{16}''$, Width $2\frac{5}{16}''$, Depth $\frac{13}{16}''$.

Bulbs—Length $1\frac{3}{8}''$, Diameter $\frac{9}{16}''$.

WEIGHT.

10 ozs.

$3\frac{3}{4}$ ozs.

0·3 ozs.

PACKING AND SPECIAL NOTES.
Batteries are packed four dozen in each of the two tin liners of case H.30 Mark IE.

PACKAGE DIMENSIONS.
Batteries in H.30 Mark IE. $16'' \times 10\frac{1}{4}'' \times 8\frac{1}{2}''$.

WEIGHT PACKED.
Batteries 34 lbs. in H.30 Mark IE.

WAISTCOAT, PROOFED COTTON

Catalogue No. NS 307.

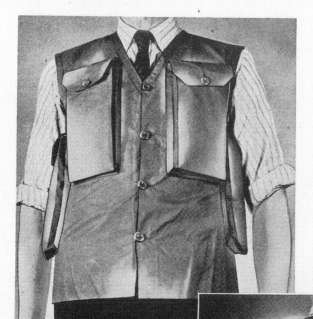

FRONT VIEW

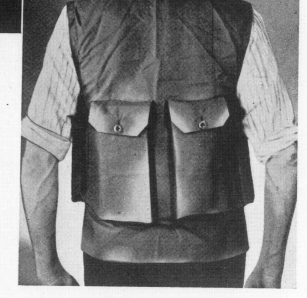

BACK VIEW

DESCRIPTION.   This device consists of a fitted waistcoat with pockets made to sizes required. Used for carrying small outfits or money.

DIMENSIONS.
Length 28″ to 30″
Chest and waist measurements vary according to individual requirements.

PACKING AND SPECIAL NOTES.
As required.
This is not a standard store, but these can easily be made to meet special demands.

●

Descriptive Catalogue

OF

Special Devices

AND

Supplies

●

COMPILED & ISSUED

BY

M.O.1. (S.P.)

THE WAR OFFICE.

Vol. 2.

1945.

INTRODUCTION

●

1. This Illustrated Catalogue Vol. II contains descriptions of various stores produced by, or for, M.O.1. (S.P.), War Office. More detailed information in regard to the items set out in this Catalogue, can be obtained, if required, from M.O.1. (S.P.), War Office, or from our representatives in the theatre in which the information is required.

2. The illustrations are intended for identification purposes only.

3. This Catalogue has been prepared in loose leaf form to facilitate the insertion of new matter or amendments.

Section I
WIRELESS SECTION

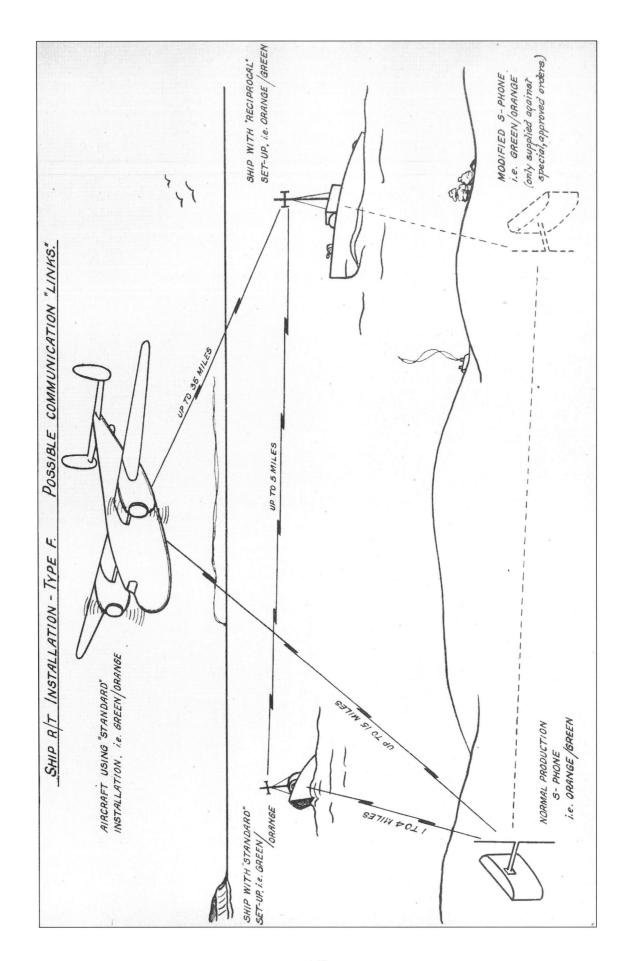

SHIP R/T INSTALLATION - TYPE F. POSSIBLE COMMUNICATION "LINKS."

AIRCRAFT USING "STANDARD" INSTALLATION. i.e. GREEN/ORANGE

SHIP WITH "RECIPROCAL" SET-UP, i.e. ORANGE/GREEN

MODIFIED S-PHONE i.e. GREEN/ORANGE (only supplied against special, approved orders)

UP TO 35 MILES

UP TO 5 MILES

UP TO 15 MILES

1 TO 4 MILES

SHIP WITH "STANDARD" SET-UP. i.e. GREEN/ORANGE

NORMAL PRODUCTION S-PHONE i.e. ORANGE/GREEN

148

MICROWAVE EQUIPMENT

★

INTRODUCTION

The use of very high frequencies to provide low power telephonic communication between ground and aircraft or ground and ships has certain definite advantages, especially with regard to security when compared with communication at more usual frequencies. It is of interest to note that:

(a) Radio energy at these frequencies will not pass through major obstacles, but requires what is almost an "optical" path for transmission and reception, consequently an intercept station must be sited on an unobstructed path from the transmitter(s).

(b) Transmission and reception uses two separate frequency channels, therefore interception would have to be accomplished with two separately tuned receivers, in order to hear both sides of a conversation.

(c) Intercept stations are very rarely provided with receiving equipment working at the extremely high frequencies used.

(d) Range is largely dependent on the height of the aerials above "ground." "Ground Range" is very limited and so reduces the possibility of interception.

Originally this equipment was designed to establish radio telephonic communication between the completely portable ground "S-Phone" and a specially equipped aircraft. The frequency of the S-Phone transmitter was fixed and the aircraft receiver had a small tuning range used when "searching" for the ground station. In the same way the aircraft transmitter worked on a fixed frequency, and the S-Phone receiver tuned over a small range.

It was found desirable for an S-Phone to work to a ship, so aircraft equipment was modified for ship use. With this arrangement the Ground Station could communicate with either ship or plane, but the aircraft could not communicate with the ship. To make this possible, a spare transmitter and receiver, working on reciprocal frequencies, was supplied with the Ship Equipment, thus with a reasonably simple changeover the ship could use the frequencies of a Ground Station, and communicate with aircraft.

It will be seen that two ships can work together if one uses the reciprocal frequencies.

To avoid stating exact frequencies, on the diagram, a normal S-Phone has been called ORANGE/GREEN — meaning it receives on ORANGE — the higher frequency and transmits on GREEN — the lower frequency, and a Standard Ship or Aircraft Installation receives on GREEN, and transmits on ORANGE.

Direction Indicators are provided with the Aircraft equipment, so that the Aircraft can "Home" on to an S-Phone.

S-PHONE

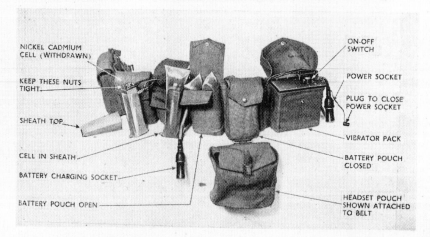

NICKEL CADMIUM CELL (WITHDRAWN)

KEEP THESE NUTS TIGHT

SHEATH TOP

CELL IN SHEATH

BATTERY CHARGING SOCKET

BATTERY POUCH OPEN

ON-OFF SWITCH

POWER SOCKET

PLUG TO CLOSE POWER SOCKET

VIBRATOR PACK

BATTERY POUCH CLOSED

HEADSET POUCH SHOWN ATTACHED TO BELT

This completely portable ground station, complete with all batteries, is designed in the form of personal equipment, to be worn by the operator. Communication is between the ground station and a ship or aircraft, fitted with special equipment.

The transmitter-receiver, housed in a cast aluminium alloy case, is held in position on the operator's chest by rings fitted to the shoulder straps, which support a cloth battery belt worn around the waist. Pockets in the belt are provided to contain the batteries and a vibrator power pack, which supply L.T. and H.T. current for the set.

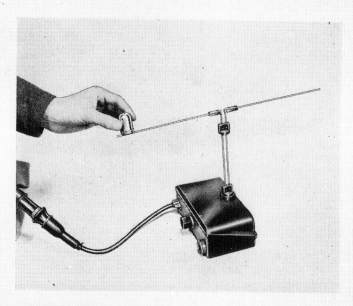

GENERAL DESCRIPTION.

Communication is carried as if over an ordinary telephone, speech quality is very similar, and as there is only one tuning control and one switch, any intelligent person is able to use the apparatus with the minimum of instruction.

Two valves are used in the transmitter, functioning as modulation (speech) amplifier and oscillator. No provision is made for adjusting the transmitter frequency, which is fixed to lie within the tuning range of the ship or plane receiver to which the ground station will transmit.

The receiver, a super-regenerative detector followed by a two-stage audio amplifier, employs three miniature valves. Receiver tuning can be adjusted by means of a knob located on the underside of the case.

A small collapsible aerial is provided which plugs into the front of the set.

The possibility of being overheard whilst transmitting is greatly reduced by the use of a microphone which restricts direct vocal radiation of the operator to within a few yards from where he is standing, when talking at a normal conversational level.

The microphone and headphone are attached to the transmitter-receiver by a flexible cable and a heavy-duty plug and socket. A similar plug and socket is used to link the battery belt and transmitter-receiver.

With the apparatus in position on the operator, it can be brought into operation merely by actuating a switch conveniently placed on the battery belt.

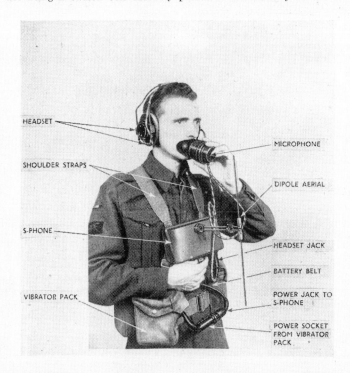

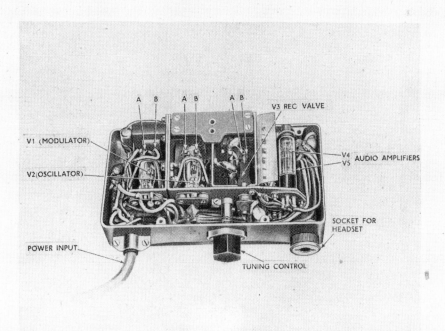

ELECTRICAL CHARACTERISTICS.

Transmitter frequency - - - 337 $\pm$ 3 Mc/s.
Transmitter Power into Aerial - - 0.1 watts approx.
Receiver tuning range - - - 370—395 Mc/s.

BATTERIES.

Lead-acid accumulators, as supplied in early models, are now replaced by Nickel Cadmium cells. New cells fully charged should give 6—7 hours operation. This will become less as the cells age. A Trickle Charger is provided.

WEIGHT AND DIMENSIONS.

	LENGTH	HEIGHT	DEPTH	WEIGHT
S-Phone -	9″	6″	3″	2 lbs.
Battery Belt -	30″	6″	2½″	17 lbs. (including batteries).

The aerial, unfolded, is 16″ long, and protrudes 8″ from the front of the set.

ACCESSORIES AND SPARES. 2 Aerials. Headset. Trickle Charger.

PACKING. The set, battery belt, spares and accessories are normally packed in a suitcase. This method of packing is suitable for all means of transport.

SIZE. 18″ x 14″ x 8″   WEIGHT. 32 lbs.

MICROWAVE EQUIPMENT
AIRCRAFT INSTALLATION
TYPE A2

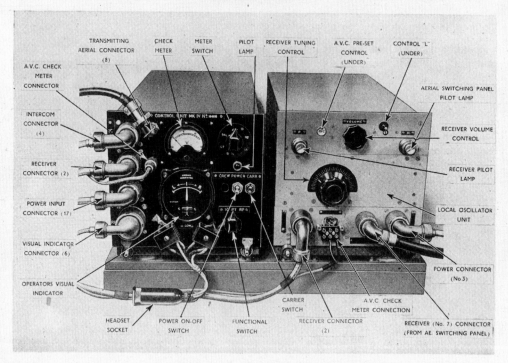

Control Unit and Receiver Panels

152

GENERAL DESCRIPTION.

. This equipment, built as a series of separate units, inter-connected by cables, is operated by one member of the air crew; the facilities available are:

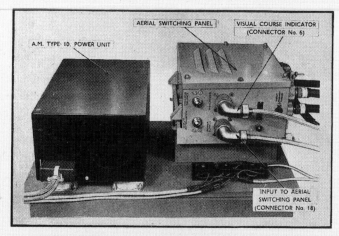

Power Unit and Aerial Switching Panel mounted as in a typical Halifax Installation

(a) When the carrier of the S-Phone is tuned in, it automatically gives a reading on a Visual Direction Indicator, enabling the pilot to "Home" the aircraft on to the Ground Station. With the aircraft flying at about 10,000 feet homing indications can be expected at about 60 miles from the ground S-Phone (Mark IV).

(b) When the range is closed to 30 to 40 miles communication can be established with the ground operator and two-way conversation carried on in a similar way and with similar speech quality to that given by an ordinary line telephone link.

(c) The speech output from the apparatus is arranged to operate into the Standard R.A.F. Inter-communication System, so that the operator using the equipment can also speak to any other member of the air crew. The other members of the air crew can, in addition, hear the conversation between the operator and the ground, but an isolating switch is provided whereby the operator can disconnect the apparatus from the I/C system, thus isolating himself on the equipment.

The Equipment consists of:—

(i) Three small rod aerials, some few inches long, mounted close together outside the aircraft.

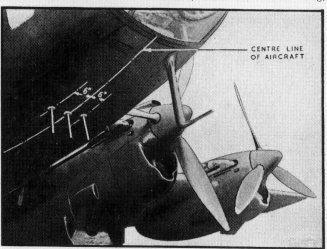

A typical Aerial Siting under Aircraft

(ii) An aerial Switching Panel, to provide electronic switching, so giving the "homing" facility. Six valves are used.

(iii) A superheterodyne Receiver employing thirteen valves.

(iv) A Control Unit — with a built-in two-valve transmitter provides facilities for connecting the apparatus to the I/C system, a speech amplifier, a check meter and a Visual Course Indicator.

(v) A Power Unit—Standard AM Type 10 for 24 volt nominal supply and Type 2A for 12 volt supply.

(vi) Pilot's Visual Course Indicator and Local/Distant Switch.

(vii) Inter-connecting cables of various lengths and dispositions, which depend on the type of aircraft. Cables, plugs, connections, etc., are of standard R.A.F. types.

(*viii*) One small rod transmitting aerial mounted some distance from the receiving aerial array.

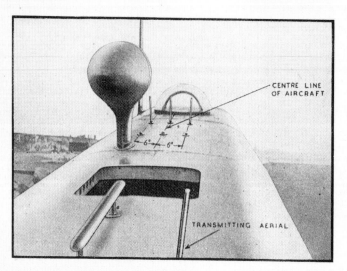

An Alternative Aerial Siting

ELECTRICAL CHARACTERISTICS.

Transmitter Frequency	380 ± 2 Mc/s.
Transmitter Power into Aerial	·5 watts (approx.)
Receiving Tuning Range	331 to 343 Mc/s.
Power Consumption (approx.)	8 amps. at 28 volts.
	16 amps. at 14 volts.

WEIGHT AND DIMENSIONS.

	WEIGHT.	DIMENSIONS.
Aerial Switching Panel	10¾ lbs.	12″ x 10½″ x 5″
Superheterodyne Receiver	23 lbs.	18½″ x 8″ x 9″
Control Unit and Transmitter	24 lbs.	18½″ x 8″ x 9″
Power Supply Unit	26¼ lbs.	12½″ x 8½″ x 5½″
Pilot's Indicating Meter and Control Switch	1 lb.	4½″ x 5½″ x 4″
Spare Indicating Meter	¾ lb.	4½″ x 3½″ x 4″
Receiving Aerials	1 lb.	10″ x 4½″ x 3″
Transmitting Aerial	5 ozs.	10″ x 2½″ x 2½″
Cables	According to the type of aircraft.	

The whole equipment is normally provided in a standard transit case, and in addition to the foregoing 100 per cent spare cables ("harness") are provided.

MICROWAVE EQUIPMENT.
SHIP INSTALLATION TYPE "F"

Microwave equipment for use in ships is built up as a series of separate units, similar to the aircraft equipment. The illustration shows one possible arrangement, but the units may be arranged in many different ways, in order to accommodate them as unobstrusively as possible in the somewhat limited space frequently available on small craft.

The Homing or Station locating facility is not provided on Ship Equipment. The transmitter and receiver normally in use work to a standard S-Phone, but a spare transmitter and receiver set to work on "reciprocal" frequencies are provided, so that by changing aerial and power supply leads, the operator can work to aircraft, or to another ship.

AERIAL PLUGS   RX "ORANGE"

RX "GREEN"

RX SUPPORT "LEG"

TX CRADLE

TX "ORANGE"

CONTROL UNIT

POWER UNIT

LOCKING SCREWS

SPARE CABLE CONNECTOR HOUSINGS

INPUT/OUTPUT CABLE ASSEMBLY

BASEBOARD

UNIT MOUNTING BAR   MOUNTING BLOCK

The Equipment consists of :—

1. **Receiver** (i) A one-valve super-regenerative detector. The aerial is coupled to the set by means of a quickly detachable plug and socket.

2. **Receiver** (ii) Mechanically the same as Receiver (i).

3. **Transmitter** (i) Two valves in a push-pull oscillator circuit. Fixed frequency.

4. **Transmitter** (ii) As for transmitter (i).

5. **Control Unit.** This links the transmitter-receiver with two independent two valve power amplifiers, housed within the unit. One amplifier is used to raise the speech output of the receiver to a level sufficient for the operation of one or more pairs of headphones.

   The other amplifier is used to increase the speech output from the microphone in order to modulate the transmitter. Both amplifiers are provided with separate gain controls.

   A meter mounted on the front panel can be switched to check H.T. - L.T. voltage and transmitter operation.

6. **Power Unit.** Standard A.M. Type 10.

7. **Aerials,** two special dipoles supplied with 50 feet of cable, are designed and built to operate on different frequencies.

8. **Interconnecting cable,** the length and disposition of which depend on the type of ship and layout adopted.

ELECTRICAL CHARACTERISTICS.

Receiver (i)	tuning range	331 - 343 Mc/s
Receiver (ii)	„ „	370 - 395 Mc/s
Transmitter (i) frequency		380 ± 2 M/cs
Transmitter (ii)	„	337 ± 2 M/cs
Transmitter power		0.75 watts (approx.)
Power consumption (approx.)		8 amps. at 28 volts

PACKING. The equipment and instructions for installing and operating are packed in a wooden crate. In this manner the equipment can be transported by road, rail or sea.

WEIGHT. (including packing)   1 cwt.   56 lbs.

COMMUNICATIONS RECEIVER
R.C.A. MODEL AR. 88.D.

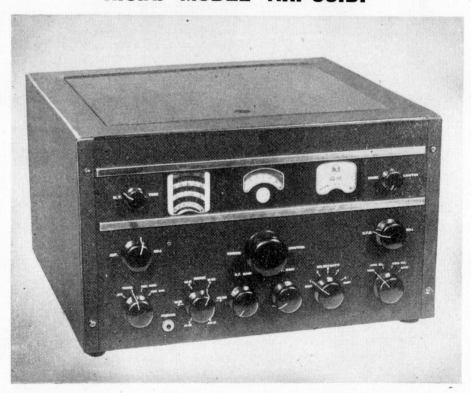

DESCRIPTION.

The AR. 88 Receiver is suitable for R.T., M.C.W. or C.W. Morse reception, on any frequency within the range of 535 to 32,000 kc/s. This range is divided into six bands. Housed in a metal cabinet it employs fourteen valves in a superheterodyne circuit, and although designed primarily for use on A.C. mains supply, it can be operated from "A" and "B" batteries or an external vibratory power pack.

Output for low impedance phones is taken to a jack socket mounted on the front panel. Ample power (2.5 watts approx.) is available for working a loudspeaker and terminals at the rear are provided for this purpose.

Rugged construction of parts and wiring has been included in the design, and this, together with voltage stabilization of the oscillator plate supply and temperature compensation of tuned circuits on all bands, ensures a high degree of mechanical and electrical stability.

Other features of the receiver include :

Mechanical Band Spread with Single Control for ease of tuning a previously logged station.

Automatic Noise Limiter which automatically limits interference to a percentage of modulation determined by the Noise Limiter Control.

Switch, for selecting any one of the five different I.F. bandwidths.

Crystal filter for ultra-sharp selectivity when required.

Twelve tuned I.F. Circuits.

Three tuned R.F. Circuits giving high image ratio on all bands.

POWER SUPPLY.

A.C. Mains of any voltage between 100—165 and 190—260; frequency 50—60 cycles. Batteries, 6 volt "A" battery for L.T. and 250—300 volt "B" battery for H.T. Vibrator Unit MI. 8319 operated from 6 volt battery.

NOTE : Batteries, and the vibrator unit are only supplied against a special order.

POWER CONSUMPTION.   100 watts.

A.F. OUTPUT IMPEDANCE.   2.5 and 600 ohms.

VALVE COMPLEMENT.

R.F. and I.F. Amplifiers	5—R.C.A. 6SG7.
1st Detector (converter)	1—R.C.A. 6Sa7.
Oscillator	1—R.C.A. 6J5.
2nd Detector	1—R.C.A. 6H6.
Noise Limiter	1—R.C.A. 6H6.
A.F. Amplifier	1—R.C.A. 6SJ7.
Power Amplifier	1—R.C.A. 6K6GT.
Beat Frequency Oscillator	1—R.C.A. 6J5.
Rectifier	1—R.C.A. 5Y3GT.
Voltage Stabilizer	1—R.C.A. VR150.

DIMENSIONS AND WEIGHT.

Width	Height	Depth	Weight
19¼"	11"	19¼"	90 lbs. (approx.)

PACKING. The receiver with instructions for operating are packed in a wooden crate, and in this manner can be transported by road, rail, sea or plane.

R.C.A. TRANSMITTER ET. 4332B
AND SPEECH AMPLIFIER

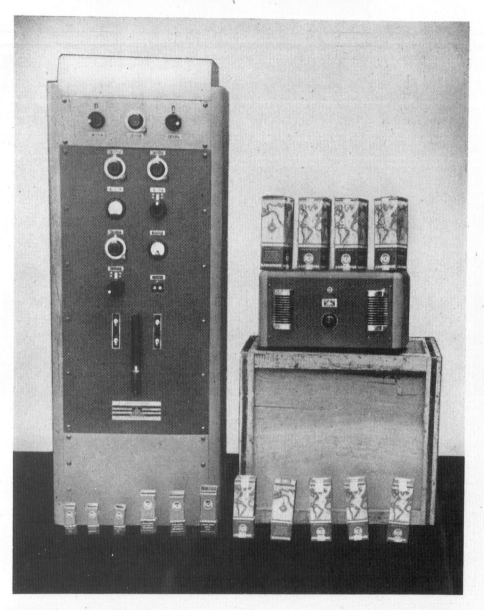

GENERAL DESCRIPTION.

The R.C.A. Transmitter has been designed for use on any frequency between 2.200—20,000 kc/s. This range is divided into three bands with separation points at 3,000 and 7,500 kc/s. selected by moving an adjustable connector lead inside the equipment. All other controls employed in tuning the transmitter are mounted upon the front panel.

For C.W. Morse transmission, the equipment is capable of high speed keying, and of transmission at either of two power levels—250 or 350 watts. The actual outputs available are somewhat in excess of these values at 20,000 kc/s. and increase with decreasing frequency to values in excess of 300 and 450 watts respectively at 3,000 kc/s.

On R.T. (Radio Telephony) the transmitter should be operated only at the lower power level. A modulation and keying indicator of the vapour-column type is provided on the front panel. With R.T. transmissions the column will become illuminated to heights varying with, and approximately proportional to, the percentage of modulation. Transmission of C.W. Morse will illuminate the column when the key is pressed.

The mechanical construction is such as to ensure great strength. All radio frequency components, except those in the aerial circuit, are mounted on the large vertically mounted chassis in the centre of the cabinet. The aerial coupling network is located on the small horizontal chassis at the top. The H.T. transformer is supported by two horizontal straps in the base of the cabinet; together with the modulator.

In order to transmit R.T. a separate speech amplifier is required. Whilst this is not normally despatched with the transmitter, it is available to special order. The amplifier is completely self-contained, housed, with its power supply, in a metal cabinet. The gain of this amplifier is adjustable by means of the volume-level control knob on the front panel.

Changing transmission from C.W. to R.T. or vice versa involves a few simple internal adjustments.

ELECTRICAL CHARACTERISTICS.

Frequency range	2,200 to 20,000 kc/s.
Power output:	
C.W.	250 or 350 watts.
R.T.	250 watts.
Type of modulation	Class B, high level.
Audio Input Impedance	500 ohms.
A.F. Response	$\pm$ 5 db. from 400—7,500 cycles.
A.F. Harmonic Distortion	5% R.M.S.
Power Input:	
C.W. Low Power	1.25 kw.
C.W. High Power	1.46 kw.
R.T. 100% modulation	1.82 kw.
Power Supply	190 to 250 volts, single phase, 50—60 cycles.
Regulation (max.)	5%.

VALVE COMPLEMENT.
Transmitter.

Oscillator	1. R.C.A.—807.
Power Amplifier	2. R.C.A.—813.
Modulator	2. R.C.A.—805.
Rectifier	4. R.C.A.—866—A.

Speech Amplifier.

Voltage Amplifiers	3. R.C.A.—1620 (or 6J7).
Power Amplifiers	2. R.C.A.—1622.
Rectifier	1. R.C.A.—504G.

DIMENSIONS AND WEIGHT.
Transmitter

Height	60"
Width	23"
Depth	22"
Weight (net)	585 lbs.

Speech Amplifier.

Height	7"
Width	15⅝"
Depth	10½"
Weight	26 lbs.

PACKING. The transmitter is despatched in a wooden crate, and when ordered, the amplifier is packed in a similar manner. This method of packing is suitable for transport by road, rail or sea.

MINIATURE COMMUNICATIONS RECEIVER
(M.C.R. 1)

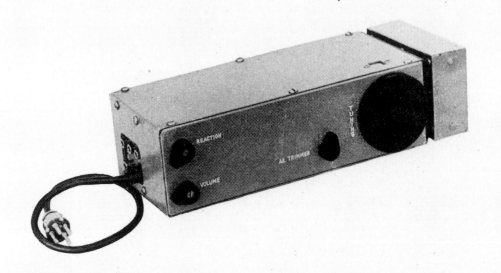

GENERAL DESCRIPTION.

The M.C.R. 1 has been developed in response to a request for a superheterodyne receiver, which is small, light in weight, capable of an exceptional performance and requires very little power for operation. In this receiver the power supply for the five miniature battery-type valves may be obtained either from a dry battery or from a mains supply (D.C. or A.C.) Four plug-in coil boxes to cover a tuning range of from 150 kc/s. to 15 Mc/s. are supplied. On one side of the case are arranged the aerial trimming, reaction, sensitivity and tuning controls, the latter provided with an internal drum scale calibrated 0—180 degrees. A regenerative second detector enables the set to be used for C.W. Morse Reception as well as telephony.

High and low tension supplies are connected when the plug on the receiver cable is inserted in a four-pin socket on the combined H.T. and L.T. battery, or to a similar socket on the mains operated power pack. Switching "ON" or "OFF" is accomplished by inserting or removing this plug. Nine pins are provided on one end of the case, these serve as electrical and mechanical connection for any one of the four coils which may be used. Each coil has a calibration chart showing the relationship between kc/s. or Mc/s. and degrees on the drum tuning scale. The mains-operated power pack, receiver and all coils are housed in separate steel boxes, finished grey cellulose.

All units have been tested for operation in temperate or sub-tropical climates, are very robust and thus able to withstand rough treatment and vibration.

The receiver is intended for use in Western Europe, an area in which good reception should be obtained from any of the medium or short-wave B.B.C. Transmitters, and in addition, the high sensitivity will allow serious listening to any other transmitter which may have considerably less power.

TUNING RANGE.

Four coil boxes having the following frequency ranges are supplied:—

(*i*) 150 kc/s. — 1,500 kc/s.
(*ii*) 2.5 Mc/s. — 4.5 Mc/s.
(*iii*) 4.5 Mc/s. — 8.0 Mc/s.
(*iv*) 8 Mc/s. — 15 Mc/s.

DIMENSIONS AND WEIGHTS —	LENGTH	WIDTH	HEIGHT	WEIGHT
Receiver with one coil box	9"	3⅝"	2⅜"	2 lb. 9½ ozs.
Battery	7½"	2⅞"	2¼"	2 lb. 5¾ ozs.
Power Pack	8¾"	3⅜"	2⅜"	3 lb. 11 ozs.
Coils "A" (3 supplied)	1⅛"	3⅜"	2⅜"	4¾ ozs.
Coils "B" (1 supplied)	1⅝"	3⅜"	2⅞"	8¼ ozs.

POWER SUPPLY.

Combined battery provides 90 volts and 7.5 volts for H.T. and L.T. respectively, or the mains-operated power pack which may be used on either an A.C. or D.C. supply of any voltage between 97 and 140 and 190 and 250. Frequency of A.C. supply 40 to 100 cycles.

POWER CONSUMPTION.

Batteries: 7.5 mA. at 90 volts H.T.
.50 mA. at 7.5 volts L.T.
Mains: 10 watts.

BATTERY LIFE.

The combined H.T. and L.T. battery will give approximately 30—40 hours service, if used for a period not exceeding one hour and then given a similar period of rest. In temperate climates, batteries should be put into service within six months from the date of manufacture. This period will be shorter in hot, damp climates.

ACCESSORIES AND SPARES.

Mains-operated power pack.
Aerial and earth wires, 30 feet and 10 feet.
Four coil boxes.
Two combined H.T./L.T. batteries.
One pair Headphones (L.R.).
Instruction card.

PACKING. The receiver, two batteries, power pack and accessories are wrapped in cardboard, then packed in a cardboard box, which in turn is placed in a tinned-steel container. This method of packing is suitable for road, rail and air transport.

CONTAINER SIZE. 9¼" x 9½" x 7⅞" **WEIGHT.** 15 lb. 14 ozs.

R.C.D. RECEIVER, TYPE 31/1
PROPAGANDA SET

GENERAL DESCRIPTION.

The R.C.D. type 31/1 is a pocket receiving set, employing three battery-operated miniature valves in a T.R.F. circuit. It is suitable for radio telephone and C.W. Morse reception, on the 25—50 metre band (6 to 12 Mcs.) The receiver and batteries (H.T.—L.T.) are housed in separate steel boxes, sprayed with grey crackle cellulose. The controls provided are " Tuning " and " Regeneration," the drum tuning scale being calibrated in metres. High and low tension supplies are connected when the receiver power cable is plugged into the correct socket on the battery box. The very sensitive telephones are of the miniature crystal deaf-aid type, which fit into the ear.

The receiver has been designed for operation in temperate or sub-tropical climates, primarily Western Europe, in which good reception should be obtainable from any of the short wave B.B.C. news transmitters. The mechanical construction is such as to ensure a high degree of durability.

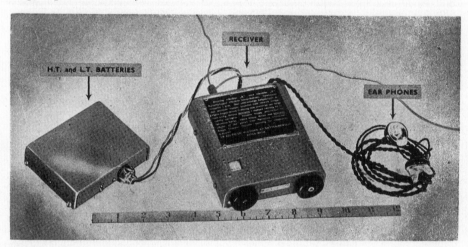

DIMENSIONS AND WEIGHT.

	Length.	Width.	Depth.	Weight.
Receiver	$5\frac{3}{8}''$	$4\frac{3}{8}''$	$1\frac{3}{16}''$	1 lb. 2 ozs.
Battery unit (including H.T. and L.T. batteries)	$4\frac{1}{4}''$	$3\frac{1}{8}''$	$1''$	1 lb.

POWER SUPPLY.

Miniature 30 V. H.T. Dry Battery.　　　Standard 4.5 V. L.T. Dry Battery.

POWER CONSUMPTION.

H.T. 0.5 m.A.　　　　L.T. 50 m.A.

BATTERY LIFE.

The H.T. and L.T. batteries will give useful service for 100 and 30 hours respectively, if used for a period not exceeding 1 hour and then given approximately the same interval of rest. Continuous operation will reduce these figures to 50.—60 hours H.T. and 8 hours L.T. In temperate climates batteries should be put into service within 6 months from the date of manufacture. This period will be shorter in hot damp climates.

ACCESSORIES AND SPARES.

Miniature Crystal Telephones, wire for aerial and earth, 2 spare L.T. batteries and 1 spare H.T. battery are provided.

PACKING.

The crystal 'phones are sealed in a small tinned-steel container; this, together with all other items, including accessories and spares, are placed in cardboard wrappers, and then packed in a cardboard box. This method of packing is suitable for road and rail transport, and may be flown, provided the altitude does not exceed 15,000 ft.

When carried at higher altitudes, or transported by sea, it is essential that the cardboard box be placed in a tinned-steel container and hermetically sealed.

SIZE WHEN PACKED. $7\frac{1}{2}''$ x $5\frac{1}{2}''$ x 3".　　　　**WEIGHT.** $3\frac{3}{4}$ lbs.

JEDBURGH SET - MODEL 46/1

GENERAL DESCRIPTION.

The Jedburgh Set is a completely portable transmitting and receiving station, primarily designed for the use of paratroops. When packed into its five webbing satchels it may be attached to the webbing harness and carried on the back of one man, and remain undamaged during a normal parachute jump. Dropping by "Leg Bag" is also very satisfactory.

The Receiver is an M.C.R. 1, drawing its power from dry batteries (see Miniature Communications Receiver (M.C.R. 1). The power to the transmitter is supplied by a tripod hand generator; consequently to work a Jedburgh Station requires at least two men, one to turn the generator, and another to key the transmitter. The equipment has been designed and tested for operation in temperate or sub-tropical climates.

Numerous factors, such as the time of day, frequency transmitted, type of aerial, etc., affect the range over which communication can be secured. However, reliable duplex (two-way) working should be obtainable between a Jedburgh Set located in Western Europe and a more powerful transmitter and receiver in the U.K.

EQUIPMENT.

A Jedburgh Station consists of the following :—

SATCHEL I, containing :

    (a) Midget Communication Receiver in protective corrugated jacket.
    (b) Coil boxes, two. (One of these is fitted on to the Receiver).
    (c) Two Batteries, each combined L.T. and H.T. in protective jackets.
    (d) Receiver Aerial and Earth-wire on bakelite card.
    (e) One Skull-cap with low impedance phones.
    (f) Spares box containing :—(i) One Valve, A.T.S. 25 (for transmitter).
                    (ii) One Valve, 1R5 (for receiver).
                    (iii) Two Valves, 1T4 (for receiver).
                    (iv) Screwdriver.
    (g) One box containing six crystals (duplicate set carried with the transmitter).
        SIZE. $10\frac{1}{2}''$ x $11\frac{1}{2}''$ x $4\frac{1}{2}''$.   **WEIGHT.** $11\frac{1}{2}$ lbs.

SATCHEL II, containing :

    (a) Transmitter with built-on key.
    (b) 75 ft. Aerial wire.
    (c) 15 ft. Aerial wire.
    (d) 75 ft. Counterpoise earth wire.
    (e) Crystal box containing six crystals.
    (f) Instruction Manual.
        SIZE. 9″ x 10″ x 6″.   **WEIGHT.** 9 lbs.

SATCHEL III, containing :

    (a) Hand Generator.
    (b) Generator handle.
        SIZE. $7\frac{3}{4}''$ x 8″ x $4\frac{1}{2}''$.   **WEIGHT.** 9 lbs.

SATCHEL IV, containing :

    (a) Tripod legs for Generator.
        SIZE. 20″ x $5\frac{1}{2}''$ x 2″.   **WEIGHT.** 4 lbs.

SATCHEL V, containing :

    (a) Two-section telescopic aerial mast Type 89 (modified) with guy lines and pegs.
        SIZE. 24″ x $5\frac{1}{2}''$ x 2″.   **WEIGHT.** $3\frac{1}{4}$ lbs.
        TOTAL WEIGHT OF EQUIPMENT. 37 lbs.

TRANSMITTER.

This is a two-band crystal controlled power oscillator, employing one valve, limited to C.W. (Morse) transmission. Provision is made for frequency doubling of any crystal between 3 and 4.5 Mc/s.

A meter mounted on the front panel can be switched to read—Aerial current, H.T. voltage or H.T. current. The whole enclosed in a metal case measures $9\frac{1}{2}''$ x 6″ x $9\frac{1}{2}''$ and weighs $5\frac{1}{4}$ lbs.

TRANSMITTER FREQUENCY AND POWER.

(Band *i*)	3—5 Mc/s.	
(Band *ii*)	5—9 Mc/s.	
Fundamental operation	3—9 Mc/s.	8—10 watts.
Harmonic operation	4.5—9 Mc/s.	7—9 watts.

RECEIVER M.C.R. I.

This is a battery-operated superheterodyne receiver, employing five miniature valves, for the reception of C.W. morse or R.T. (radio telephony) transmission. The tuning control is provided with an internal drum scale calibrated 0—180 degrees. Nine pins, located at one end of the metal case which houses the receiver, provide electrical and mechanical connection to the coil box. The tuning range, 2.5—8.0 Mc/s. is covered by the two plug-in coils, each of which has a calibration chart showing the relationship between frequency and degrees on the drum tuning scale.

High and low tension supplies are obtained from a dry battery. The Receiver, including one coil box, measures 9" x 3⅝" x 2⅜" and weighs 2¼ lbs.

TUNING RANGE.

Two coil boxes are supplied :
  (*i*) 2.5 Mc/s.—4.5 Mc/s.
  (*ii*) 4.5 Mc/s.—8.0 Mc/s.
   Dimensions of coil boxes are; 1⅛" x 3⅜" x 2⅜".

GENERATOR.

The generator is a hand-driven double-wound D.C. machine which provides power for operating the transmitter. Housed in a metal case, it has three detachable telescopic legs and a detachable handle.

Assistance in determining the correct speed of rotation is given by a meter, which is mounted on the case and connected internally to read L.T. voltage. The complete generator weighs 11½ lbs., and with legs fully extended is 27" high. In later models the meter has been replaced by a voltage regulator, thus simplifying the operation of the generator.

POWER SUPPLY.

Transmitter, generator revolving at 90 r.p.m.
   H.T. 320 volts D.C. at 60 mA.
   L.T. 6.3 volts D.C. at 1.2 amps. (2.6 amps. maximum).
Receiver, combined dry battery.
   H.T. 90 volts at 7.5 mA.
   L.T. 7.5 volts at 50 mA.

BATTERY LIFE.

The combined H.T. and L.T. battery will give approximately 30—40 hours service, if used for a period not exceeding one hour and then given a similar period of rest. In temperate climates, batteries should be put into service within six months from the date of manufacture. This period will be shorter in hot damp climates.

PACKING. When packed in a lightweight wooden crate the Jedburgh Set may be transported by road, rail, sea or air.

THE NICHOLLS SET, R.C.D. TYPE 48/1

This set is designed on similar lines to the Jedburgh Station, being packed into five satchels weighing 16 lbs. 9 ozs., 9 lbs. 12 ozs., 9 lbs. 11 ozs., 4 lbs. 3 ozs., and 4 lbs. 7 ozs. Total 44 lbs. 10 ozs.

In this case the M.C.R.1 is provided with four plug-in coils covering frequencies from 150 kc/s. to 15 Mc/s.

The transmitter is identical to that used in the Type 3 Mk. II equipment and covers frequencies from 3 to 16 Mc/s. with a power output of 11 watts.

JEDBURGH SET - MODEL 46/1

TRANSCEIVER TYPE A. MK. III.

GENERAL DESCRIPTION.

This is the third of a series of lightweight transceivers—primarily designed to be packed in and used from a small suitcase. The present model, together with either a box of spares or a Battery Power Pack, has been sent out in a small case, but an alternative and now preferred packing is as shown in Fig. 1.

In the larger of the two containers is the transceiver with its own built-in A.C. Mains power unit (Fig. 2) and in the smaller is the Spares Box and Battery Power Pack. When A.C. Mains are not available a large capacity 6 volt battery of the automobile type should be used and provision made for keeping it fully charged.

FIG. 1.

THE TRANSMITTER.

This is a two valve crystal controlled transmitter having a frequency coverage of 3.2 to 9.0 Mc/s in two wave bands. Transmission is C.W. only, at speeds up to 200 words per minute. Provision is made for the frequency doubling of crystals between 3.2 and 4.5 Mc/s providing outputs of 6.4 to 9.0 Mc/s.

A meter mounted in the front panel facilitates tuning up and the matching of the transmitter to the aerial.

Frequency Coverage: Band 1. 3.2 to 5.2 Mc/s.
                          Band 2. 5.0 to 9.0 Mc/s.

Supply: From built-in power unit or 6 V. Battery Pack.
           (a) 270 volts at 50 mA.
           (b) 6.3 volts at .75 Amp. (1.65 A. with Rec. heaters).

Power Output: (a) Average Fundamental Power 5 watts.
               (b)   ,,   Harmonic   ,,   3.25 watts.

THE RECEIVER.

This is a four valve superheterodyne receiver which utilises the oscillator valve of the transmitter as the L.F. amplifier in the receiver.

Frequency Coverage: Band 1. 3.2 to 5.25 Mc/s.
                          Band 2. 5.2 to 8.55 Mc/s.

Supply: From the built-in power unit or battery.
           (a) 250 volts at 35 mA.
           (b) 6.3 volts at .9 Amp. (1.65 A. with Trans. heaters).

Maximum Output: 100 milliwatts.

A.C. POWER UNIT.

Mains Supply A.C. only: 100-130 volts.   200-250 volts.   40-60 c/s.
Consumption: (a) Transmitter 39 watts key down.
                           26   ,,   key up.
           (b) Receiver 30 watts.

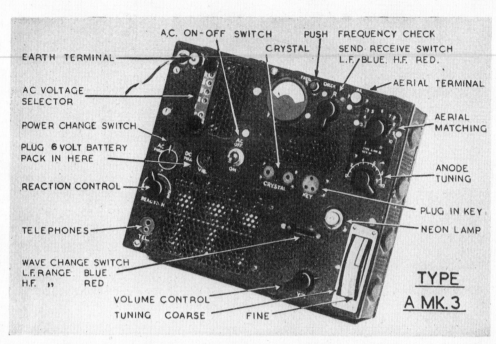

EARTH TERMINAL

A.C. ON-OFF SWITCH

AC VOLTAGE SELECTOR

POWER CHANGE SWITCH

PLUG 6 VOLT BATTERY PACK IN HERE

REACTION CONTROL

TELEPHONES

WAVE CHANGE SWITCH
L.F. RANGE BLUE
H.F. „ RED

PUSH FREQUENCY CHECK
CRYSTAL
SEND RECEIVE SWITCH
L.F. BLUE. H.F. RED.

AERIAL TERMINAL

AERIAL MATCHING

ANODE TUNING

PLUG IN KEY

NEON LAMP

TYPE A MK.3

VOLUME CONTROL
TUNING COARSE FINE

FIG. 2.

BATTERY POWER PACK.

Supply: 6 volt accumulator, automobile type of largest available ampere hour capacity. This battery is only supplied on special order.

Consumption: a) Transmit: 6.5 amps (key down)
            3.8 amps (key up)
        b) Receive: 4.7 amps.

SPARES BOX.

Spare valves, fuses, mains plug pins, together with morse key, telephones, crystals, aerial and earth wires, etc., are supplied.

DIMENSIONS AND WEIGHTS.

1. **Combined Transmitter/Receiver and A.C. Power Unit.**
   Size: $9\frac{1}{4}''$ x $7\frac{1}{2}''$ x $3\frac{1}{4}''$.   Weight: 8 lbs. 4 ozs.

2. **Battery Power Pack.**   Size: $7''$ x $3\frac{1}{2}''$ x $2\frac{3}{4}''$.   Weight: 4 lbs. 4 ozs.

3. **Spares Box.**   Size: $7''$ x $3\frac{1}{2}''$ x $2\frac{3}{4}''$.   Weight: 2 lbs. 2 ozs.   **Total Weight:** 14 lbs. 10 ozs.

4. **Watertight Containers.**   a) Size: $11\frac{1}{2}''$ x $9\frac{1}{2}''$ x $4\frac{1}{2}''$.   b) $9''$ x $5\frac{3}{4}''$ x $7''$.
   Weight: 14 lbs. 8 ozs.   11 lbs. 5 ozs.

PORTABLE TRANSMITTING AND RECEIVING EQUIPMENT, TYPE B. MK. II.

GENERAL DESCRIPTION.

This is a completely portable transmitting and receiving station, capable of working from A.C. Mains or from a 6 volt accumulator. The whole (apart from accumulator) together with a box of spares has been sent out in a suitcase, but is now despatched in two watertight containers as shown in Figs. 1 and 2.

In the larger container is the transmitter and receiver and in the smaller is the power pack and spares-box. When A.C. Mains are not available a large capacity 6 volt battery of the automobile type should be used and provision made for keeping it fully charged. Suitable batteries in watertight containers (Fig. 2) and battery chargers are available to special order.

The pedal generator which is being designed to operate the B. Mk. III Set will, with the special adaptor cable, run the B. Mk. II without any modification to the set.

(a) POWER PACK AND SPARES BOX

(b) TRANSMITTER AND RECEIVER

| SIZE. | (a) 13″ x 10″ x 6″ | FIG. 1. | WEIGHT. | (a) 25 lbs. |
| | (b) 13¼″ x 11½″ x 6″ | | | (b) 22 lbs. |

THE TRANSMITTER.

Two valves are employed, an oscillator-doubler driving a Class C amplifier, crystal controlled. Provision is made for frequency doubling. Plug-in tank coils cover 3.0 to 16 Mc/s. A multi-range meter on the panel measures voltages and currents and facilitates tuning.

Size: $9\frac{1}{2}$ inches x $4\frac{1}{4}$ inches x $4\frac{7}{8}$ inches. Weight: 7 lbs. 8 ozs.

Supply: (a) 500 V. at 60 mA.   Frequency Coverage: Coil L1 3.0 to 5.25 Mc/s.
      (b) 230 V. at 18 mA.   ,, L2 4.5 to 7.5 Mc/s.
      (c) 6.3 V. at 1.1 amps.   ,, L3 6.5 to 10.0 Mc/s.
                                   ,, L4 9.0 to 16.0 Mc/s.

Power Output: (a) Fundamental 20 watts.   Valves: EL32.
              (b) Second Harmonic 18-20 watts.   6L6G.
              (c) Third   ,,   15-20 watts.

WATER-TIGHT PACKING

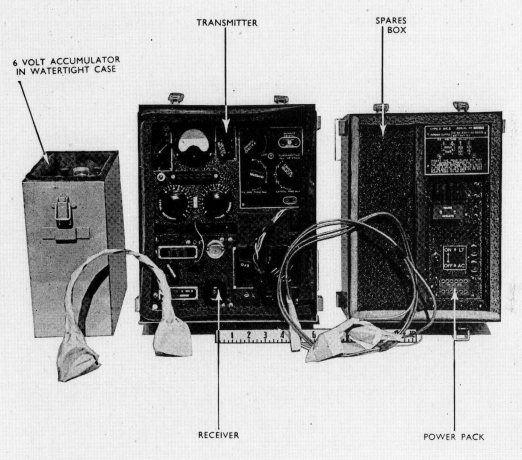

FIG. 2.

THE RECEIVER.

This is a four-valve seven-stage superheterodyne receiver essentially designed for C.W. reception. A three-wave band selector gives a coverage of from 3.1 to 15.5 Mc/s.

Size: $9\frac{1}{2}$ inches x $4\frac{1}{2}$ inches x $4\frac{7}{8}$ inches.   Weight: 6 lbs. 12 ozs.

Valves: 7Q7, 7R7, 7Q7, 7R7.   Intermediate Frequency: 470 Kc/s.

Sensitivity: 1-3 microvolts for 10 milliwatts   Selectivity: 1 Kc/s. 3 dB down.
            output at 1,000 c/s.   9 Kc/s. 20 dB down.

Max. Output: 50 milliwatts into 120 ohm telephones.

COMBINATION POWER PACK.

Size: $10\frac{3}{4}''$ x $4''$ x $5''$.   Weight: 12 lbs. 8 ozs.

A. A.C. Mains.

Supply: 97-140 volts.   190-250 volts.   40-60 c/s.
Consumption: (a) Transmit, 70 watts.   (b) Receive, 40 watts.

B. Battery Supply.

6 volt accumulator of the largest available ampere-hour capacity.
Consumption: (a) Transmit, $9\frac{1}{2}$ amps.   (b) Receive, $4\frac{1}{2}$ amps.
A spare vibrator is fixed inside.

SPARES BOX, containing:

Aerial wire, earth wire, transmitting key, telephone headset (LR), 12 fuses, 4 spare valves, screwdriver, mains pins and adaptors and tank coils.

DIMENSIONS AND WEIGHTS.

Watertight Containers: (a) Size: $13''$ x $10''$ x $6''$.   Weight: 25 lbs.
(b) Size: $13\frac{1}{4}''$ x $11\frac{1}{2}''$ x $6''$.   Weight: 22 lbs.

HAND GENERATOR, BATTERY CHARGER NO. 2

This equipment comprises a generator with built-in gear box, a detachable handle and two table clamps.

When the handle is fitted—keyway and left-hand screw—and the table clamps firmly attached to a rigid support, the handle can be rotated at 80 to 100 turns per minute, when the generator will charge a 6 volt battery at 2·5 to 3 amps.

PACKING. Watertight steel container.   **SIZE.** $6\frac{3}{4}'' \times 5'' \times 8\frac{1}{2}''$ **WEIGHT.** 10 lbs.

THE PEDAL GENERATOR

This battery charger consists of a collapsible tripod stand of cycle tubing to which is fitted a cycle saddle, pedals and a chain to drive an attached generator via a ten-toothed sprocket and a totally enclosed 8 to 1 step-up gear box.

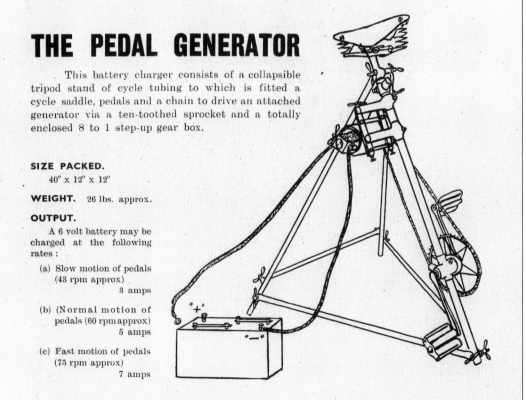

SIZE PACKED.
$40'' \times 12'' \times 12''$

WEIGHT. 26 lbs. approx.

OUTPUT.

A 6 volt battery may be charged at the following rates :

(a) Slow motion of pedals (43 rpm approx)
 3 amps

(b) (Normal motion of pedals (60 rpm approx)
 5 amps

(c) Fast motion of pedals (75 rpm approx)
 7 amps

CYCLE ADAPTOR CHARGER

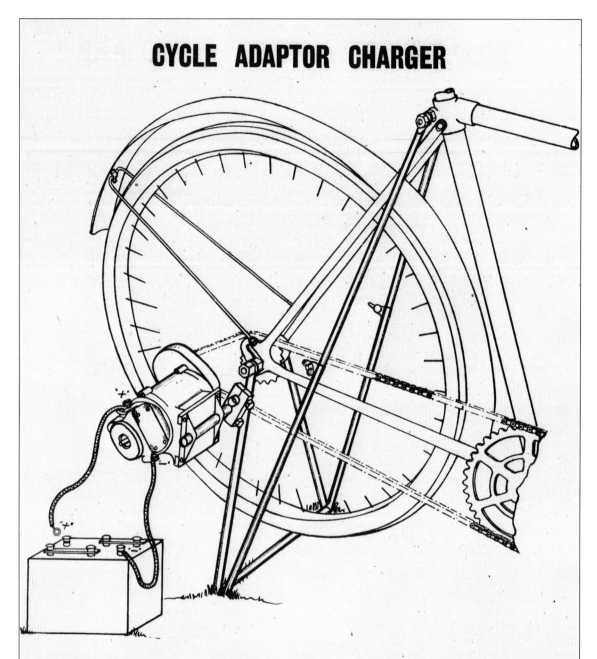

This cycle attachment consists of :

(a) A light collapsible stand of steel tubing which raises and supports the cycle and to which the generator and gear box are attached.

(b) A generator—rated 20 watts 6—8 volts 3 amps. driven via a totally enclosed 8/1 step-up gear box built on to the generator, and driven by a 10 tooth-sprocket from the chain of the cycle.

(c) Double spring extension links for lengthening the cycle chain, and a circlip for locking the free wheel.

SIZE. Tubing folded 24″ x 13″. Generator 10″ x 7″ x 6″.   **WEIGHT.** 13 lbs.

GENERATOR OUTPUT.

6—8 volts at 3—10 amps according to the speed at which the generator is revolved.

When charging at 4 to 5 amps, the pedals turn easily, and this rate can be maintained over long periods with very little fatigue to the operator.

PETROL DRIVEN BATTERY CHARGER
(TYPE RB 8)

ENGINE	4 Stroke.	**PETROL CONSUMPTION**	$\frac{2}{3}$ pints per hour.
WEIGHT	82 lbs.	**SIZE**	Height 20″. Baseboard 28″ x 15″.
GENERATOR OUTPUT	6—7 amps. into a 12 volt battery.	**PACKING**	Wood crate.

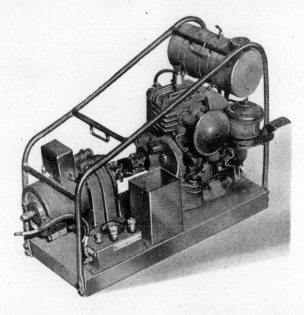

STEAM DRIVEN GENERATOR

FURNACE AND BOILER

Height 40″.   Diameter 16″.   Weight 20 lbs.
Fuel Consumption 15-20 lbs. wood per hour.
3-4 lbs. coke per hour.

ENGINE AND GENERATOR

Dimension 15″ x $5\frac{1}{2}$″ x $7\frac{1}{2}$″.   Weight 30 lbs.
Steam pressure 30 to 35 lbs. per sq. in.
Water Consumption 1 gall. per hour.
Generator output 6-8 volts at 4 amp.

PACKING

The whole equipment together with spares packs
into the furnace.

MAINS CHARGER, HEAYBERD TYPE AD25

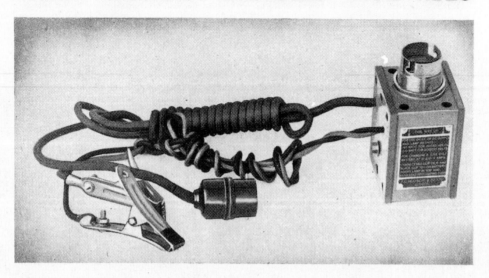

2 to 12 volt batteries may be trickle-charged with the AD.25 from either A.C. or D.C. Mains of voltages from 90—250.

If the mains are 90 and 120 volts a 60 watt lamp is inserted in the holder, and if 200—250 volts a 100 watt lamp may be used.

Charging rate ·2 to ·4 amp.

MAINS CHARGER, HEAYBERD TYPE AD3

This charger is used for charging 2, 6, or 12 volt batteries from the mains, but only when the Supply is A.C. 200—250 V or 100—200 V 40—100 cycles.

Output 1½ amp. maximum.

Section II
SMALL BOAT SECTION

SLEEPING BEAUTY

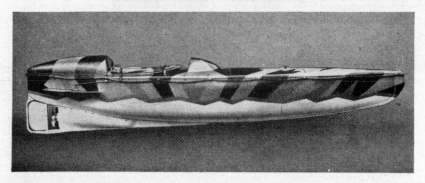

GENERAL DESCRIPTION.

General. Length approximately 12 feet 8 inches, beam 27 inches, weight 600 lbs. complete with batteries, bottles and paddles, but not including pilot, oxygen apparatus, gear and cargo.

Electrically Propelled Range. 12 sea miles at full speed, or 40 miles at cruising speed, in still water. Full speed 4.4 knots. Cruising speed 3.1 knots. Operation planning range 30 miles at 3 knots.

Controls. Single stick control operating rudder and hydroplanes.

Instruments. (i) One magnetic compass, shipped in a binnacle.
(ii) One depth gauge registering to a depth of 50 feet.
(iii) One watertight 8-day aircraft clock.
(iv) One watertight H.P. luminised air gauge.

Cockpit Cover. One watertight cockpit cover fitted with zip fastener and extra flap closed by pops, making the craft entirely splashproof when running as a surface canoe.

Mast and Sails. One wooden mast, length 6 feet, above the deck, divided into two parts to lie along the top deck. A lug sail, area 36.0 square feet of parachute silk, is folded with the yard and stowed in the stowage locker in the stern cowling.

Cargo. Two types of underwater charges for Sleeping Beauty operations are being considered, both being neutrally buoyant during the time of transport underwater.
(i) Containing $3\frac{1}{2}$ lbs. of explosive
(ii) Containing $2\frac{1}{2}$ lbs. of explosive
or
(iii) Type A. Mk. III wireless transmitter and receiver, batteries and aerial.

Motor. 24 volt (0.5 H.P.) C.A.V. type, with direct drive to propellor.

Headguard. A collapsible headguard is permanently fitted to the craft which can be erected by the pilot before proceeding under water in enemy harbours.

SUPPLY POSITION. Now in full production. Mast and sails, will, in future only be supplied if specially requested.

WELMAN

GENERAL DESCRIPTION.

The Welman is a "one man submarine." The controls are very similar to, and as simple as those in a modern motor car. It has a reasonable range and releases its charge from inside the craft and can travel a considerable distance from the target before the charge is detonated. When compared with the canoe, the Welman has obvious advantages as it is mechanically propelled, has a smaller silhouette and can submerge and consequently disappear at will.

OPERATIONAL USES.

Special Operational Uses.

(a) The charge container may be used for carrying up to 600 lbs. of normal stores.

(b) The driver can land, and submerge or surface his craft from shore by means of an airline and bottle.

(c) The craft may be used for reconnaissance.

(d) The craft may be used for launching mobile mines or placing limpets.

(e) The craft may be used as a beacon for assisting major operations.

Transportation of Craft.

(a) By parent Submarine.

(b) By Flying Boat or Aeroplane.

(c) By any small vessel capable of handling 2 tons.

GENERAL SPECIFICATION AND PERFORMANCE.

DIMENSIONS.

Overall Length (including Charge) 20' 2"	Overall Length (without Charge) 16' 10"
Overall Height (Tip of Skid to top of Hatch) 5' 9"	Maximum Overall Width 3' 6"
External Diameter of Hull 2' 7"	Freeboard 1' 2"

RANGE.

22 miles at Fast Speed, 33 at Cruising.

SPEED.

With charge fitted—Slow—1.5 knots   Cruising—2.1 knots   Fast—3 knots   Full—3.5 knots

N.B.   With the charge released the above speeds are slightly increased.

DEPTH.

Normal Operational—Down to 75′   Maximum—300′

NAVIGATIONAL INSTRUMENT.

Blind Flying Gyro Direction Indicator.   Aircraft Type.

CHARGE.

Total Weight—1,190 lbs.   Actual Weight of Explosive—450 lbs.

WEIGHT.

In air without Charge fitted—4,600 lbs.

MOTOR.

2½ H.P. Electric.

WELFREIGHTER

GENERAL DESCRIPTION.

The Welfreighter is a submersible surface craft designed for running considerable distances on the surface, but capable, in case of emergency, of diving and running under water.

In rough weather the craft is virtually undetectable. In calm weather, particularly in day time, when it may be necessary to submerge the craft, it can be submerged to a depth of 50 feet for up to 20 hours.

The craft can be operated by only one man, and the total crew consists of four men. The general lay-out of the craft consists of a living compartment embodying the conning tower and the boot, and a second compartment which is termed the Engine Room. A semi-collapsible dinghy is super-imposed on the engine hatch.

When running on the surface, the craft is driven by the main Diesel engine and a large propellor. When under water the two small propellors drive the craft.

OPERATIONAL USES.

The Welfreighter is primarily designed to land Agents and stores in areas in which it is impossible to use larger or more conspicuous craft.

It is possible to land two Agents and one ton of stores, using for the operation the Welfreighter's own semi-collapsible dinghy. The craft can also be used as a submersible home for operational personnel, and it can be used to maintain forward bases, and to transport two Sleeping Beauties and their crews to an advanced base.

GENERAL SPECIFICATION AND PERFORMANCE.

Overall length	37' 3"	Main Engine	Gardner 4LK 42 h.p.
Overall Width	7' 0¾"	Fuel	Pool Gas Diesel Oil.
Draft of craft, surface trim	5' 6"	Weight of stores	1 ton (approx.)
Operating depth	0—50'	Crew	Pilot and Co-Pilot.
Weight of craft	13 tons 5 cwt.	Passengers	Two

Surface speed, full revs.   6 knots.

Section III
CAMOUFLAGE SECTION

CAMOUFLAGE
SECTION

As man acquired defensive methods, and became more and more civilised, his instinctive desire to hide as a means of preservation gradually dwindled, and finally disappeared. It was modern warfare that reawakened these lost instincts, and brought him again the imperative need of concealment.

Therefore the art of camouflage has been developed to give protection to the soldier and his equipment. In the same way, camouflage has been introduced into this Organisation for the purpose of safeguarding the Agent proceeding to the 'field.' It supplies his correct clothing to the smallest detail. It provides means of disguise, so that he can pass unnoticed amongst hostile acquaintances. It aids him in the concealment of the necessary equipment, which has to accompany him, and it facilitates the infiltration of arms and explosives into the country in which he has to work so that he can organise and carry out operations against the enemy. It provides him with every aid in order that he can fit himself into the existing background.

THE CAMOUFLAGE SECTION,

is divided into the following categories :—

(a) The introduction of a "shell" over stores in order to transport in bulk. For example, in an operation during 1943 some 20 tons per month were camouflaged in this manner, success depending on the variety of the represented commodities in order to confuse the Gestapo.

(b) The more complicated method of hiding each article in a tin or package as an extra precaution to the outer "shell" and with each tin or package fitted with a liquid container or false bottom carrying a quantity of the purported commodity. If needs be this "shell" can be used to get articles already camouflaged to a destination, e.g., a broken spar carried ashore containing cans of putty concealing plastic explosive.

(c) The camouflage of devices, where standard or special charges are disguised as innocent vehicles such as oil cans, coal or stones.

(d) The introduction of camouflage into booby traps such as tins which explode when opened, or the innocent military manual left lying on a desk.

(e) The camouflage of wireless sets can be divided into two categories; firstly, that of a carrier as described in Category A, or secondly as a permanent camouflage where the wireless set is in constant use, such as a Calculator, or an ordinary receiving set.

(f) The concealment of small articles which are needed to be carried by the agent upon his person, e.g., codes, microscopic photographs and messages, hidden in pens, pencils or wallets, etc.

(g) In this Section the agent's clothing is dealt with, particular importance being placed on the necessity for ensuring that everything he wears or carries fits in with his cover story.

(h) This Section shows how the agent's physical appearance can be altered, either temporarily or permanently by make-up, disguise, plastic surgery, or other means, and how he can change his personality so that he can move about freely without fear of recognition.

(i) It is often necessary to use methods of camouflage as laid down by the Armed Forces, as in many cases operations are carried out by small military or naval parties. The principles involved in disruptive painting are explained in this section, which shows how objects are so painted to break up their shape and to help them to become immersed into their background. This method applies mostly to small craft and the personal equipment of the men taking part.

(j) The camouflage of tyrebursters. This is done by three different methods, illustrations of which are appended to the text.

(k) All the labels and printing matter necessary to complete the fake commodities as described in the previous sections, are produced by the Printing and Art departments. This also includes production of armlets for invading forces, insignias for foreign uniforms and the printing of codes.

(l) Photographic Section exists chiefly for the purpose of producing the necessary photographs for faked documents. It is also responsible for the illustrations required for the various catalogues and technical journals.

(m) MISCELLANEOUS. Included in this section are all the smaller and more unusual items of camouflage which cannot be properly classified under any of the above headings.

While it is not possible to include in a catalogue of this nature all the many and varied camouflage items that have been produced, it will be found that the above sections cover all the main branches of camouflage work, and any items not included vary only in details from the chief principles set out in the succeeding pages.

"SHELL" OVER STORES

The introduction of a "shell" over stores is used for camouflaging single units of bulk stores such as arms, ammunition, food, etc. Where possible this principle is aided by additional tricks of subterfuge such as the introduction of a liquid container in tin flagons, or drums, but in the majority of cases, the camouflage consists of only the outer covering. A list of articles that have been used is appended below:

Bricks, Barrels, Plaster Bandages, Plastic Bottles, Bottles of Mineral Water, Drums of Pitch, Drums of Size, Driftwood, Drums of Paint and Oil, Fishboxes, Fish Barrels, Food Tins, Plaster Logs, Plaster Vegetables, Papier Mache Oil Bottles, Soap Powder Cartons, Food Cartons, Skittles, Ships' Spars, Stones, Tunney Fish and Water Carriers.

DRUMS OF OIL, PAINT, etc.

Different types and sizes of metal drums are designed to represent normal commodities in the countries concerned. They are used for the concealment of arms, ammunition, explosives, and are painted and stencilled to appear as paint, tar, tallow, creosote, herring oil, etc. As illustrated, these drums can be fitted with a bung-hole, and a section inside the drum is filled with the liquid which it is supposed to be carrying, so that it will stand scrutiny when a dip stick is inserted into the drum.

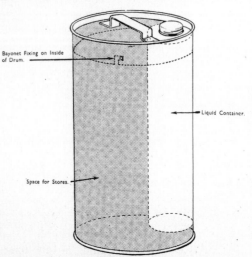

Bayonet Fixing on Inside of Drum.

Liquid Container.

Space for Stores.

FISH BARRELS.

A fish barrel of a type fairly common to most countries is used for shipping of arms and ammunition. A metal drum is filled with the stores, sealed down with pitch to protect from damp, and then placed in the barrel. It is packed round on all sides with rock salt, or cod roe (fertilizer) and the barrel top is then nailed on and banded.

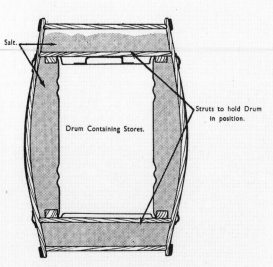

Salt.

Drum Containing Stores.

Struts to hold Drum in position.

METAL FLAGONS.

Metal Containers of various types and shapes are used for concealment of ammunition, small stores, grenades, crystals, money, etc. A great range of tins and labels of all countries is kept in stock. Below is an illustration of some of the tins used, but as almost any type of label can be copied and the tin produced, it is not necessary to give an illustration of them all. Liquid containers etc., are fitted to each tin so that when shaken it appears to be full of the purported contents.

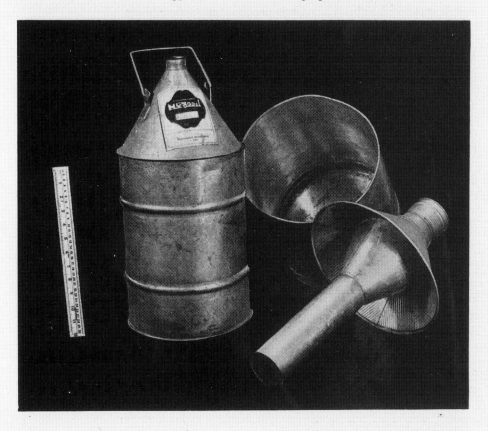

PLASTER LOGS.

A range of plaster logs designed for shipping arms and ammunition. The arms are packed in cardboard containers and sealed to protect from damp. They are then built into dummy logs made of plaster, which are modelled on actual types of trees common to the countries to which the shipments are being made. The plaster is then painted and garnished with moss, green lichen, or other tree fungi.

Wooden logs with a hollow cavity in the centre are also used for concealment of stores and ammunition. See illustration below.

PACKING CASES.

A series of packing cases in wood and cardboard designed to represent commodities in everyday use in the countries concerned. Arms and ammunition are sent out in these boxes representing such articles as china and glassware, jam, tinned foods, electrical goods, mineral waters, etc. These cases are designed to fit the Standard Dump Unit and variations are made to the outside appearance by means of cross members, handles, wire banding, stencils, and destination labels. In some instances the box is given a coat of paint or stained according to the type required.

PLASTER VEGETABLES AND FRUIT.

Vegetables such as potatoes, swedes, parsnips, etc. and tropical fruit are made of plaster or papier mache and used for the concealment of ammunition, Plastic explosive, Incendiary material, etc. The result is an excellent imitation of the actual vegetable or fruit. This type of device when filled is useful for depositing ammunition in dumps and mixed with real vegetables or fruit until distributed.

For the far East, fruit are produced. These include: Pommegranates, Paw Paws, Pineapples, Mangoes, Coconuts, Sweet Corn, etc.

DRIFTWOOD AND SPARS.

Driftwood, such as old railway sleepers, and struts in bridge building, are made with a cavity, and are used for the concealment of Sten guns and ammunition. To guard against the effects of dampness, the stores are first packed in tin containers, and then placed in the pieces of wood.

The same principal is used in the construction of ships' spars, except that the entry to the concealment chamber is from the bottom instead of from the side.

CEMENT BAGS.

Bags of cement are used for carrying arms and ammunition. The arms are packed into tin containers around which a plaster shell resembling cement hardened by damp or water, is modelled. The whole is then put into a cement bag, which is printed and aged to look like the genuine article.

FISH BOXES.

A fish box of normal type is used for packing arms and ammunition. The arms are first packed in a sealed tin box, placed in a fish box with a salt or fish covering, and a wooden lid nailed or banded down.

The boxes are made from new wood if actual fish boxes are unobtainable. They are aged with paint, dyes, and various solutions of fish and oil.

"DOUBLE SHELL" CAMOUFLAGE

The term "double shell" camouflage describes the method of introducing arms, ammunition, and other stores into a foreign country in the disguise of normal merchandise. These stores are first packed in a manner to ensure that they do not rattle or otherwise expose the camouflage, and then these packages are packed into cartons, tins, etc., appropriate to the commodity under which they are being disguised.

An example of this "double shell" packing is as follows:—

It is required to send grenades to Norway. Each grenade is greased and packed into a tin which is an accurate copy of a current brand of Norwegian fishcakes. Each tin is specially constructed with a liquid container which is filled with an appropriate amount of water. Special attention is paid to weight. The tin is correct as to size and label, and sounds genuine when shaken.

The tins are scaled by the same method that the fishcake manufacturer would use, and packed in reproductions of his crates.

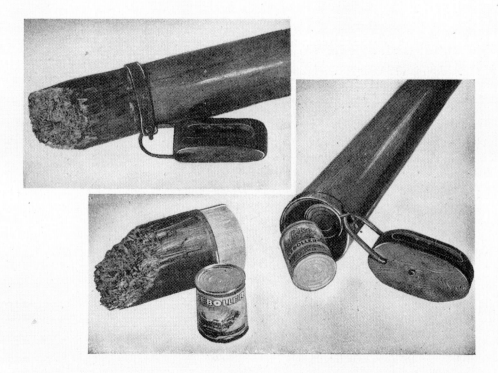

Obviously careful selection of commodity containers is necessary to ensure that (a) weight of packages is similar to real goods, (b) that weight for space is closely related, i.e., it would be wasteful of space to send rifle ammunition in tins of tobacco on account of the small number of rounds which could be packed in, say, a half-pound tin, and still keep the weight down to that of the original quantity of tobacco.

A complete variation of "double shell" camouflage can be employed in the following way:—

A reproduction of a broken ship's spar is constructed of wood. It is hollow and provision is made for it to be opened to contain a considerable volume of stores. Inside the spar may be packed grenades, etc., which have been concealed in plaster reproductions of vegetables or other camouflage.

The hollow spar is waterproof and may be left on a beach or collected by a "beachcomber" who, of course, will be a person connected with the particular operation. He can distribute the camouflaged articles as necessary or keep them concealed in the spar.

For the purpose of "double shell" camouflage a comprehensive range of foreign boxes, tinned goods and lables are kept in stock, covering the following countries:—

Norway, Hungary, Italy, Germany, Belgium,
Denmark, Holland, France, Portugal, Japan.

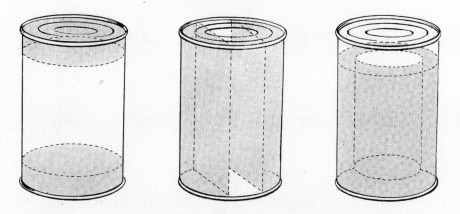

THE SHADED PORTIONS ILLUSTRATE THREE TYPES OF LIQUID CONTAINER.

CAMOUFLAGE OF EXPLOSIVE DEVICES
(Including Booby Traps and Anti-Personnel Incendiary Devices)

This section explains the camouflage of devices where standard or special charges are disguised as innocent vehicles. The following list gives examples of some of the methods used : Bridge limpets filled with plastic explosive and made to represent rusty nuts and bolt heads, Incendiary Cigarettes, Explosive Coal, Dummy Fishplates for railway lines, Explosive Oil Cans, Explosive Rats, Wooden Road Blocks filled with plastic explosive, Explosive Wood Fuel, Chianti Bottles and Clogs, Lifebelts, Driftwood, Ships' Fenders. Explosive Tins and Containers and various devices for the Far East, including Ornamental Carvings cast in TNT and coloured to represent wood or porcelain.

Also included in this section are Incendiary Briefcases, Suitcases, Attache Cases and various types of boxes, all of which are protection against anyone other than the owner opening the vehicle. Some of these have already been included in the first volume of M.O.1. (S.P.) Catalogue, but it is felt advisable to again include them in this volume. Those already described are marked with an asterisk.

RUSTY BOLTS OR NUTS.

A hollow wooden imitation of an iron bolt or nut is made and is painted to give it the appearance of rusted iron. Two horse shoe magnets are fixed inside the bolt. When the device is to be used a General Purpose Charge is clipped into position in the bolt. Initiation is by means of a Pencil Time Fuse and No. 27 Detonator. The assembled device is then fixed by means of the magnets on to the target to be attacked.

EXPLOSIVE COAL.

A hollow cast of a piece of coal is made in two sections. The interior is filled with plastic explosive, in which a 1 oz. Primer, Field, is set. The two sections are then clamped together and the join sealed. The coal is finished off with a coating of black shellac which is garnished with coal dust. A length of dowelling keeps the passage to the Primer clear until the insertion of the initiation unit. Initiation is by means of a match headed safety fuse to which a No. 27 Detonator is crimped, or by means of a length of safety fuse with a No. 27 Detonator crimped on one end and a Copper Tube Igniter crimped on the other end. The match end is dusted over with coal dust prior to operational use.

WOODEN LOGS, EXPLOSIVE.

This device can be made in two ways. Firstly, the log can be hollowed out from one end. Secondly, the log can be split in two, and hollowed out. In both methods the log is filled with P.E. and a 1 oz. Standard Field Primer set in it. Initiation is by means of a short length of safety fuse with a No. 27 Detonator crimped on one end and a Copper Tube Igniter on the other end. A length of dowelling keeps the passage to the Primer clear until the insertion of the initiating unit. The log can be used in many ways, particularly as fuel for boilers, furnaces, etc. An illustration is shown above.

CHIANTI BOTTLE.

The Chianti bottle is made of thick celluloid, and is in two sections, see photograph. The lower section is bowl shaped, the top section represents the neck and shoulders of the bottle, and has the base of the neck closed by means of a diaphragm of celluloid so that the neck may be filled with wine to complete the camouflage when the bottle is assembled. Each section is filled with P.E. A C.E. pellet is set in the top section, but must be at an angle in order to permit the maximum length for the insertion of a detonator and "L" delay. The "L" delay is inserted through a hole in the base when required operationally. An A.C. delay may also be used to initiate the charge, but a P.T.F. is too long.

When filling is completed, the two sections are fixed together and the joint sealed with acetone and buffed up, the inside of the celluloid having first been treated with transparent green paint, so that when the two portions are fixed together the whole takes on the appearance of green glass as used in wine bottles. Next the raffia cover is attached to the bottle together with authentic labels. The finished effect is that of a genuine bottle of Chianti.

EXPLOSIVE PUMP.

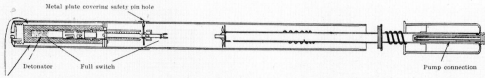

Metal plate covering safety pin hole

Detonator   Pull switch

Pump connection

Two sides of explosive cylinder flattened,
to allow the passage of air.

1. Using slightly shorter stroke than usual the pump will pump air into your tyres.
2. When the piston is screwed into the pull switch the device is then ready to operate as a booby trap.

A hollow brass cylinder filled with explosive and fitted with a pull switch, is pushed inside the barrel of a bicycle pump. The piston rod is shortened but air can still be pumped into the tyres, two grooves on the side of the cylinder acting as air passages. A nut is soldered on to the top of the Pull switch, and a screw is fixed on the end of the piston.

When required to operate as an explosive device, the piston is screwed on to the pull switch, and the safety pin withdrawn. This latter operation is done by removing a small brass name-plate from the side of the pump, pulling out the pin, and replacing the name-plate.

The enemy's pump is replaced by the explosive one and his tyres deflated. When he uses the pump the device operates.

EXPLOSIVE FOOD TIN.

This tin is of the lever lid type and is partly filled with P.E. A pressure release switch is set vertically in the tin. A lug attached to the lid engages the shoulder of the release switch. Initiation is by means of a spring snout attachment with a No. 27 detonator set in a 1 oz. field primer. The safety pin in the release switch is pulled out through a small hole in the side of the tin. When the lever lid is prised open the lug releases the shoulder of the pressure release switch which operates and fires the P.E. The tins are made in varying designs and sizes with authentic labels attached. The device can be left in damaged houses, food dumps, billets, etc.

INCENDIARY SOAP.

A hollow cast is made of a cake of soap. The cavity is filled with pure metallic sodium and the joint is carefully sealed up with soap, so that the join cannot be seen. When the soap covering of the sodium wears thin through use, moisture seeps through causing it to ignite and burn fiercely. This device can cause a great deal of injury to the hands or face.

INCENDIARY SHAVING BRUSH.

A normal shaving brush handle is hollowed out and filled with pure metallic sodium. A small hole is bored in the stub of the hairs of the brush to allow water to seep through, and when the brush is used the sodium is ignited by contact with the water.

CIGARETTES, INCENDIARY, PACKING OF

Incendiary cigarettes are illustrated in Section II Special List NS 302 (Vol. 1. M.O.1. (S.P.) Catalogue).

This illustration shows how a normal cigarette may be used as a message carrier, the message being rolled up into a small tube and inserted into the partly emptied cigarette. The tobacco is then replaced, sealing up the ends of the cigarette.

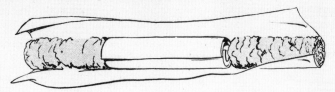

Illustrated above are two top labels from Greek Cigarette packets. The incendiary cigarettes are packed as if they were normal cigarettes and the usual Goverment seal pasted round the packet.

EXPLOSIVE BOOK.

The Explosive Book is a booby trap which may be placed on any flat surface preferably among other books on a table top.

The inside of the book is cut away in order to leave sufficient space for a lb. or more of P.E.

Initiation is by means of a Fuse, Anti-Removal (Air Armed) to which is fitted a Type 6 Burster. The back cover is cut away and reinforced with sheet metal if necessary so that the fuse may be held rigidly flush with the outer face of the cover. The covers are fixed so that any attempt to open the book will cause lifting of the volume and immediate action of the fuse.

The book is camouflaged with any suitable book jacket, which is removed prior to " placing " the booby trap.

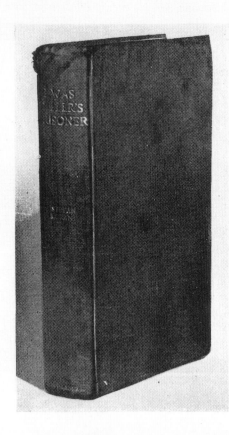

ENGINEER'S OIL CAN.

A Continental type of oil can as shown in the illustration is used, with a small liquid container built around the oil filling well, so that when the cover is pulled back it gives the impression that the can is full of oil. The remainder of the oil can is filled with P.E. in which is set a 1 oz. Primer, Field, or a No. 6 C.E. Pellet enclosed in a close fitting metal container with which is embodied a guide tube leading to the spout of the can. Initiation is by means of a Pencil Time Fuse fitted with a No. 27 Detonator. For operational use, the spout of the can is removed, the P.T.F. slipped down the guide tube until the detonator fits into the Primer or C.E. Pellet. The spout is then replaced. As the device is quite innocent looking it can be left by the Student beside machinery without causing undue attention. The delay should not be too long as an oil can is liable to be used frequently.

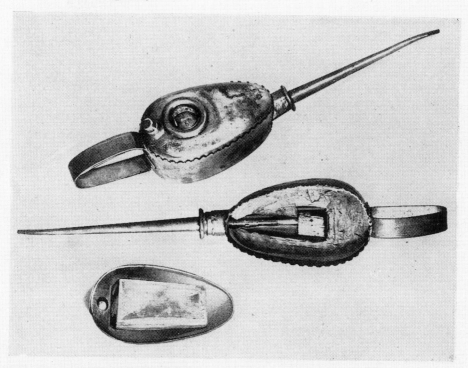

WOODEN ROAD BLOCKS.

A tarred wooden road block of normal size is made with a hollow interior which is filled with P.E., into which is set a 1 oz. Field Primer. Initiation is by means of a short length of safety fuse with a No. 27 Detonator crimped on one end and a Copper Tube Igniter crimped on the other end. A length of dowelling keeps the passage to the Primer clear until the insertion of the initiation unit. The whole is tarred and aged to resemble a worn road block which may be found in any pile or dump of wood.

RATS, EXPLOSIVE.

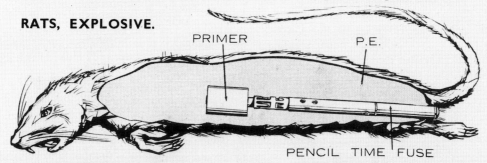

PRIMER   P.E.

PENCIL TIME FUSE

A rat is skinned, the skin being sewn up and filled with P.E. to assume the shape of a dead rat. A Standard No. 6 Primer is set in the P.E. Initiation is by means of a short length of safety fuse with a No. 27 detonator crimped on one end, and a copper tube igniter on the other end, or, as in the case of the illustration above, a P.T.F. with a No. 27 detonator attached. The rat is then left amongst the coal beside a boiler and the flames initiate the safety fuze when the rat is thrown on to the fire, or as in the case of the P.T.F. a Time Delay is used.

SHIPS FENDER.

This device containing a charge of 10 lbs. P.E. will detonate if upwards of 150 lbs. crushing pressure is applied.

It comprises a thin metal cylinder containing the charge which is initiated by Tyre Bursters, the whole being camouflaged as a ship's fender.

Method of Initiation. The side stitching forming a running loop, may be eased open with the fingers, revealing the metal cylinder. On removing outside and inside lids at BOTH ends, eight pockets will be visible. Insert Brass Priming Caps to Tyre Bursters provided in Accessories Box. Smear the THREADS and HEAD of each cap with Luting Compound and cover with protective strip of Adhesive Tape. It is necessary to ensure that no Luting Compound enters the interior of the Tyre Burster. Place a prepared Tyre Burster in each pocket and replace inner and outer lids carefully to both ends, securing by passing the thin metal strips through the brackets on the outside of the container and turning back. Carefully replace charge inside jute cover, draw taut by the running loop —pulling from the rope end of the "fender." Knot loop close to stitching and cut off superfluous string. Make good the stitching if necessary, with the needle and string provided.

Important. These devices are to be identified by the KNOT tied at the junction of the rope and the "fender."

TORCH ANTI-PERSONNEL GRENADE

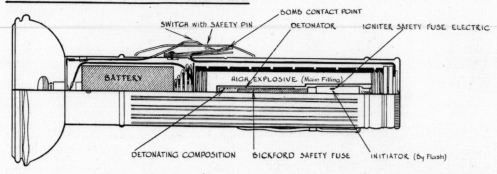

SWITCH with SAFETY PIN — BOMB CONTACT POINT — DETONATOR — IGNITER SAFETY FUSE ELECTRIC

BATTERY — HIGH EXPLOSIVE (Main Filling)

DETONATING COMPOSITION — BICKFORD SAFETY FUSE — INITIATOR (By Flash)

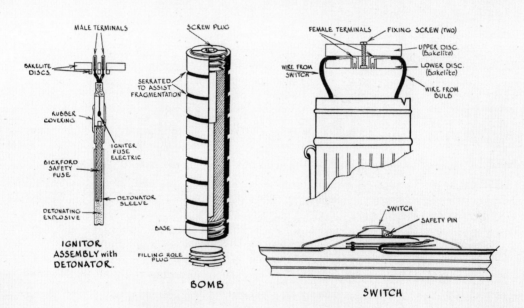

MALE TERMINALS — SCREW PLUG — FEMALE TERMINALS — FIXING SCREW (TWO)

BAKELITE DISCS — SERRATED TO ASSIST FRAGMENTATION — WIRE FROM SWITCH — UPPER DISC (Bakelite) — LOWER DISC (Bakelite) — WIRE FROM BULB

RUBBER COVERING — IGNITER FUSE ELECTRIC

BICKFORD SAFETY FUSE — DETONATOR SLEEVE

DETONATING EXPLOSIVE — BASE

IGNITOR ASSEMBLY with DETONATOR. — FILLING HOLE PLUG

BOMB

SWITCH — SAFETY PIN

SWITCH

TORCH, ANTI-PERSONNEL GRENADE.

A German pattern torch of the Daimon variety is used as an explosive device. Two of the three batteries normally present in the torch are removed, their place being taken by a cylindrical, deeply grooved bomb filled with Baratol. Initiation is by means of an igniter safety fuse, electric, crimped on to a length of safety fuse which has a No. 27 detonator crimped on the other end. The delay is from 4—5 seconds. The normal switch on the outside of the torch has been adapted so that current can flow to the torch bulb, or, after removal of a small safety pin, to the igniter safety fuse, electric. This safety pin prevents accidental initiation prior to operational use.

CHINESE STONE LANTERNS.

In the ordinary way the originals are made of solid stone, weighing anything up to half-ton. Camouflage Section have reproduced these Chinese Lanterns in light wood with a veneer of plaster and resembling in every way the original.

The device is divided into five separate compartments each of which can be filled with H.E. and fitted with delayed action fuse or anti-removal switch, and can be assembled as in illustration, or unassembled as if the lantern had been knocked over. This is the reason why the lantern is made with arming devices in all five sections.

BALINESE CARVINGS.

These are faithful reproductions of the famous Balinese wood carvings, but in this case they have been cast in solid H.E. and coloured to represent wood, sandstone or porcelain. Each head is mounted on a wooden base and equipped for initiation by a time delay. It is intended to use these through native agents posing as hawkers frequenting the quaysides, and selling them to Japanese troops about to embark.

JAP SAUCE TIN.

The illustration shows a reproduction of a Japanese tin which contains Shoyu Sauce.

This type together with the many brands of Kerosine tin which are in common use for carrying water and food in all parts of the Far East have been adapted either as explosive devices (fig. 2) or for the concealment of W/T sets and stores.

FIG. 1.

Japanese ammunition boxes have also been put to similar use, but with the addition of carrying an anti-removal switch.

EXPLOSIVE OIL TIN

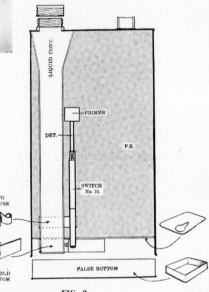

FIG. 2.

*INCENDIARY BRIEFCASE (Single Lock).

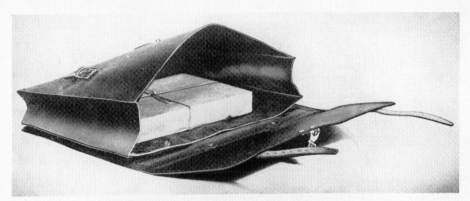

The external appearance is that of an ordinary Briefcase. A camouflaged parcel inside the case contains a thermit charge, battery and arming switch. The electric wiring is concealed in the lining of the case. One quilt of potassium nitrate is provided to assist in combustion of documents. The lock is converted to act as a switch.

Another switch, under a patch of rexine inside the case, takes the place of the right hand lock on double lock types.

The arming switch is set to "ON" position. To close and open the case safely, the switch under the patch of rexine must be depressed to its full extent and held thus while the outer lock is manipulated. If this is not done the charge will fire when the external lock is moved.

*INCENDIARY ATTACHE CASE.

The external appearance is that of an ordinary case. One camouflaged parcel inside the case contains a thermit charge, battery, and an arming switch. The electric wiring is concealed under the lining of the case. Two quilts of potassium nitrate are

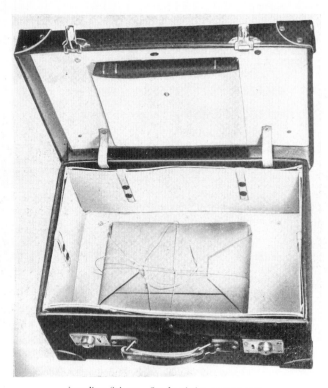

Incendiary Suitcase. See description on next page.

provided to assist in combustion of documents. The locks are converted to act as switches and control the firing of the charge.

The arming switch is set to "ON" position. To close and open the case safely the knob of the right-hand lock must be pressed and held to the right. If this is not done the charge will fire when left-hand knob is moved.

*INCENDIARY SUITCASE.

External appearance is that of an ordinary suitcase. Internally there are two camouflaged thermit charges, one in the lid, the other in the bottom of the case. The electric battery and wiring are concealed under the camouflage and lining of the case. Five quilts of potassium nitrate are provided to assist combustion of documents. The locks are converted to act as switches and control the firing of the charges.

The arming switch incorporated in the lower thermit unit is set to the "ON" position. To close and open the case safely the knob of the right-hand lock must be pressed and held to the right. If this is not done the charges will fire when the left-hand knob is moved.

CAMOUFLAGE OF WIRELESS SETS

The size and shape of wireless receiving and transmitting sets used in the field, and the fact that they are mostly required to be assembled ready for use, presents a difficult concealment problem but, as the following list shows, a large number of articles have been successfully used to conceal wireless sets :—

Artist's paint box.
Blocks of granite.
Bundles of faggots.
Bathroom scales.
Car batteries.
Concrete posts used in fencing.
Cement sacks.
Driftwood.
Domestic wireless sets, continental type.
Electrical testing meter.

Portable gramophone.
Geyser.
Munro adding machine.
Paint and oil drums.
Rocks, rubber, tin, papier mache.
Rubber armchairs.
Vacuum cleaners.
Vibro massage sets.
Workman's tool boxes.

Each item is either "manufactured," e.g., made with Papier Mache, Plaster, etc., or, in the case of bathroom scales and other mechanical objects, the machinery is replaced by the wireless set, and the outside appearance remains as the original innocent domestic appliance.

The following examples and illustrations are typical of wireless concealment devices :—

BUNDLES OF FAGGOTS.

BUNDLES OF FAGGOTS—Cont.

This type of concealment is useful for country districts. Care must be taken to ensure that the faggots correspond to the kind of trees found in the neighbourhood. A rope aerial (see Aerials) can be used to bind round the bundle of faggots.

The construction of the bundle is shown in the illustration below. The first operation is to gather a real bundle of sticks, and then to select those which are to be used for the centre, and cut out the middle of each stick. Holes are bored in the end of the box and the short ends of sticks firmly secured into them. The outer casing of sticks is nailed into the box. In the field the agent can alter the bundle by placing more locally gathered sticks on the outside, and binding them on with his aerial.

MUNRO ADDING MACHINE.

This machine is manufactured in America, but it is in common use on the continent.

The machine is used to conceal the A. Mk. II wireless set. If the vibrator pack is required it must be sent under separate camouflage.

When the set is fitted into the machine it is still possible to operate the keys, but the machine does not work. This latter fact would help to substantiate a cover story that the machine was being taken for repairs if an agent was stopped in the street.

DOMESTIC WIRELESS SETS.

Domestic wireless set cabinets constructed to appear identical to those in use on the continent can be very satisfactorily used as a concealment for an agent's wireless set. The outside controls are dummy and the agent's set is hidden in the false case.

PORTABLE GRAMOPHONES.

The A. Mk. II wireless set fits conveniently into a continental type gramophone. By removing the gramophone motor, substituting a dummy spindle to carry the turntable, and cutting away the sound horn inside the gramophone, enough room is provided to take the four packs of the A. Mk. II wireless set.

This concealment is only for carrying purposes and the wireless set must be taken out of the gramophone and assembled for working. Wherever possible the gramophone is made to play and appropriate records are supplied. Plates below show details.

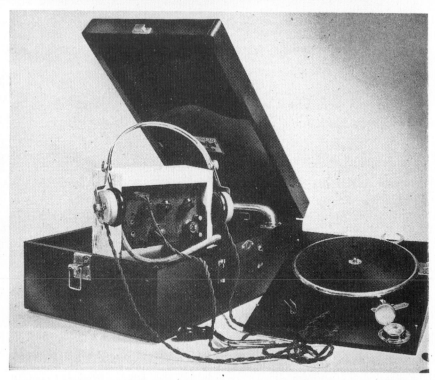

VACUUM CLEANER.

The plates below show the method of concealing the four packs of the A. Mk. II wireless set, crystals and spares in a continental type Electrolux cleaner and its carrying case.

The cleaner can be "plugged in" and although not actually operating as a cleaner the noise produced will give all the appearance of it doing so.

If an agent was stopped while carrying the cleaner in the street it would be normal to tell a story that it was being taken for repair, or to be sold.

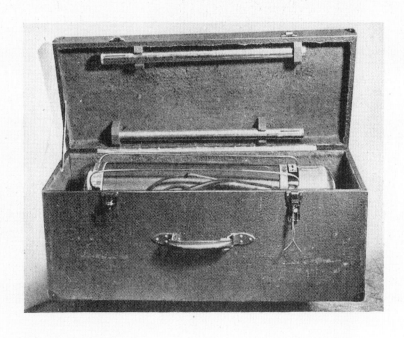

AERIALS.

A good aerial always improves the performance of a wireless set, and an agent can make use of one with little fear of detection if it is concealed in a rope clothes line or window sash cord.

The illustration on the left shows aerial disguised as a tendril in its natural surroundings.

The illustration below shows the finished clothes line aerial. This aerial is made by twisting the rope strands over the aerial: a rope making machine can be adapted to do this work. In the case of the window sash cord, the centre core of the cord is withdrawn and the wire threaded back in its place.

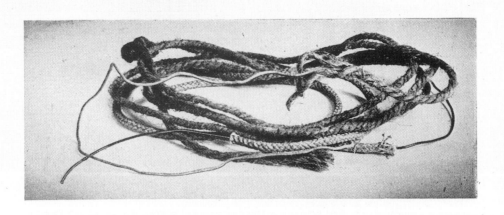

ROCKS.

These are devices for depositing a wireless set on beaches or in open country.

A papier mache shell is constructed and is lined inside with a tin case which conforms to the outline of the rock at the top and is flat at the base. See the plate below. The shell is realistically painted and finished to blend with the geological

types of the district in the country in which operations are being carried out, providing they are used with discretion to fit into their correct surroundings.

These rocks are weather proof when finished and quite safe to leave in an appropriate place without fear of detection or damage to the wireless set.

Hollowed out spars or blocks of driftwood are also successfully used for concealing wireless sets out-of-doors.

RUBBER ARMCHAIR.

This device is constructed like a balloon. When it is inflated with a pump it has the outline of an ordinary armchair. The wireless set can be placed under the seat.

The effect is perfected by covering the chair with a loose cover, placing a cushion on the seat and the chair can be used in the normal way. Care must be taken to keep it normally inflated. When deflated the chair folds up to a package about 15 ins. by 9 ins. Rocks and Boulders can also be produced in the same way. This type of camouflage takes up very little space and is easily manipulated.

CONCEALMENT OF M.C.R.'s

The following pages of illustrations showing various devices used for the concealment of Miniature Communication Receivers.

Antique German Clocks copied from originals, and suitably aged and painted are illustrated on this page. On the right, showing the front view, and below, the back view, with concealment chamber sufficiently large enough to accommodate an M.C.R.

Above are illustrations, left to right, of Paper Punch, German Water Bottle and a Belgian Tea Can. Each of these items are sufficiently large to conceal an M.C.R. In the case of Water Bottle and Tea Can, a small liquid container is included to complete concealment.

The above illustrations show three further methods of adapting ordinary articles into concealment devices for M.C.R.'s. Left to right, German Manual, German Bible in case and Brandy Flask. The illustrations below show normal appearance of these articles.

ARTICLES CARRIED BY A STUDENT

This section could very well be a catalogue in itself as even the many articles mentioned in the following pages do not in any way cover the whole field of material which comes under this heading.

Almost anything which a person carries or makes use of professionally, by way of trade, for personal convenience or toilet purposes, can be adapted for concealment.

This section covers all types of articles but by no means all varieties, and for simplicity it has been divided into sub-sections.

No. 1 sub-section deals with those concealments which are possible in the actual personal clothing and contents of the pockets of the average man.

PERSONAL ARTICLES.

The following is a short list of some of the articles which have been adapted :—

Collar stud	Pocket torches
Collar stiffener	Pen knife
Coat button	Pipe
Cigarette holder	Pipe cases
Door key	Pencils
Fountain pen	Shoe trees
Finger ring	Shoulder paddings
Pocket petrol lighter	Shoe heels and soles
	Spectacles

The following examples show what can be done with these articles :–

Collar Stud. A metal collar stud with a celluloid back can be used for concealing micro prints. The celluloid back is removed, and the print placed in the cavity. The celluloid is replaced and secured with a small application of Seccotine.

Necktie. A necktie can conceal a small code printed on silk. The code is secured to the back of the tie with two small press studs. This method is used in order that the code may be very speedily used and replaced. A tie adapted in this manner is worn quite normally and without any bulkiness showing.

Door Key. A door key has been successfully adapted for the concealment of small microprints. The shaft of the key is drilled to about three quarters of its length, and a small stud is made which fits into the hollowed shaft by means of a left handed thread. See illustration.

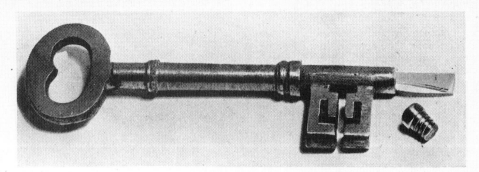

TOILET ARTICLES.

In the following list are some of the toilet articles which have been used for concealment purposes, and which form some of the personal equipment of a Student.

Bath salts.	Folding mirror.	Razor.	Manicure accessories.
Razor box.	Sponge.	Shaving soap.	Toilet soap.
Shaving stick.	Talcum powder.	Toilet roll.	Toothpaste.
Lipsticks.			

Examples from this list are given below.

Sponge. A suitable place in the sponge is chosen, and a hole is cut to conform to the natural texture of the sponge. A small amount of the sponge fibre is cut away from the inside to leave sufficient room to insert a message or code printed on silk. The object inserted in a sponge must necessarily be of a soft nature in order not to make a hard lump and to avoid a rustling sound which would be made by paper.

The cavity in the sponge is closed up by replacing a small sponge plug and securing with Seccotine or by stitching.

Toilet Soap. It is necessary to procure or copy a cake of soap common to the district where the Student is proceeding.

The piece of soap is carefully split open and the centre hollowed out. Pins are used to help to keep the two halves together. When the object for concealment is in place, the soap is pressed together. To render the joint unnoticeable a little moisture is rubbed round the joint, or the soap is used in the normal way.

Toothpaste in Tubes. These tubes have a number of uses. The Student naturally requires toothpaste appropriate to the country to which he is proceeding. Some of the "brands" which are made up by the Camouflage Section are shown below. Glass-frosting ointment is also dispatched under this cover.

For concealment purposes the tubes are completed with the supposed makers' trade marks, etc., and the top of the tube is filled with toothpaste. If the object to be concealed requires to be damp-proofed (e.g. a code printed on silk), it is inserted in a rubber balloon. The object is placed in the tube, packed with a little cotton wool

213

and the end of the tube is folded over in the normal way. This device is safe enough because the toothpaste can be used and should arouse no suspicion.

Shaving Cream in Tubes. This method is exactly similar to the toothpaste tube, except that there is a larger concealment space. Examples are shown.

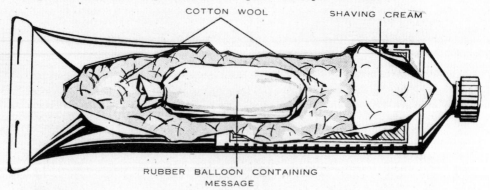

COTTON WOOL   SHAVING CREAM

RUBBER BALLOON CONTAINING
MESSAGE

BRUSHES.

The following is a list of some of the brushes used for concealment :—

Hair brushes, celluloid backs, wooden backs, and swivel sided. Shaving brushes. Clothes brushes. Tooth brushes. Nail brushes. Shoe brushes. Paint and distemper brushes. Wire brushes.

These are used for concealment of codes, money, documents, etc. There are two principal methods used for brushes. When the brush is used to carry money, etc. to the field and is not re-used, the back of a celluloid brush, for example, is removed, money is packed inside the cavity, and the brush sealed up. The brush must be split open to extract its contents. If the brush is for use on a number of occasions the swivel sided brush described on the next page is an example of the type of brush supplied.

The following are some descriptions of typical brush concealments.

Celluloid Hair brush and Shaving brush. In the illustration below is shown a complete toilet set in a leather case. The case itself has a concealment pocket and the

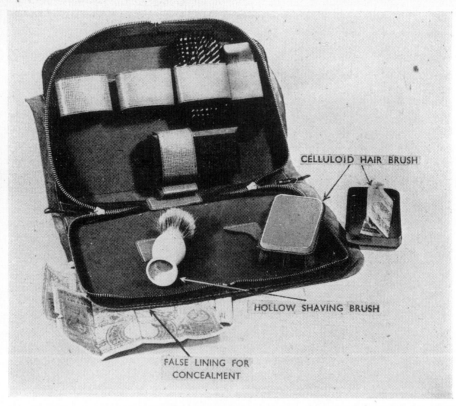

CELLULOID HAIR BRUSH

HOLLOW SHAVING BRUSH

FALSE LINING FOR
CONCEALMENT

hair brush is of the celluloid back type. The shaving brush is hollow as shown. These three devices are for use only once each, because each article must be forcibly opened to extract the hidden contents.

Swivel type Hair brush. The photograph shows the working of the swivel sided hair brush. The cavity is approximately 3 inches x 2 inches x ⅜ inch.

Shaving brush. This brush is also for quick and frequent use. The bristles are held in place by a tight metal ring which clamps them to the handle. This brush must not be confused with the type, shown in the illustration on the previous page, which can only be used once.

Tooth brush. A celluloid handled tooth brush can be used for concealment of small micro prints. The handle of the brush is drilled, the print inserted and the hole sealed by softening the celluloid with acetone and smoothing off on a buffing wheel. To extract the message the handle of the brush must be broken.

Various types of Leather Goods can be used for the concealment of Codes, Money, Documents, etc. A list of these is given below.

LEATHER GOODS.

1. Brief cases.
2. Cycle Saddle bag.
3. Cigarette cases.
4. Card cases.
5. Handbags, ladies'.
6. Needle cases and housewives.
7. Pocket chess set.
8. Razor strop.
9. Suit cases, various types.
10. Tobacco pouches.
11. Pocket note books, various types.
12. Toilet cases, various types.
13. Wallets, Photo and Money.
14. Writing cases, various types.
15. Leather belts and braces.
16. Hairbrush case.
17. Toolbags.

Two methods are used in the camouflage of Codes, Documents, etc.

1. Where the article is used only once for transporting Money and Documents to the Field, it can be sealed and ripped open when needed.
2. In the case of Codes when the article would have to be used many times, a concealed flap device is incorporated in the design so that the Code can be readily accessible.

Brief Cases. These are of Continental design in various sizes and colours, having double sided partitions, with fake sewing along the top. Partitions are glued together after the Documents have been inserted.

Suitcases. Varying types of Continental Suitcases are used for the concealment of Codes, Documents, Money, etc. In some cases the handle is also used as a concealment device for small articles. The double-bottomed suitcase as shown below is constructed so that a sliding panel is held in position by threaded rivets, which when unscrewed allow the panel to be withdrawn. The cavity exposed is about $\frac{1}{2}$ inch deep and covers the area of the bottom of the suitcase. From these measurements it can be seen that this type is extremely useful for large amounts of money.

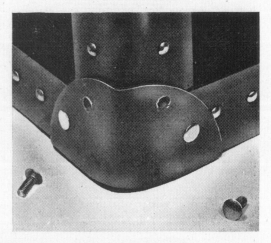

In the double sided type (top illustration) an inner casing is made to lift out exposing a shallow cavity on all four sides.

A Handle made in metal and constructed in two parts is held together by threaded rivets; a nut is soldered on to the inner side of the bottom half, thus facilitating the removal of the two parts, and easy access to the article concealed therein.

See illustration opposite.

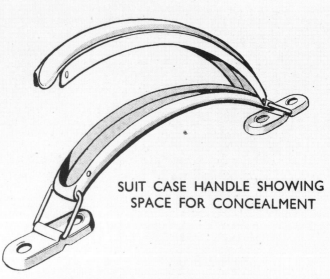

SUIT CASE HANDLE SHOWING SPACE FOR CONCEALMENT

Ladies Handbags. These handbags are stocked in various designs and colours. An opening concealed in the fold at the bottom of the bag gives access to the hidden compartment, which is between the lining and the outer covering. This allows easy insertion and withdrawal of the Code, etc., which is concealed therein.

Razor Strop. In this case the Razor Strop handle is used for the concealment of small messages and Micro-prints. The handle is opened up, and the message inserted in the padding. The handle is then re-sewn.

Needle Cases and "Housewives." Needle cases and "housewives" being quite normal things to carry, are used for the concealment of silk codes and messages. The concealment is in a false lining. Cotton reels, Woolcards, needles, scissors, etc., used for the contents of the housewife are authentic. Labels are printed copies of originals.

Spools and reels of cotton or silk can also be used as further carrying devices for Drugs, Micro-prints, etc.

Leather Belts. Double sided belts of varying colours and design, with Grip-on buckles are used for the concealment of micro-prints. When the buckle is removed, the open end is revealed, giving quick and easy access to the hollow centre of the belt where the Micros and Prints are inserted.

Braces. The leather connecting piece between the two braces can be unstitched and used for the concealment of Micros and Prints. Continental designs are used as far as possible.

Wrist Straps can also be used on the same principle.

STATIONERY.

A selection of stationery articles which form part of the normal equipment of a writing desk have been adapted for the concealment of Codes, Money, Documents and Tablets. Included in this list are book-ends, uncut books, desk blotters of both the flat and curved varieties, fountain-pens, inkstands, message-carrying pencils, pencil boxes, penknife handles, rubber stamp pads, sealing wax and rubbers.

Uncut Books are a quick and easy method of concealing silk and paper Micro-prints. These books are authentic copies of current volumes on sale in the countries of origin. The codes are inserted between the uncut leaves at the back of the book, and a few pages at the beginning of the book are cut purposely to give the impression that the book is being read.

Rubbers and Sealing Wax are used for the concealment of B, K and L tablets. A cavity is bored in the centre of each of these articles, the tablet inserted, and the article buffed up to remove any sign of the join.

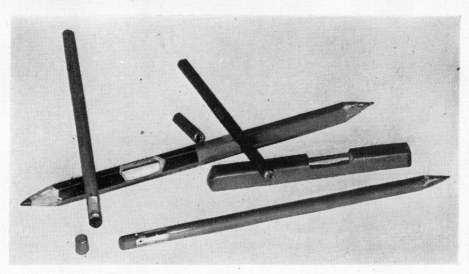

MATCHES, FOREIGN.

A large stock of various types of foreign matches is carried for the personal use of Students in the Field. These can be adapted with false bottoms for concealment purposes where required, but normally they are issued as part of the Agent's cover story. Below is appended a list with illustrations of the various types of match boxes and the countries of origin.

French.
Allumettes soufrées.
  „   amorphés.
  „   de sûreté.
  „   gitanes.
Casque D'or.
Drapeaux.
Timax.
La Cocarde.

Dutch.
Gaai.
Molen Lucifers.
Oehoe.

Italian.
Allumettes 120.
S.A.F.F.A.

Portugal.
Nau.
Patria No. 2.
  „   No. 3.

Norway.
Nitedals.
Hjelpestikker.

Japan.
Eagle matches.
Two Lion matches.

Poland.
Polski Monopol.

U.S.S.R.
Lenin matches.

Sweden.
Sakerhets tandstickor 222.
  „   „   Swallow.
Kampion.

Spain.
Compania Arrendataria.
Phosforos de papel.

Denmark.
H.E. Gosch safety.
  „   paraffin.

Germany.
Schubert.
Haushaltungsware.
Welt-Holzer.

Denmark

France

Thailand

Norway

Japan

Holland

Germany

BATTERIES, ELECTRIC.

Various types and makes of foreign batteries have been used from time to time for the camouflage of codes, etc. Types such as the three cell flat battery, three separate unit round type, the single unit three volt battery, and the large bell battery are used.

These carry labels authentic to the country where they are to be used, e.g., Pile Wonder, Energo and E.V.D., some of which are illustrated.

The three cell flat battery of the usual type is the one most frequently used. The centre cell is removed and replaced with a thin tube of the same size and it is connected up in series by means of a wire so that current still flows through the circuit. Therefore the light is generated by the two outside cells. The empty cell is used for the concealment of Micro-prints, Codes, Money, etc.

In the three cell round battery shown in the illustration the centre unit is hollowed for carrying purposes. The large bell batteries consist of a hollow shell with a small battery to provide the light, fixed in the top of the casing, and the remainder of the space used for concealment. As the concealment space is larger, this type of battery is particularly useful for carrying Wireless crystals, etc. These are, of course, used in conjunction with the Torch itself.

RAZOR BLADES.

Various types of razor blade covers are printed and issued with blades for the general personal equipment of the Agent. Some of the types are listed below :—

French.	German.
Gibb's Mince	Bohm
Parker	Golf
Hurrah	Einloch
Ile de France	Rotbart
Kiss	Fasan Gold
	Robuso
	Punktal

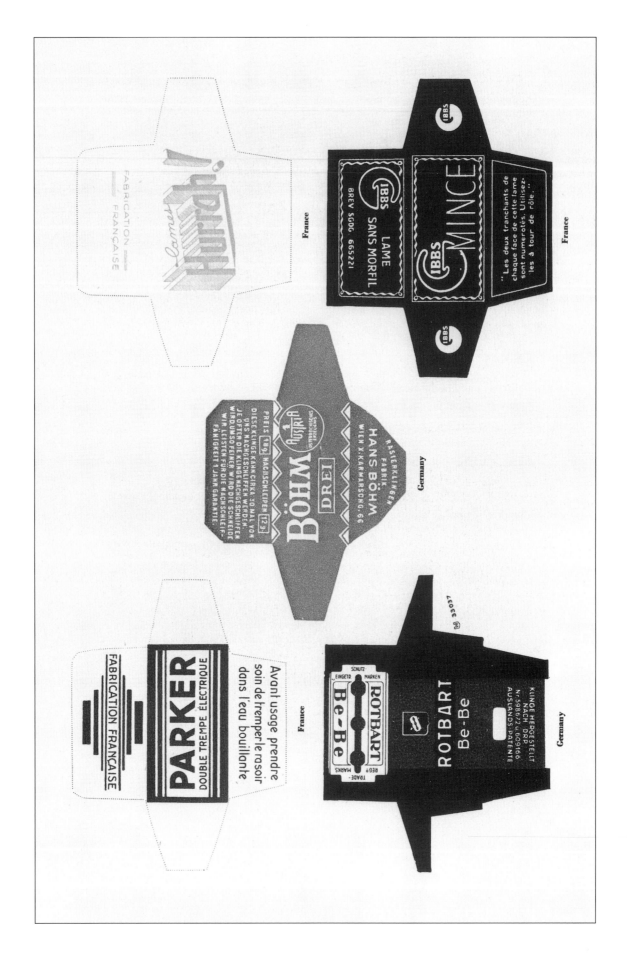

Cigarette Cases and Wallets. Two types of Cigarette Cases, showing concealment devices.

Photo Wallet as used for concealment of codes, etc.

WORKMANS' TOOLS AND EQUIPMENT.

Articles of this kind give us great scope for the concealment of documents and money. These are necessarily controlled by the cover story of the Agent, for instance, a carpenter would have chisels, planes, and hammers, whilst an engineer would carry an oil-can, files, pliers, etc. Naturally, all the tools possible for concealment are not listed below as they cover such a wide field and almost anything of any size can be used for the concealment of codes and money.

Among tools that have been used are the following :—

Blow lamp
Builders' level
Car Dynamo
Car jack
Dentist's Drill
Dentist's chair head-rest
Drawing instruments case
Cycle oil-tin
Engineer's oil-can
Grinding wheel
Oil-stone
Scythe-stone
Hammers
Screwdrivers
Chisels
Mallets
Planes
Drillstands

Illustrated on this page is a carpenter's kit of tools made for the concealment of small stores, money, or documents. The top illustration shows where the tools have been hollowed out to provide concealment cavities.

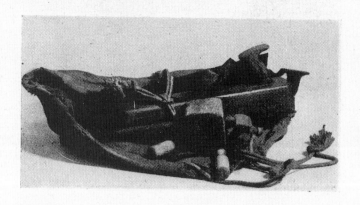

CIGARETTE PACKETS.

A variety of foreign cigarettes and packages is kept in stock for personal use of Agents in the Field, or as concealment devices for small articles or Micros, or Incendiaries. (See Vol. 1. M.O.1. (S.P.) Catalogue, Section II, N.S. 302).

The illustrations below show several packets in the made up state. And opposite are examples of foreign packing illustrated in colour.

French.
Gauloises Blue.
  „   Buff.
  „   Green.
Gitanes.
Golden Gate.
Deka.

Norwegian.
Gold Flake.
South State.
Marmara.
Golden West.

German.
Overstolz.
Privat.
Merkur.
Juno.
Cairo.
Milde Sorte.
Reemtsma Sorte.
Club.
Röth Handle.
Hoco.

Belgian.
Vega.

Greece.
Papastratos.
Arista.

Italy.
Stella.

Thailand.
Pratu Chai.

Japan.
Aeroplane Cigarettes.

PIPES.

As used for carrying small messages and codes.

223

Deka

Germany
Balkans

France

CIGARETTENFABRIK

Josetti

BERLIN S O

Warum ist Juno rund?

Weil nur dieses Format
die beste gleichmäßige Durchlüftung der
Cigarette und damit die ungewöhnlich
reine Geschmacksbildung der feinen

Juno-Mischung

gewährleistet.

Aus gutem Grund ist Juno rund!

JOSETTIJUNO
CIGARETTEN

Josetti

JUNO
o/M.rund

JUNO 9

Germany

MISCELLANEOUS.

The following is a list of articles that can be adapted for camouflage and can be carried by the Student personally, but cannot be classified under a general heading. The list includes:—Electric bulbs, candles, crucifixes, corks, cotton reels, electric irons, fishing floats, hollow faggots, gas-masks, life-jackets, musical instrument cases, mouth-organs, medical kits, piano-accordions, toys, thermos flasks, walking-sticks, and wine bottles.

Corks. A normal cork as used in a wine bottle is used for the concealment of small codes and micro-prints. The cork has a hollow centre with a sliding panel.

Cotton Reels. The cotton reel is composed of two parts, firstly, the outer casing which comprises one end and the body of the cotton reel around which the thread is wound, and secondly the removable centre shaft which is attached to the other end. When the reel is taken apart the silk code is wound round the centre shaft, and the reel is then re-assembled.

225

CLOTHING

The clothing and outfitting of a Student can be said to be the final "finishing" process before he proceeds to an assignment. It is the cloak which must conceal from the enemy and the people with whom he associates in the Field, that he is other than a native of the locality, or a bona fide traveller. All his clothing and equipment must fit completely the cover story and status of the Student. It is obvious that a Student posing as a mechanic would arouse suspicion if under his veneer of dungarees and dirt, he was found to be wearing silk underclothes and a fine linen shirt.

This is a simple example, apparent to anybody, but the tell-tale points about clothes, patterns of shirts, underwear, toilet articles, etc., etc., are innumerable and require minute attention to ensure that no article is supplied to a Student which would disclose to an expert examination, that it is other than genuine and of the type appropriate to the owner.

The task of providing all the necessary variety of items of the correct type is formidable.

The following list shows a typical outfit for a male and female Student proceeding to the Continent.

Male.

Two Suitcases.
Two pairs Shoes, one brown, one black.
One pair Slippers.
One Hat.
One pair Gloves.
Two Face Gloves.
Two Towels.
One Comb.
One Toilet Case.
Two Sponge Bags.
One Nail Brush.
One Clothes Brush.
One Shoe Brush.
One Hair Brush.
One Overcoat.
One Raincoat, with or without camel hair lining.

One Working Suit or Sports Suit.
One Town Suit.
Six Shirts, poplin and/or woollen.
Three pairs Pants.
Three Vests.
One Pullover or Slipover.
One Scarf.
Two pairs Pyjamas.
One Dressing Gown.
Six pairs Socks.
One pair Braces.
One pair Suspenders.
Three Ties.
One dozen Handkerchiefs.
One Belt.
One Wallet.
One pair Cuff Links.

Female.

Two Suitcases.
Two Costumes, one Town, one Sports.
One Overcoat, Sports or Travelling.
Three pairs Shoes, one Sports, one Walking, one Dress.
One pair Slippers.
Six pairs pure Silk Stockings or three Silk, three Lisle.
Three Slips.
Three pairs Knickers.
Two Nightgowns or Pyjamas.
One Woollen Dress.
One Silk Dress.
One Woollen Blouse.
Two Silk Blouses.
One twin set Cashmere Jumper and Cardigan.

One Corset.
Two Brassieres.
Two pairs Gloves.
Two Handbags, one Sports, one Dress.
One Raincoat.
One Scarf, Silk or Wool.
One dozen Linen Handkerchiefs.
One Dressing Gown.
Two Towels.
One Face Square.
One Toilet Case.
One Nail Brush.
One Hair Brush.
One Clothes Brush.
One Shoe Brush.

In addition there are special extras for those proceeding to join the Maquis. They have a choice of taking the following items, over and above, or in lieu of some of the foregoing.

One Rucksack with or without frame or haversack.
One Canadienne Jacket, or Leather Jacket, or Wind Jacket, or Anorak, or Sheep-skin waistcoat with or without sleeves.
One pair Corduroy or Whipcord Trousers, or Plus-fours, or Breeches.
One Cap or Beret.
One pair Ski or Mountain Boots studded with clingers, or Fleece Lined Boots.
One pair Leather Gauntlets, or Fur Lined Gloves, or Woollen Gloves, or Ski Gloves in leather or proofed material.
One Boilersuit or Dungarees.
One Balaclava Helmet.
One Ski Cap.
One pair Ski Trousers.
One Ski Jacket.
Three pairs Oiled Woollen Ski Stockings and/or three pairs Golf Stockings with elastic tops or turnovers.
Three pairs Long Woollen Pants.
One Rubber Water Bottle.

Many Students have to be equipped for countries where ski-ing is a necessary method of travel, and therefore they frequently require complete ski-ing outfits. Similarly, seamen's outfits are often called for, and there are other less frequent special demands, not the least of which is the supply of enemy uniforms in a variety of ranks and services, complete down to the smallest detail.

To deal with the provision of this variety of requirements, a comprehensive range of men's clothing and personal equipment is held. The stock is comparatively large, because in addition to variety, there is the consideration of sizes to take into account. To give an idea of the volume of turnover, the number of articles issued in one month during 1944 was 8,665. The stock figure in that month was 20,040 articles.

No stock of women's clothing is held because fashion changes by district, and it has been found practicable to deal with women by selecting patterns for dresses, etc., from current foreign newspapers and periodicals appropriate to the country to be visited. The patterns, etc., are copied by selected tailors and suppliers. Individual "shopping" for each woman student is necessary by this method, but it works well and results in complete satisfaction of the Student's requirements.

Continuous difficulty is experienced in obtaining suitable men's garments. This is to be expected, because clothing of normal British manufacture would not pass as Continental on even casual examination. Contact has been made with civilian firms in this country who were either importers of genuine Continental articles of clothing, or who manufactured goods for Continental sale and who still carry Continental tailors and cutters on their staffs.

Resort has had to be made to copying many articles. By the most careful attention to details, to weaves of materials, dyes, buttons, cottons, finish, shape, cut, trimmings and all the numerous characteristics of clothing apparent to an expert, garments can be produced which are almost impossible to distinguish from Continental manufacture.

Clothing is issued without any makers' or retailers' marks, or marks showing sizes, because clothing may be traced back to the supposed supplier, and he may disclaim any knowledge, or even condemn the Student by his assurance that he never stocked any such article. There are exceptions to these rules on some occasions, because it is necessary as part of a Student's cover story that he be definitely associated with some town or district or firm, and then copied markings must be reproduced on his clothes. This process is difficult as it necessitates weaving trade marks, etc. A considerable amount of genuine Continental second-hand clothing has also been obtained from refugees.

Despite the difficulties of supplying the Student's necessities on the basis that he must be properly equipped, it is the policy and practice to go further in assisting the mission. It is a principle that if the Student has complete confidence in his outfit, that very confidence is one of the finest tonics to his morale that could be administered. Every thing is done to ensure that he is satisfied as well as properly outfitted according to his cover story.

Most of the clothing is new when taken from stock, but before it is issued to Students it is "aged" to produce the correct appearance of wear according to the Student's cover story. The appropriate state of wear can be perfectly similated by the experienced men who do this work. Any article of equipment can be treated, but it is a skilled operation.

Final touches (as illustrated), are provided for the outfit in the form of watches, cigarette cases, wallets, penknives, fountain pens, etc., belts, purses, lighters, housewives, toilet and handbags as appropriate. All these items are procured through laborious and careful exploration of likely channels. Most of these items are found in the hands of pre-war importers or refugees, and some are obtained from other Government Departments.

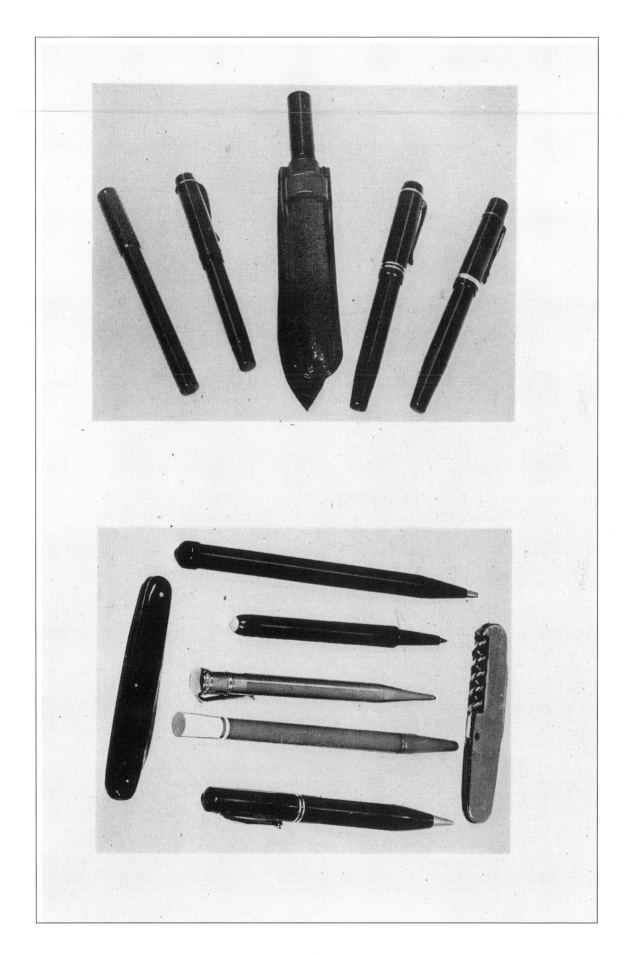

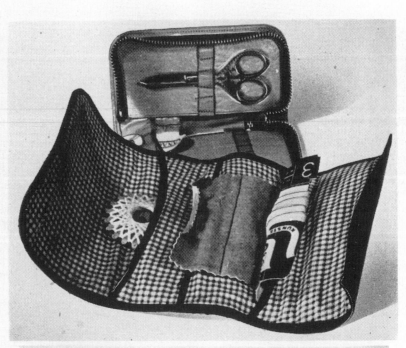

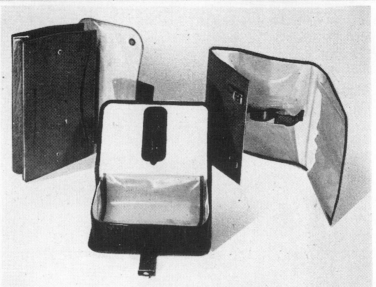

SUITCASES AND BRIEFCASES.

The illustrations show the different types and sizes of suitcases and briefcases issued.

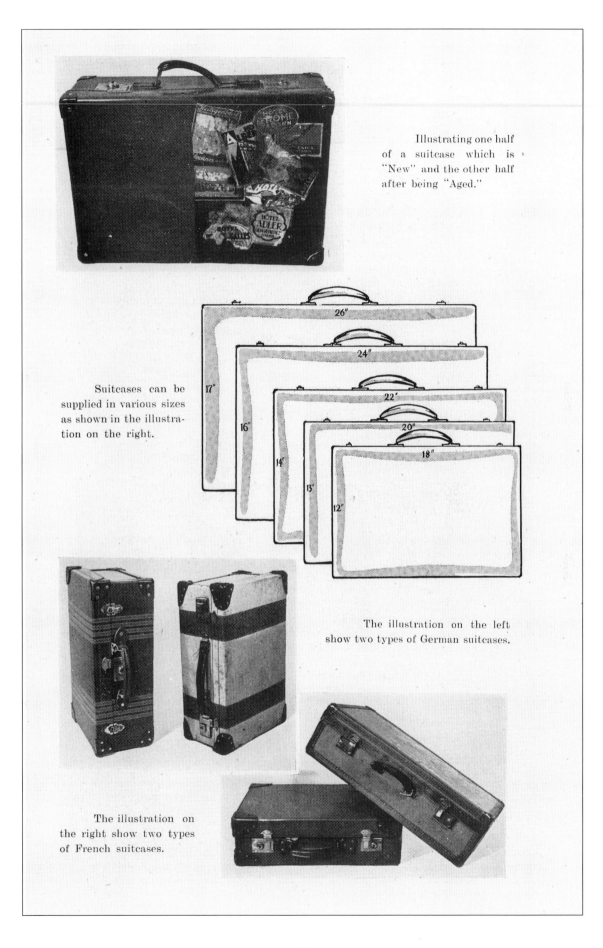

Illustrating one half of a suitcase which is "New" and the other half after being "Aged."

Suitcases can be supplied in various sizes as shown in the illustration on the right.

The illustration on the left show two types of German suitcases.

The illustration on the right show two types of French suitcases.

SECTION H.   # MAKE-UP

The Make-Up Department affords facilities for disguise and personal camouflage of the Student. It is a process that cannot be hurried and sometimes involves weeks of specialized treatment including plastic surgery and dental operations.

Make-up can be considered in three distinct classes:

- (i) **Temporary**—as a measure of emergency camouflage.
- (ii) **Semi-permanent**—to cover the period of a short operation in the Field.
- (iii) **Permanent**—to obtain a complete change of personality which will last him indefinitely.

TEMPORARY MAKE-UP.

This can be applied quite effectively by the Student himself and has proved most useful in the Field to persons who require a quick change for a short period. Illustrations 1 and 2 show what can be done with a little shading, a theatrical moustache and a pair of glasses.

No. 1.

No. 2.

SEMI-PERMANENT MAKE-UP.

This requires more time and can be accomplished only by someone who has received instructions in make-up. Illustrations 3 and 4 show one type of semi-permanent make-up where the most obvious feature of the man is his bald head. This has been obviated by the use of a toupee. Illustrations 5, 6 and 7 show the method of measuring a man for a wig or toupee. Illustrations 8, 9 and 10 show how to take correct measurements for spectacles.

The illustrations 11, 12, 13, 14, 15 and 16 show the use of gum pads and nose plugs, and the following instructions describe how impressions can be made. These instructions are given for the benefit of Students who cannot avail themselves of local wig makers, opticians and dentists and who would have to rely on the Make-Up Department supplying them with their needs. If the instructions are carried out with care all the Students' requirements can be met with first class results despite the distance between themselves and the Make-Up Department.

Impression Trays (illustration 17).

A fair range of impression trays should be available, ten uppper and ten lower are suggested. With this range any size jaw may be dealt with. The size of trays can only be determined by experience and good judgment. Rehearse on a friend. Judge the size and shape, insert the tray and see how it fits. Make sure the tray is

No. 3.

No. 4.

large enough and see that there is a good clearance round all the teeth, and if necessary, bend to ensure that the muscle attachment or soft tissue are not displaced.

Impression Composition.

A composition is preferable to plaster for making impressions, as it is less "messy" and is much less unpleasant for the Student. Also impression-taking from some people induces intense salivation which floods the floor of the mouth and any attempt to take a good plaster impression with the mouth filled with saliva is a waste of time. The saliva mixes with the plaster and is inclined to crumble it. "Stents Red" should be used and this is the procedure for this and the majority of compositions that set by cooling.

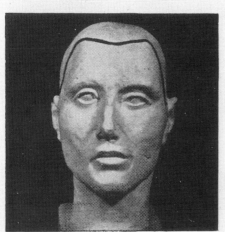

No. 5.

Place the composition in a bowl of hot water and when sufficiently pliable, knead well and pass once or twice through a Bunsen flame to dry it and ensure that it is of a uniformly soft consistency. Make it into a roll and press in the previously warmed tray. Warming the tray ensures that the composition will adhere to the tray when removing from the mouth. Smooth out all wrinkles and dip in hot

No. 6.

No. 7.

235

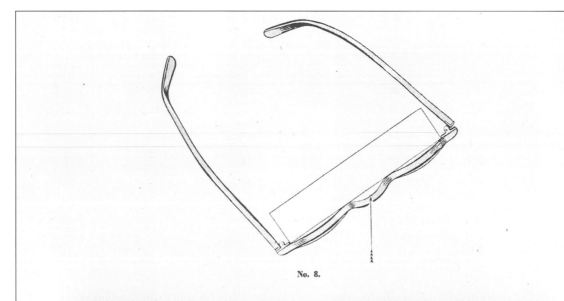

No. 8.

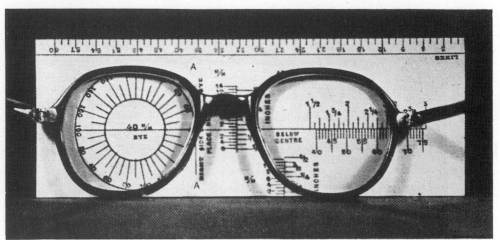

No. 9.

No. 10.

236

water, test on the side of the face to make sure it is not too hot, then place it in the Student's mouth. Illustrations 18 and 19 show how to insert the tray for the bottom impression. When in position hold down with the left hand and with the right hand manipulate the cheeks. Allow approximately five minutes for setting and remove carefully. Follow the same directions for the upper jaw, illustrations 20 and 21. For the casting, use a fairly stiff mixture of plaster, well shake down and allow to set, place in warm water and remove the composition. This should leave a perfect mould of the Student's mouth. This is now ready for the dental surgeon and if the necessary care has been taken he should be able to produce the required pads.

SKIN DYES.

It is impossible to supply a fast dye for the skin, but there are several means of staining the skin for three or four days. Powder blocks can be supplied in three colours,

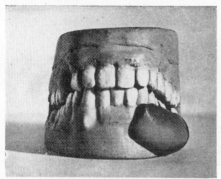

No. 11.

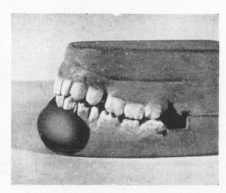

No. 12.

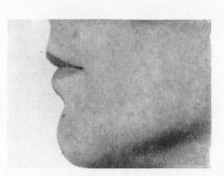

No. 13.

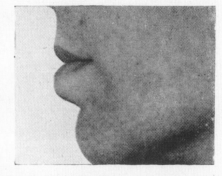

No. 14.

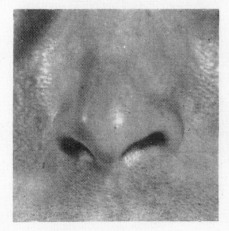

No. 15.

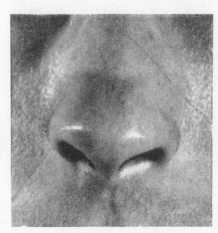

No. 16.

brown, black and green. These blocks can be impregnated with dimethyl phthalate as a repellant for mosquitos.

Mepacreme, after approximately a dozen doses, will turn the skin a yellowish colour, turning into a fairly deep brown as the doses are continued.

Carotene is the pigment of carrots and if taken internally will produce a staining of the body.

One grm. of silver nitrate in 100 c.c. of water and 100 c.c. aqueous alcohol sprayed through a glass nozzle will, after exposure to strong sunlight, produce a very strong dark brown stain that would last approximately three days in Far East climates.

Permanganate of Potash, using two teaspoonfuls to a half pint of water and applied to the body with a cotton wool pad, will produce a brown stain that will last approximately two days.

The following is a prescription for the production of a walnut dye:—

| Green Walnut Hulls | ... | 17 drams | Alcohol | ... | ... | 8 drams |
| Alum | ... | ... | 1¼ drams | Water to make | ... | 3 ozs. |

No. 17.

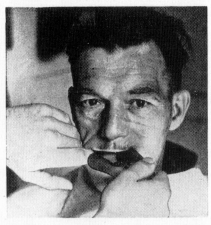

No. 18.

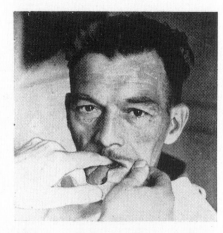

No. 19.

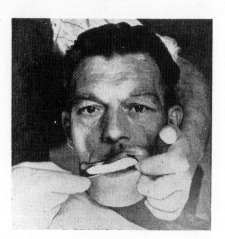

No. 20.

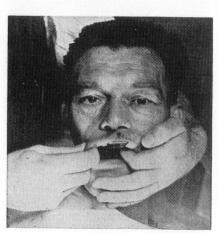

No. 21.

238

Triturate the first two ingredients in a mortar, add the alcohol and let stand for four days. Filter and apply with cotton wool pad.

Wrinkling Cream is the name given to an ointment used for giving an aged appearance to the skin. It does not actually wrinkle the skin but produces an unhealthy pallor.

Plastic noses and wigs can be supplied for distant use. For example, a white crew operating a native craft could be very easily disguised in order to give the impression of natives if seen from a distance.

Contact lenses are a useful camouflage for a person who has to wear very thick pebbles in his spectacles. They may also be used to give the impression of a wall eye or a blind eye, and if sufficient time is given they can be produced to alter the colour of the eyes.

PERMANENT CAMOUFLAGE.

This can only be accomplished by alteration to the features and the removal of scars, which naturally has to be carried out by a qualified plastic surgeon. Appointments for permanent make-up and the necessary arrangements for the operation are made through the Make-up Department, but it must be remembered that sufficient time must be given otherwise the application will have to be refused. An eminent plastic surgeon and his staff are at our disposal and have carried out a great number of operations.

Some examples are shown in the following illustrations of what can be accomplished by facial surgery.

Illustration 22 is a rebuilt broken nose.

Illustration 23 shows the result of treatment of an unusually large and prominent nose.

In illustration 24 the nose has been operated on to alter a typical Jewish character. This type of face presents a particular problem because there is something about the cheek bones, that although characteristic, cannot be clearly defined and the surgeon finds it impossible to make any alteration to the bones. The nose can be camouflaged by skilled surgery and the face can be altered to eliminate the outstanding facial characteristics of the race of the owner.

No. 22.

No. 23.

No. 24.

Tattoo marks are most difficult to remove. The process is long and painful and recourse to removal is not recommended. By far the most satisfactory treatment has been found to be re-tattooing with larger and more elaborate designs. Skillful blending can achieve amazing results and this method has the advantage of speed and there is much less discomfort to the subject.

The dental surgeon can achieve practically any alteration to the teeth and mouth. The methods used are many, but some examples can be given. Gum pads are within his province and their uses have already been described. False teeth can of course, be provided or existing dental plates altered. Gold teeth should be removed. A hollow gold tooth in the form of a cap to slip over an existing tooth can be carried in a pocket ready for immediate use.

This article gives only examples of some methods of each type of personal camouflage. This important subject is one to which any Student should give most careful consideration, and the best results will always be attained by co-operation between the subject and the make-up man.

FIELDCRAFT AND CAMOUFLAGE

The principles of Camouflage as used by the Armed Forces very rarely apply to the specialised forms of camouflage which are adopted for our specific purposes, where no attempt is made to render the object difficult to observe, but to present it openly to view as an entirely different object but usually of an innocent character; but there are occasions when we have to consider camouflage entirely from a Fieldcraft angle.

The aim of camouflage is to render the object inconspicuous and difficult to recognise; let us consider, therefore, the qualities which make an object CONSPICUOUS. These may be classified as under:—

(a) Movement.

(b) Colour: differentiation from the surrounding objects which form its background.

(c) The general tone or texture of the object.

(d) The form that the object takes: the contrast of light and shade.

(e) The outline compared with its surroundings.

(f) The form of the object's shadow.

It is obvious that the more one can eliminate the contrasting elements of an object with its background the more difficult it will become to recognise. Therefore the fundamental steps towards effective camouflage are:—

1. Absence of movement.

2. Colour resemblance.

3. Matching of tone and texture.

4. Destruction of the object's shape.

5. Disruption of the outline.

6. Elimination of its shadow.

Showing contrast of colour to background.

Showing nature's addition to disruptive pattern emulating immediate background of coral.

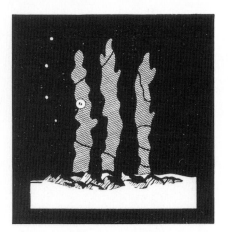

Showing additional coloration blending with coral and background and the elimination of shadow against broken ground.

SMALL CRAFT.

We are all familiar with the common sight of buildings, vehicles and ships painted in coloured designs. Disruption, as this patterning is called, functions to prevent or delay the recognition of an object by painting only. When the surface of an object is covered with these irregular patches of contrasting local colours and tones, they assist the object so covered to blend into the existing background. The pattern is so designed that the shape of the object becomes disrupted or broken up. Set patterns can be supplied, but the study of the colour and tones used must be left to the user, who must make a careful analysis of the colours and tones in the location in which he is to operate, and have his paints carefully matched. Disruptive painting is not foolproof camouflage, but it is definitely an aid. Climatic conditions vary so much that apart from a guide as to the patterning, no hard and fast rules can be made.

An example of nature's method of fitting into existing background, i.e., a moth on tree.

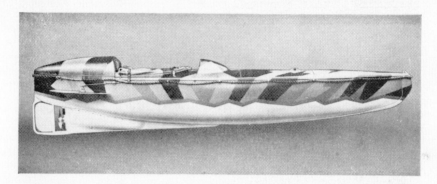

This method is chiefly used by us for the camouflage of small craft. Operating in water, the question of texture does not arise so long as the coloration matches the condition of the operation. The disruptive painting takes care of this, and also the breaking-up of the shape, and as far as possible the elimination of the shadow.

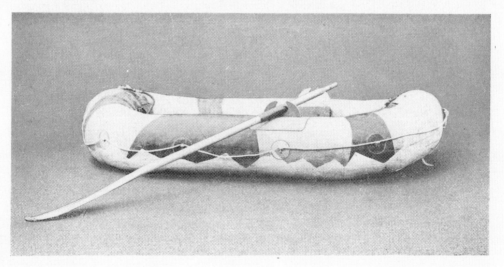

241

CLOTHING.

Military operational clothing is also treated with these patterns. As these are generally needed for jungle warfare, the colours used are dark green and black. Colour is also applied to faces and hands. Suitable "pancakes" can be supplied in various shades of black, green and brown. (See Make-up Section).

CONTAINERS.

Parachute containers are painted in disruptive patterns according to the season, plus local coloration. This is only used as a temporary measure where the container has to be hidden quickly and for a short while.

A more elaborate form of camouflage is obtained in the form of rubber sheets representing tree trunks which are wrapped round the container, giving the impression of a fallen tree. If the cells have to be carted away to some distance in order to be unpacked, they can be painted to appear as common objects, such as drums, logs, kegs of butter, etc.

Holdsworth containers having first been coated with a plastic paint to conform with local geological conditions, are also painted with a disruptive pattern to give the requisite tone and texture to the surface.

Similar containers made from papier mache and produced as rock boulders are also obtainable. These containers are exact reproductions of various rock formations (See Section E) and embody all the six principles as laid down by camouflage. They are light to carry, and are guaranteed damp proof.

Container with rubber open

Container with rubber closed.

Keg of Margarine.

Wooden Log.

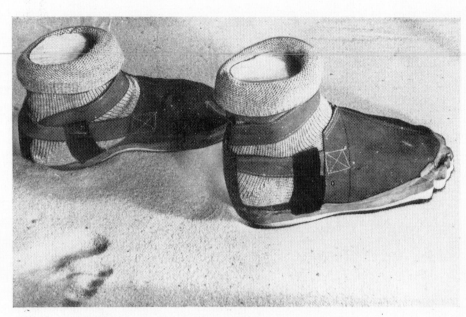

FIG. 1.

SNEAKERS.

Sneakers are in the form of a sandal carrying a sole bearing the imprint of a Japanese shoe or native foot.

They were devised for use in raiding parties for operations in the Far East.

They are easy to wear and the track left by the wearer leaves faithful imprints, thus hiding all traces of the intruders having been other than Japanese or local natives.

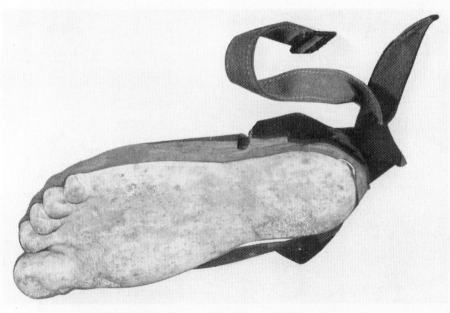

FIG. 2.

FIG. 3.

JAPANESE BOOTS.

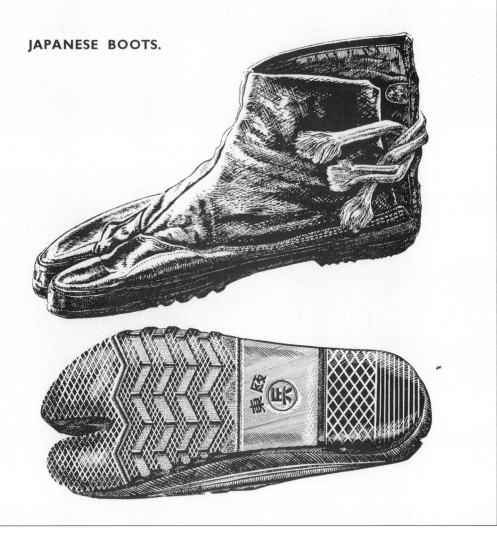

OBSERVATION POSTS.

Various types of light portable observation posts are made for special operations. These are easily erected and afford enough room to hide two people. The above illustration shows an observation post treated with foam (Pyrene) to represent snow. Visibility is good from the interior while the exterior blends into the existing background.

Sniper Suits can be provided for any location. The illustrations show one made of teak leaves for tropical use.

CAMOUFLAGE OF TYREBURSTERS

Three methods of Camouflage of Tyrebursters have been used; 1. Complete concealment of the device in a shell representing a stone, a lump of mud, or animal dropping. 2. Concealment of the Tyreburster in a cloth bag representing a stone. 3. Disruption in colour of the Tyreburster taped and painted.

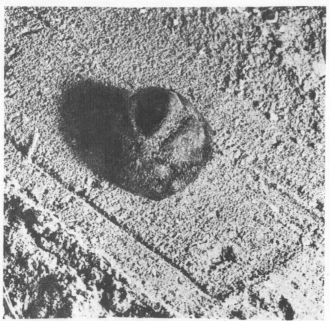

COMPLETE CON-CEALMENT, No. I.

This type of camouflage is obviously the most satisfactory because, in the case of stones, if the geological conditions of the place of operation are studied carefully the article fits completely into its own background, and in the case of animal droppings the disguise is such that it will not attract undue attention because it is one of many objects with which the eye is unconsciously familiar.

Tyreburster as Mule's Dropping.

Tyreburster, left to right, Flintstone, Sandstone, Dry mud.

CONCEALMENT IN CLOTH BAGS, No. 2.

The illustrations below show the method of concealing tyrebursters in bags. The bags are made of rubberised canvas and are painted to resemble stones to tone with the geological colours of the locality in which the tyrebursters are to be used. The shapes of the bags differ in order to achieve a variety of outlines.

This is a "quick camouflage" method, and is a handy one because the space occupied by the actual camouflage material is very small.

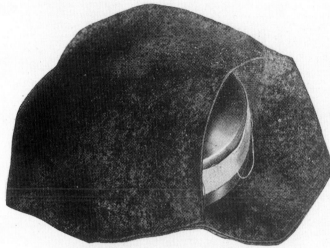

Tyreburster in cloth envelope. (Closed).

Tyreburster in cloth envelope. (Open).

TAPED TYREBURSTERS.

The metal tyreburster is completely covered with adhesive tape, a flap is left at the bottom so that the lead plug can be removed and the detonator replaced. The whole is then painted with a disruptive pattern and coloured to conform with the geological type of the district. No paint can come into contact with the working parts, and apart from being a further precaution against damp, this type of painted burster takes up less space in packing.

Tyreburster semi-camouflaged i.e. covered with adhesive tape and painted disruptive patterns.

PRINTING
DEPARTMENT

All the labels and printing matter necessary to complete the fake commodities as described in the previous sections are produced by the Printing and Art Department.

This also includes the production of armlets for invading forces, insignias for foreign uniforms and the printing of codes.

The following pages give some idea of the assortment of work produced.

Above is reproduced a sample of a German food tin label.
On the right is shown a Portuguese sardine tin
label, which is normally printed on "Flexglas".

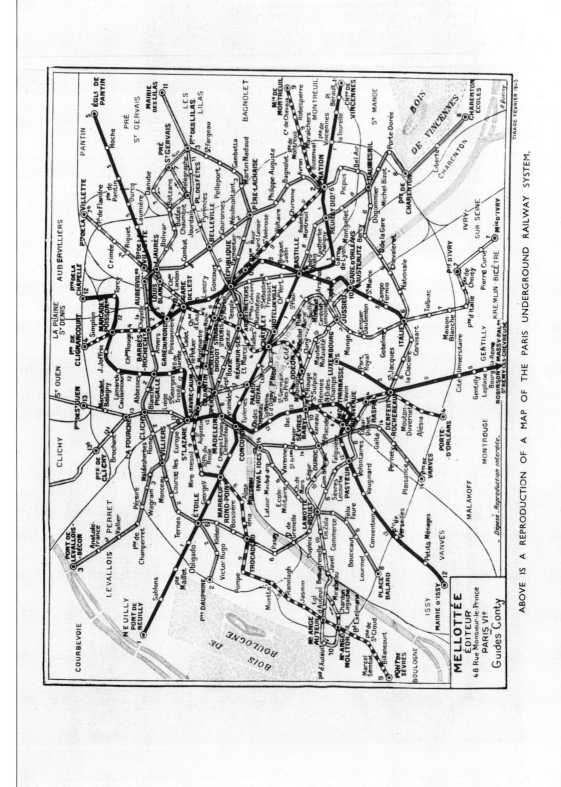

ABOVE IS A REPRODUCTION OF A MAP OF THE PARIS UNDERGROUND RAILWAY SYSTEM.

Above is a reproduction of a Norwegian Brisling tin label.

Three Italian labels, used in the production of explosive Chianti bottles.

The label below has been copied from an original tin of Belgian lighter fuel.

It is printed on a type of transfer paper called "Flexglas" which adheres to the tin after it has been immersed in water. By this process it is possible to give the exact appearance of tin printing without the use of elaborate plant.

Two examples of German Labels:—
Above : German Tinned Preserves Label.
Left : German Bell Battery Label.

HOTEL SRPSKI KRALJ SKOPLJE TELEFON 291

VLASNIK V. AVRAMOVIĆ

GRAND HOTEL DE LA POSTE

ROUEN

On this page are shown some reproductions of Continental luggage labels, which, when suitably aged, are attached to trunks, suitcases, etc., to give a genuine appearance or to bear out a cover story.

HÔTEL de PARIS

SAINT-TROPEZ VAR

PENSIONE ITALIA

CAPRI - MARINA GRANDE

IMP. G. BOURGEADE, PARIS

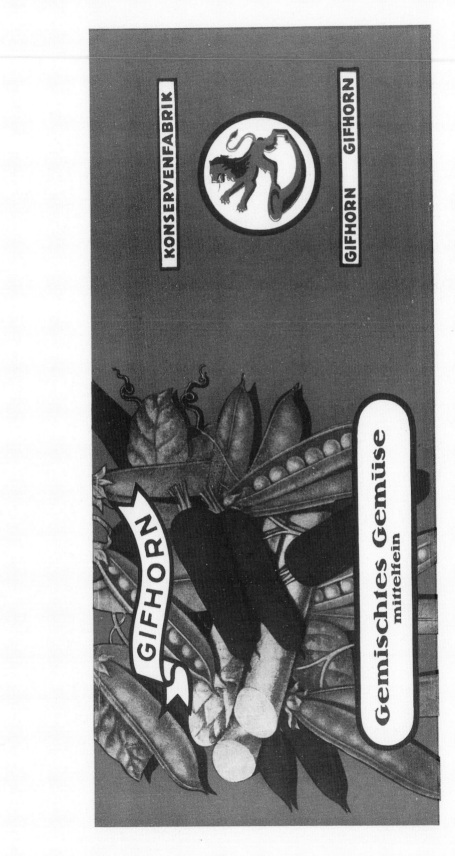

Above is a reproduction of a German vegetable tin label. The tins can be used for all normal types of concealment, such as ammunition, money, messages, codes, etc.

INDEX OF SPECIAL DEVICES AND SUPPLIES

Volume I

Volume II